THE OTHER MISSILES OF OCTOBER

PHILIP NASH

EISENHOWER,

KENNEDY,

AND THE

JUPITERS,

1957–1963

THE

OTHER

MISSILES

OF OCTOBER

THE UNIVERSITY OF NORTH CAROLINA PRESS / CHAPEL HILL & LONDON

The paper in this book meets the guidelines for permanence and
durability of the Committee on Production Guidelines for Book
Longevity of the Council on Library Resources.

Library of Congress Cataloging-in-Publication Data
Nash, Philip.
The other missiles of October: Eisenhower, Kennedy, and the Jupiters,
1957–1963 / Philip Nash.
      p.   cm.
Includes bibliographical references and index.
ISBN 0-8078-2339-2 (cloth: alk. paper).—ISBN 0-8078-4647-3 (pbk.: alk.
paper)
1. United States—Foreign relations—1953–1961.   2. United States—
Foreign relations—1961–1963.   3. Cuban Missile Crisis, 1962.
4. Jupiter missile—Government policy—United States.   5. United
States—Military policy.   6. United States—Politics and
government—1953–1961.   7. United States—Politics and
government—1961–1963.   I. Title.
E835.N37   1997
327.73047'09'046—dc20   **327.73**   96-43691
                                                                       CIP

01   00   99   98   97   5   4   3   2   1

Chapter 2 appeared in a different form as "Jumping Jupiters: The U.S.
Search for IRBM Host Countries in NATO, 1957–59," *Diplomacy and
Statecraft* 6 (November 1995): 753–86. Portions of Chapter 5 appeared
in different form as "Nuisance of Decision: Jupiter Missiles and the
Cuban Missile Crisis," *Journal of Strategic Studies* 14 (March 1991):
1–26. Both are reprinted here by permission of Frank Cass and Co., Ltd.

FOR SOO

CONTENTS

ILLUSTRATIONS

MAPS

TABLES

ACKNOWLEDGMENTS

In writing this book, I have been fortunate in countless ways.

I am grateful for the financial support of the Department of History and Contemporary History Institute at Ohio University; the Nuclear Age History and Humanities Center at Tufts University; the U.S. Air Force Historical Research Agency; and the U.S. Arms Control and Disarmament Agency.

Like countless others, I also benefited from the support, activities, and declassified documents of three absolutely indispensable institutions: the Cold War International History Project, the National Security Archive, and the Nuclear History Program.

The final stages of this project were made possible by a generous fellowship from the Charles Warren Center at Harvard University, where my colleagues were the friendliest and most helpful imaginable: Petra Goedde, Susan Hunt, Tom Knock, Tim Naftali, Daniela Rossini, and Rafia Zafar. I shall miss them all.

Other friends and colleagues who provided support and encouragement, shared insights or documents, or read and commented on the manuscript in various forms are Barton Bernstein, Alan Booth, Dave Broscious, Bill Burr, Nur Bilge Criss, John Gordon, Matt Grant, Lon Hamby, Jim Hershberg, Lisa Howell, Phillip Karber, Wolfgang Krieger, Uwe Nerlich, Leopoldo Nuti, Chester Pach, Mike Ruhl, Mark Sonntag, Marc Trachtenberg, Jan van der Harst, Hallie Willard, Philip Zelikow, and one anonymous reader.

I also thank many archivists—especially David Haight, June Payne, Maura Porter, and Regina Greenwell—for their efficient service.

Moreover, I have learned firsthand why so many people speak so highly of the University of North Carolina Press. In particular I have had the privilege of working with Lew Bateman, Grace Buonocore, and Pam Upton, whose professionalism and patience have made these last steps a pleasure.

Three friends and colleagues deserve special thanks. Brent Lundy's friendship, a great source of strength for me during this project, has survived the ultimate test—his having read my manuscript. I hereby promise to give his "important work" on civil defense at least a quick skimming when he finishes. John Gaddis has been a far better mentor than I deserve. His sense of humor, patience, and encouragement of young scholars are truly admirable, and I cannot thank him enough. The faculty and students of Yale University are fortunate to be welcoming him. And Marty Sherwin, who sparked my interest in nuclear history many years ago, has encouraged and helped me ever since. All three have my lasting gratitude.

I would also like to thank the Nashes—Caroline, David, Erik, Fletcher, and Gerald, whose love and good humor over the years have meant more to me than they will ever know.

Finally, my wife, Lu Soo Chun, has been everything—best friend and companion, critic, scholar, editor, and inspiration. There are the many who have helped make this possible, and then there is Soo. It is to her that I dedicate this book.

ABBREVIATIONS

ABC	American Broadcasting Company
AEC	Atomic Energy Commission
BBC	British Broadcasting Corporation
BNSP	Basic National Security Policy
CENTO	Central Treaty Organization
CIA	Central Intelligence Agency
DCI	Director of Central Intelligence
DEFCON	Defense Condition
DOD	Department of Defense
ExComm	Executive Committee, National Security Council
FRG	Federal Republic of Germany
FY	Fiscal year
IAF	Italian air force
ICBM	Intercontinental ballistic missile
IRBM	Intermediate-range ballistic missile
JCAE	Joint Committee on Atomic Energy
JCS	Joint Chiefs of Staff
JFK	John F. Kennedy
MAP	Military Assistance Program
MLF	Multilateral Force
MRBM	Medium-range ballistic missile
MSP	Mutual Security Program
NAC	North Atlantic Council
NATO	North Atlantic Treaty Organization
NBC	National Broadcasting Company
NEA	Bureau of Near Eastern Affairs
NSAM	National Security Action Memorandum
NSC	National Security Council
ONE	Office of National Estimates

PAL	Permissive Action Link
PCI	Partito Comunista Italiano, Italian Communist Party
POL	Petroleum, oil, and lubricants
PPS	Policy Planning Staff, Department of State
PSAC	President's Science Advisory Committee
QRA	Quick Reaction Alert
RAF	Royal Air Force
RFK	Robert F. Kennedy
SAC	Strategic Air Command
SACEUR	Supreme Allied Commander, Europe
SALT	Strategic Arms Limitation Talks
SEATO	Southeast Asia Treaty Organization
SHAPE	Supreme Headquarters, Allied Powers Europe
SLBM	Submarine-launched ballistic missile
SNIE	Special National Intelligence Estimate
TAF	Turkish air force
UN	United Nations
USAF	United States Air Force
USAFE	United States Air Forces Europe
USIA	United States Information Agency
WSEG	Weapons System Evaluation Group

THE OTHER MISSILES OF OCTOBER

INTRODUCTION

Elaborate military arrangements of this nature,
once put in hand, have consequences. They
produce counter measures on the other side.
People come to depend on them as essential
elements of their security. In the end it becomes
difficult to consider their withdrawal or to make
them the subject of negotiation.
George F. Kennan, BBC broadcast, December 1957

By 5 March 1962, the last of them were finally operational. On fixed, unprotected sites above ground, forty-five Jupiter intermediate-range ballistic missiles (IRBMs)—thirty in Italy, fifteen in Turkey—stood ready, pointed at the sky. Nine feet in diameter and sixty feet long, with a large metal skirt shielding the engine, each was rather conspicuous, gleaming white, resembling an enormous crayon or the "Washington Monument," as a U.S. congressman would later recall. On the side of each Turkish Jupiter was painted a Turkish flag and an insignia consisting of a large arrow and, in a none-too-subtle indication of what this thing was for, a mushroom cloud.[1]

Italian crews tended the missiles in their country, while in Turkey the U.S. Air Force did the honors as the Turks finished their training. In case of a serious alert, crews would pump their IRBMs' fuel tanks full of a liquid oxygen-kerosene mix. Although originally intended to be kept in separate concrete "igloos" in USAF custody—in accordance with U.S. law—and mounted only at the last minute, the W-49 thermonuclear warheads already sat atop the missiles to quicken their reaction time.

In case of hostilities, responsibility for launch rested with NATO's military chief, the Supreme Allied Commander, Europe (SACEUR), who first had to seek approval from both the U.S. and host governments. Upon receipt of that dual go-ahead, SACEUR would send launch orders down a special chain of command to the launch control officers at each three-missile launch position. These officers, one Italian or Turk and one American, each with a necessary launch key, would together fire their three Jupiters after a fifteen-minute countdown. The missiles would then roar toward their predetermined targets—the Soviets' own IRBMs, stationed in the western USSR—traveling up to seventeen hundred miles (fifteen hundred nautical miles) in under eighteen minutes. Once over their destinations, the W-49s in their nose cones would each detonate with a force of 1.44 megatons, more than one hundred times the destructive power of the atomic bomb that had incinerated central Hiroshima seventeen years earlier. The Jupiters, purveyors of such unimaginable havoc, were finally in place, part of NATO's strategic deterrent, ready for war, after a difficult deployment process that had lasted more than four years.

They would be dismantled and carted off within thirteen months, one of the shortest operational life spans for a Western strategic delivery system in the nuclear age.

Despite their brief existence and little-known place in the history of the U.S. nuclear arsenal, the Jupiters caused major diplomatic headaches for Presidents Dwight D. Eisenhower and John F. Kennedy. The missiles were a knotted thread connecting two of the most important events in the Cold War: the launch of the Soviet space satellite *Sputnik* and the Cuban missile crisis. Their deployment was a major NATO defense policy that repeatedly demanded the involvement of top U.S. officials, from the president on down.

Along the way, the Jupiter story was at times marked by irony. Although throughout this period U.S. officials would remain interested in permanently deploying some kind of medium- or intermediate-range missiles in Europe, they intended the first-generation IRBMs like the Jupiter as interim weapons, to fill the need for strategic ballistic missiles until more sophisticated intercontinental and submarine-launched missiles were ready. With all the delays in deployment, however, most of the Jupiters did not join the arsenal until the more modern systems did—virtually a case of instantaneous obsolescence. Equally ironic, President Eisenhower briefly considered using the Jupiters as diplomatic bargaining chips but then went ahead and deployed them. Three years later, after proceeding with the deployment in Turkey despite several recommendations to the contrary, President Kennedy ended up using the Jupiters as bargaining chips in the Cuban missile crisis.

The missiles with so little military worth had, in the end, proven to be of significant political value.

Despite the many existing studies of the Cuban missile crisis, the Eisenhower and Kennedy foreign policies, and the role of nuclear weapons therein, the six-year story of the Jupiter deployment and removal has never received a full-length treatment. This study attempts to fill that void and to illuminate further a key period in U.S.-Soviet and U.S.-NATO relations. It does so relying heavily on documents from a variety of U.S. collections, many of them only recently declassified.

The Jupiters, for all their capacity to annihilate, did not exactly impress American policymakers, neither at the time nor in retrospect. "It would have been better to dump them in the ocean," Eisenhower once complained, "instead of trying to dump them on our allies." His secretary of state, John Foster Dulles, said it would be "quite wrong to assume that Europe want[ed] these missiles." And Ike's last defense secretary, Thomas Gates, in turn declared them "more symbolic than useful."[2]

Similar views were held by their successors. To Kennedy's secretary of defense, Robert McNamara, the Jupiters were "a pile of junk"; to national security adviser McGeorge Bundy, "worse than useless." Dean Rusk, JFK's secretary of state, recalled, "We joked about which way those missiles would go if they were fired." And President Kennedy himself commented during the missile crisis that the Jupiters "had become more or less worthless." In a more heated moment, he is alleged to have called them simply "those frigging missiles."[3]

One might gather from such comments that these were all officials who had had nothing to do with deploying or maintaining the Jupiters overseas— and one would be wrong. Those with such harsh words for the missiles, and many of their colleagues, in fact played active roles in making them strategic reality. The fundamental question that arises is the focus of this book: Why? Why did successive presidents initiate and perpetuate a policy about which they had serious doubts from the start, doubts that only deepened with time?

This book also seeks to answer related questions: Why and how did the successive administrations deploy these missiles? Why did some NATO members receive them while others did not? What were the rationales for and criticisms of the deployment? What role did the Jupiters play in the origins, development, and settlement of the Cuban missile crisis? How were they removed thereafter? How do the Jupiter policies fit into assessments of the broader Eisenhower and Kennedy foreign policies?

Approaching such questions should shed light on several significant aspects of recent U.S. foreign policy. These include how nuclear weapons, while never detonated in war after August 1945, were used as political tools; how bilateral, alliance, and superpower relationships intermingled unpredictably; and how concerns about credibility could lead presidents perfectly capable of sound decision making to pursue policies against their better judgment.

EISENHOWER'S

IRBM OFFER

TO NATO

1957

1

WE CANNOT DENY
THEM TO OUR ALLIES

The Joint Chiefs of Staff have observed that the
interdepartmental activity in connection with
preparation of subject papers [for the upcoming
NATO summit] is somewhat precipitous, if not
slightly frantic. They are convinced that, in the
current atmosphere, commitments may be made
which will provide cause for regret at a later date.
JCS chair Twining to Defense Secretary McElroy,
21 November 1957

The Sputniks are the bows and arrows of
tomorrow. You Americans will find something
to top them.
Senior official, Turkish Foreign Office,
December 1957

The governing body of the North Atlantic Treaty Organization (NATO), the North Atlantic Council (NAC), held another of its semi-annual ministerial-level meetings on 16–19 December 1957, but this time it was something special. For the first time since the alliance was founded in 1949, the heads of the member governments—save Portugal's dictator, Antonio Salazar—would themselves represent their countries. It was the greatest gathering of leaders in Paris since the Versailles Conference of 1919. President Dwight D. Eisenhower and other alliance leaders felt this grand occasion necessary as a response to the October launch of the Soviet space satellite, *Sputnik*. Although the Eisenhower administration at first dismissed it—one official calling it "a silly bauble"—*Sputnik* had quickly cast a pall over the alliance because of its grave implications for Western security.[1] Here in Paris, two months after the Soviet breakthrough, was a widely publicized event that Eisenhower and others hoped would restore the West's sagging morale.

Adding to the drama was the mild stroke Eisenhower had suffered on 25 November. For several days, as his subordinates anxiously discussed the murky issues of disability and succession, it looked as if Ike would not go to Paris. The frustrated president, for his part, established his ability to attend the conference as a test of whether he would remain in office or resign. "I'm going to take this trip if it kills me," Eisenhower declared. "This is my job. I *am* going to run this damn show." Luckily, he made a speedy recovery, and just six days before the meeting was to start, doctors declared him fit to attend. Still, he flew across the Atlantic at low altitude to minimize the strain on his heart. In his condition, he seemed to embody the frailty of the alliance itself as *Sputnik* continued to orbit overhead.[2]

On the first day of the summit, Eisenhower and Dulles joined the other heads of government in the Palais de Chaillot, around a large table with the four-pointed NATO emblem at its center. After the ailing Eisenhower delivered brief words of encouragement, his secretary of state, John Foster Dulles, tabled the U.S. proposals. Chief among them was the U.S. offer, as Dulles put it, "to make available to other NATO countries intermediate-range ballistic missiles, for deployment in accordance with the plans of SACEUR," NATO's military commander.[3]

A precedent for NATO conferences had produced a first for NATO policy: for the first time, NATO would have the opportunity to deploy ballistic missiles capable of delivering nuclear warheads deep inside Soviet territory. This chapter traces the history of the Eisenhower administration's decision to make the IRBM offer and the allies' agreement, in principle, to accept. It then attempts to assess both the decision itself and the process by which U.S. officials arrived at it.

ORIGINS OF THE FIRST OFFER

"The decisions which we make today in the fields of science and technology," the late Solly Zuckerman once wrote, "determine the tactics, then the strategy, and finally the politics of tomorrow."[4] He might have written these words about U.S. intermediate-range ballistic missiles (IRBMs) in the 1950s, for the Eisenhower administration's decision to offer them to NATO Europe was influenced by its decision to build the systems in the first place. With a range of seventeen hundred miles the missiles could not, with some exceptions, reach targets in the Soviet Union from U.S. or U.S.-controlled territory. The missiles embodied a "technological imperative": their very specifications meant they almost certainly required bases in friendly countries relatively near the USSR—as well as the agreement of those countries and whatever that might entail.

No real program to produce an IRBM existed until 1955. Early that year, the Technological Capabilities Panel (or "Killian Committee") of Eisenhower's Science Advisory Committee concluded that a ballistic missile with a seventeen-hundred-mile range could be developed with greater ease, speed, and certainty than could its intercontinental counterpart (ICBM). The panel recognized that the envisioned proximity of IRBM sites to the Soviet Union would increase their military vulnerability and that "political considerations" might place "certain limitations" on their establishment abroad. But for the purpose of countering the Soviets' own prospective IRBM, increasing the United States' chances of achieving a ballistic missile capability, and "further strengthening [its] striking power," the panel recommended that the United States develop an IRBM.[5]

President Eisenhower responded by approving an IRBM program, but at this stage his administration considered its international political implications only in limited terms. In August 1955, Eisenhower and U.S. Air Force chief of staff Nathan Twining questioned whether overseas bases for IRBMs would be available in the long term, while Secretary Dulles cited the bases' "doubtful" nature as a reason to pursue the ICBM concurrently. The following month, Dulles's undersecretary, Herbert Hoover Jr., wondered whether allies would host IRBM bases at all. But despite such doubts, the National Security Council (NSC) omitted the deployment problem in directing the State Department to study the IRBM program; policymakers seem to have been concerned only with what impact a Soviet ICBM or IRBM would have if the United States had no equivalent capabilities.[6]

The resulting study endorsed the IRBM program, and Dulles's concern about the deployment issue did not prevent him from staunchly supporting the missile's prompt development. Eisenhower, too, focused on obtaining the missile and not on the implications of its deployment. By December 1955, he was "absolutely determined not to tolerate any fooling" with the two missile programs. The United States simply had "to achieve such missiles as promptly as possible," he said, "if only because of [their] enormous psychological and political significance." The "United States had to have a reliable missile system quickly," he reportedly insisted, "even if he had to run the project himself." Therefore, the president directed "that the IRBM and ICBM programs should both be research and development programs of the highest priority above all others." Thus the development of an IRBM—in reality two nearly identical IRBMs, the air force "Thor" and the army "Jupiter," soon objects of a controversial rivalry—proceeded with a renewed sense of urgency.[7]

Officials at lower levels, particularly in the U.S. military, did devote some attention to deployment at a fairly early stage. The air force, ultimately given control of both IRBM types, formulated plans by early 1956 calling for placement of eight fifteen-missile squadrons in Great Britain. It no doubt selected this host for several reasons. It was well suited geographically, a safe distance from NATO's front line, and yet well within IRBM range of the western USSR. It was the only U.S. ally that had already joined the nuclear club, a fact that minimized fears of proliferation, and the two countries even before 1955 had begun discussing joint production of an IRBM. The possibility of distributing IRBMs more widely among other NATO allies and sharing control over nuclear weapons with them occurred to military and State Department officials, as did the possibility of protests by such allies over a U.S.-U.K. IRBM deal that excluded them. Despite this, the infant IRBM deployment program remained a bilateral Anglo-American endeavor.[8]

Through 1956, however, no explicit, sustained effort to negotiate IRBM deployments in Britain materialized. In July, air force secretary Donald Quarles raised the issue "very informally" with top British defense officials, whose "initial reaction was rather favorable." And yet, while low- and mid-level discussions continued through the end of the year, by October the Eisenhower administration had decided not to pursue an agreement for the time being, apparently because of bureaucratic squabbling and the significant financial burden involved in deployment. Defense Department difficulties in formulating a deployment plan further hampered progress.[9]

The Suez crisis of October–November 1956 propelled the IRBM issue to the highest level of decision making. Suez caused the greatest rift in the Anglo-American "special relationship" since the end of World War II and shook the whole Atlantic alliance to its foundations. Both Washington and London eagerly desired to patch things up, especially after Prime Minister Anthony Eden, who had presided over the Suez disaster, resigned in January 1957. His replacement, Harold Macmillan, was an old friend of Eisenhower's, having served as his British political adviser in North Africa during World War II. Thus a solid personal relationship now cleared the way for reconciliation, as well as cooperation on the deployment of IRBMs.[10]

THE FIRST OFFER: BERMUDA, MARCH 1957

Eisenhower and Macmillan quickly agreed to meet in March in Bermuda. The meeting's most important objective, the State Department argued in a paper approved by Dulles, was "to restore confidence in the Anglo-American relationship without detracting from the achievement of U.S. policy goals in other areas." For public purposes, this required "reaching the optimum number of agreements with the British on specific U.S.-U.K. problems of a type which [could] be made public." The British were of like mind.[11]

The particular IRBM deployment plan that would help meet these mutual goals emerged first from high-level military discussions in December of the previous year and then from talks between the countries' defense ministers at the end of January. The United States would hand over to the British four fifteen-missile squadrons, with Thor tentatively the chosen system, by the end of 1960; the warheads, in accordance with legal requirements imposed by the McMahon Act, would remain in U.S. custody. A joint decision would be required for launch, effectively giving each partner a veto.[12]

Eisenhower and Macmillan met in Bermuda on 21–24 March 1957. As agreed beforehand, numerous other issues, such as Cyprus, nuclear testing, and the Suez Canal, occupied the agenda. When the IRBM issue arose, the president made it clear that the deployment was dependent on successful development of the missile, an achievement then still only in prospect. He also understood that the IRBM might be superseded in the future by improved missiles of some type. For these reasons, Eisenhower wanted to avoid a detailed, binding agreement for the time being. Rather, in what the president later called "a commitment of signal importance," the two leaders agreed in principle to deploy four IRBM squadrons in Britain. "Certain guided missiles," the conference communiqué inconspicuously stated, "will be made available by the United States for use by British forces." Immediately after the conference, pending successful development, Eisenhower approved corresponding production of four squadrons of IRBMs.[13]

The British had several incentives to accept IRBMs, apart from sharing the desire to restore amicable relations. First, the U.S. IRBMs would appear at least five years before their own IRBM, the "Blue Streak," promised to and would thus satisfy the need for missiles in the meantime. Indeed, the deployment of U.S. systems might yield design information useful in Blue Streak development or, conversely, permit cancellation of Blue Streak altogether at a significant savings. Second, the missiles also fit in nicely with the Macmillan government's new defense strategy, taking shape at this same moment in the form of the "Defence White Paper." The British equivalent of Eisenhower's "New Look," this strategy called for conventional force reductions and an offsetting reliance on nuclear weapons, and the Thors would facilitate it. Third and most important from their standpoint, the British saw an IRBM deal as a wedge with which they could finally reestablish the formal nuclear partnership with the Americans that the latter had dissolved in 1946.[14]

As for the United States, it too had multiple reasons for making the Thor offer, apart from the pressing needs of alliance politics. First, the Eisenhower administration remained interested in deploying a *strategic* nuclear missile— that is, one capable of hitting, and thus deterring, the Soviet Union—as soon as possible. The IRBMs still promised to be the first such systems available, so the question remained not whether but where to deploy them. Second, more specifically, IRBMs might deter the Soviets from repeating the sort of nuclear missile rattling in which they had engaged during the Suez crisis. Third, defense officials continued to believe that Britain would be the best country in which to deploy them. And fourth, the Thors might convince the British to abandon Blue Streak. This would indirectly strengthen Western defense by preventing wasteful duplication and preserving British funds for conventional forces, while it would also head off what might become a fully independent British missile capability.[15]

The United States had, in short, a variety of political and military reasons for making the IRBM offer. For the man who mattered most, however, the political reasons carried much greater weight. Eisenhower had summarized his view of the IRBMs during the conference, explaining, according to official minutes, that the weapon was "one of tremendous psychological importance, although he was inclined still to discount its military significance." It appears from the context that Eisenhower was also speaking of missiles in general, as he did on other occasions, and that he meant more the psychological benefit of producing and having missiles than of deploying them abroad. Nevertheless, the key fact remains: Eisenhower still supported the deployment of IRBMs for political reasons—first, to develop a ballistic missile to facilitate the deterrence of Soviet *threats* as soon as possible, and second, to help repair the Anglo-American relationship.[16]

Senator William Knowland (R-Calif.) raised the issue of reaction in the rest of the NATO alliance in a meeting held upon Eisenhower's return from Bermuda. Dulles "thought there would be some but not great difficulty," because the United States already had nuclear weapons in Europe and because Britain was the best site for IRBMs. The president added that the United States should rely on indigenous crews for nuclear weapons whenever possible, by which he may have implied that additional IRBMs should be more widely deployed in western Europe. But Dulles's response was a little weak, for he neglected three points. First was the important difference between IRBMs and existing nuclear systems in NATO, namely, that the IRBMs could reach the Soviet Union proper. Second was the issue of joint control, which the British could now expect and which others might envy. And third, the other allies might not agree that Britain was the best site. One wonders how much serious thought Dulles, or any other senior official for that matter, devoted to this interaction of relations with Britain and relations with other NATO countries on the IRBM issue. Dulles's deputy undersecretary Robert Murphy had raised the question in January. He opposed making the IRBM offer until they "had more time to consider the best way to proceed with IRBM deployments in general, not only in the United Kingdom but elsewhere in the world." Such considerations thus did occur before Bermuda, but as in 1955, they had no effect. The United States offered IRBMs to Great Britain only—and Great Britain accepted.[17]

ORIGINS OF THE SECOND OFFER

Ike thought Bermuda had gone well. It "was by far the most successful international conference that [he] had attended since the close of World War II," he later recalled, one that did "much to restore Anglo-American understanding." Prime Minister Macmillan agreed. Yet one of the summit's main substantive accomplishments, the tentative IRBM agreement, made little headway toward finalization for some time thereafter.[18]

Although the United States had a draft IRBM agreement ready by mid-April, several issues combined to delay fulfillment of the Bermuda agreement into the fall of 1957. These included the costs, estimates of which soared during this period, and how they would be distributed; the manner in which the United States would provide the Thors, whether by sale or lend-lease; British interest in extending their range and ultimately perhaps equipping them with British warheads; physical control of the missiles; the conditions under which they would be used, including their relationship to NATO and its plans; target selection; and the timing of the agreement. The Thor was still in its development stage, and at least the U.S. side felt there was time to resolve these issues. But neither the U.S. nor the British government was determined to fulfill the Bermuda agreement immediately. Rather, each was content to allow detailed, third-level negotiations to proceed at a modest pace. The result was that by October 1957, six months after Bermuda, a formal IRBM agreement was still not in sight.[19]

Just as the Suez crisis had done the previous year, however, the launching of the Soviet satellite *Sputnik* provided a spark that reignited the issue of Thor deployments in Britain and, more important, led the Eisenhower administration to extend the IRBM offer to NATO as a whole.

The nuclear histories of the Eisenhower administration and NATO itself up to this point help make this multilateral IRBM concept easier to understand. Ike's declared national security strategy from the beginning, the New Look, had asserted that nuclear weapons would be considered conventional weapons. Similarly, the nuclearization of NATO had been under way since the early 1950s, with nuclear weapons being formally incorporated into alliance strategy in the key documents MC 48 (1954) and MC 14/2 (1957). "Nuclearization of the alliance," of course, meant that nuclear sharing of some sort was virtually unavoidable. At the December 1956 ministerial meeting of the NAC, several members had asked the United States to make available to the alliance nuclear weapons and short-range delivery systems for them. The Eisenhower administration agreed in April 1957 to do so under joint, "dual-key" arrangements. With the principle of progressive nuclearization thus firmly established, one cannot see a NATO IRBM offer as something completely new. The recent precedents no doubt led some officials to see it as the next logical step, if not just more of the same. An IRBM offer in fact was a departure in significant ways, but increasingly nuclear U.S. and NATO strategies provided an environment conducive to it, one that made it seem less extraordinary.[20]

With this trend in the background, the Soviets caused a sensation on 4 October 1957 by successfully launching *Sputnik*, by any measure a major event in the history of the Cold War. The breakthrough represented many things for the Soviets, including a major propaganda coup, proof of their technological sophistication, and most important, confirmation of their ICBM capability, which they had first demonstrated in August. For most Americans, *Sputnik* came as a rude wake-up call, one that would have lasting effects on everything from education and the space program to domestic politics and national self-confidence. For Ike, it also brought a sharp dip in his popularity, some severe public criticism, and sustained pressure to do more for national defense.[21]

In NATO Europe, *Sputnik* severely exacerbated what had become, by 1957, a fundamental problem confronting the Atlantic alliance: that even as NATO increased its dependence on nuclear weapons, European members increasingly doubted the reliability of the U.S. nuclear deterrent. Suez had made matters worse, especially in London and Paris; and then came *Sputnik*, which compounded the dilemma further because Soviet ICBMs could now threaten the United States itself with annihilation. If the Red Army attacked toward the Rhine, would the United States use its nuclear weapons and risk suicide, or let Europe fall in hope of surviving? Suddenly called into question, to an unprecedented degree, was nothing less than the credibility of the U.S. strategic guarantee, the foundation of Western defense in the Cold War. The already existing pressure on Washington to restore this credibility, perhaps through nuclear sharing, had swiftly mounted.[22]

One thing *Sputnik* had not changed was Eisenhower's general attitude toward IRBMs; indeed, the satellite only had a reinforcing effect. At an NSC meeting on 10 October, Ike "felt that such matters as deployment . . . were completely secondary to the determination by the United States to fire a 1,500-mile missile and hit something." He "stressed once again the great political and psychological advantage of the first achievement of an IRBM and an ICBM" and noted that the NSC had agreed from the beginning that such considerations outweighed the purely military ones.[23]

However, *Sputnik* had infused Ike's views of the IRBMs and of the nation's security in general with a greater sense of urgency. Although he refused to panic, as some others did, he realized he had to take steps to meet the new Soviet challenge. Thus when Macmillan, shortly after *Sputnik*, suggested that the time had come when progress could be made toward pooling efforts, for example, "in such things as nuclear weapons [and] ballistic missiles," Eisenhower and Dulles arranged another meeting with the prime minister, this time in Washington, to begin planning the allied response.[24]

The immediate origins of the NATO IRBM offer are not perfectly clear, but it seems that NATO's military chief, the Supreme Allied Commander, Europe (SACEUR), General Lauris Norstad (USAF), placed the idea before the administration sometime in October. Norstad had been surveying alliance defense policy for months and saw a need to counter the emerging Soviet IRBM threat against Europe and generally modernize NATO's forces. More important, he also wanted to satisfy emerging French interest in IRBMs. The French air force was, and would remain, ambivalent about these conspicuous "asparagus" dotting the countryside. Despite this, the French chief of staff, General Paul Ely, had raised the issue back in July with the departing JCS chair, Admiral Arthur Radford. Alluding to the U.S.-U.K. Thor proposal, Ely asked whether France could also obtain IRBMs, in order to avoid the costs of an indigenous program and better deter the Soviets from launching a limited war in Europe. The French followed up on 23 September with an aide-mémoire requesting the initiation of bilateral talks on the subject. After reviewing it during the next few months, the Joint Chiefs as well as the State and Defense Departments approved the concept of providing IRBMs to France, although not at the expense of the Thor deal with Britain. Thus, to match Soviet IRBMs, modernize NATO's deterrent, and meet the French request, Norstad hit upon the idea of providing IRBMs (minus their U.S.-controlled warheads) to the allies. This would be part of a larger program in which they would also gain the technical know-how necessary to produce, ultimately, their own missiles.[25]

Norstad's IRBM idea reached the White House at the right time, because his relatively narrow motivations merged with the broader motivation of Eisenhower and Dulles—restoring strategic credibility—to give it life. This is clear from a key meeting Eisenhower and Dulles held on 22 October, in which they discussed Macmillan's visit scheduled to begin the following day. The secretary of state, not surprisingly in light of the strategic implications of *Sputnik*, said it was now time to complete the Thor agreement with the British. But the context in which he expressed this opinion was new and

President Dwight D. Eisenhower (left) and Secretary of State John Foster Dulles. Their deep concern over U.S. strategic credibility in the wake of Sputnik *led them to offer nuclear missiles to the NATO allies under dual control. In their haste, they scarcely considered what the reactions might be on either side of the Iron Curtain. (National Park Service; courtesy Dwight D. Eisenhower Library)*

striking. What now concerned Dulles most was the condition of the entire Western alliance, particularly with regard to the nuclear question. Whereas Macmillan would want to play up the bilateral "special relationship," Dulles argued that whatever emerged from the visit had to demonstrate U.S. interest in all its allies. He sensed that they felt themselves caught between an increasing dependence on nuclear weapons and exclusion from decisions about their use.

These considerations led Dulles, first, to advocate creation of a NATO "nuclear stockpile." This concept, which General Norstad and then the French had originally proposed in 1956, envisaged a joint stockpile of nuclear weapons of several types, including tactical, aircraft- and artillery-delivered, and air defense, pre-positioned for NATO's use. Second, Dulles "felt it was time to close up the IRBM agreement with Britain and then to extend it to other countries." "We cannot," he continued, ". . . tell our alliances in effect that these new weapons are becoming conventional weapons, and at the same time tell them that they cannot have such weapons. . . . Now is the time for a decision in this matter—the alternative is that the alliance will fall apart." Not only did Dulles feel constrained by the New Look, but he also believed, with remarkable conviction, that the very survival of the alliance rested on this question. The president agreed, hoping to use the Macmillan meeting as an occasion to tell the American people more about "the significance of these weapons," to educate them that they were becoming conventional and that the United States could not deny them to its allies. For Eisenhower and Dulles, the logic of heavy U.S. reliance on nuclear weapons, and more important, the strains they thought *Sputnik* had placed on the alliance, pointed to a single solution: nuclear sharing with NATO Europe. IRBMs, having already been offered to Britain and constituting the earliest possible counters to Soviet strategic missiles, would be the obvious choice for thus recoupling American and European security.[26]

In addition, an important side effect of the March 1957 Bermuda offer was now making itself felt: the commitment to Britain had created pressure to extend the deployment to NATO. The administration was well aware of this problem. As we have seen, Dulles had been exposed to it at the time of Bermuda. The French confirmed its existence within months when they expressed interest in the missiles. In July, Dulles had shown that he grasped the logic involved, commenting publicly that rather than share nuclear weapons bilaterally, it would be "more appropriate" to do so, "if possible, as a NATO matter, which would not involve drawing lines of distinction . . . between different allies. That becomes an invidious process." It was an astute description, unfortunately, of the very course Dulles was helping to steer. The problem was not one of recognition, but one of action. Dulles realized the danger in letting the special relationship result in special treatment, but he failed to act on that awareness before it was too late. He had thus initially pursued a policy that now, several months later, helped make the extension of that policy difficult to avoid.[27]

THE EISENHOWER–MACMILLAN MEETING, OCTOBER 1957

Prime Minister Macmillan arrived in Washington for three days of talks on 23 October. According to the minutes of their meetings, he and Eisenhower agreed that "the whole free world" needed "a 'shot in the arm'" and "ways to rid itself of its state of semi-paralysis" in the wake of *Sputnik*. Eisenhower and Dulles again expressed their concerns about Anglo-American nuclear exclusivity and its effects on the other allies, emphasizing the widening gap between their substantial dependence and their lack of authority. The British shared these worries, and with the "Declaration of Common Purpose" they issued afterward, the two leaders approved intensified cooperation extending beyond the Anglo-American relationship, indeed even beyond NATO to other alliances such as SEATO. The declaration also hinted vaguely at increased multilateral nuclear cooperation, but it contained nothing about IRBMs per se. The most tangible result of the meetings was "the great prize" Macmillan had most wanted: Eisenhower's agreement to seek amendments to the McMahon Act to allow greater sharing of nuclear information between their two countries. The leaders also agreed to establish a "study group" that they clearly intended to expedite the Thor deployment to Britain, although a formal agreement would not be signed until February 1958.[28]

The declaration also suggested, finally, that the regular December meeting of the NAC in Paris, at which the entire Western alliance could continue the discussion, might "be given a special character." What this meant became plain shortly thereafter when NATO secretary-general Paul-Henri Spaak publicly proposed that, for the first time in the pact's eight years of existence, the heads of government themselves attend the meeting. Spaak had been in Washington at the same time and discussed the notion with Macmillan, Eisenhower, and Dulles. Although publicly they credited Spaak with the idea, it was Dulles who had hatched it, even before the Macmillan visit. Such a summit, he had argued, would "almost compel constructive thinking and planning," and Eisenhower agreed that it might give NATO "a lift." It would also become, as Robert Divine notes, "the main American diplomatic response to *Sputnik*."[29]

THE ROAD TO THE NATO SUMMIT, NOVEMBER–DECEMBER 1957

Attendance by the heads of government, of course, would render the conference a high-profile affair, one sure to attract close attention on all sides. That was part of the intent behind it. However, it was just as likely to raise expectations as well. Thus in a manner vaguely reminiscent of the Bermuda conference, once the Eisenhower administration decided to transform the December meeting into a major event, the most important opportunity for demonstrating alliance cohesion as unanswered *Sputniks* circled the planet, it felt compelled to lend the meeting substance of some sort in order to produce the desired psychological effect. From SACEUR, General Norstad, Eisenhower had heard in late October that the United States would "need some good 'fill in' material" at the conference. Robert Murphy touted the

IRBM offer because of the "political benefit": "Psychologically, we needed some specific action which could be taken at the . . . meeting to dramatize the defense posture of NATO." This sort of thinking tended, beyond the merits of the IRBMs themselves, to reinforce the decision to make the NATO offer.[30]

As the proposal emerged in early November, few if any dissenting voices were heard in or around the administration, certainly none in the top ranks. While they might differ over details, State, Defense, and the Joint Chiefs of Staff all seem to have supported it, as did officials then completing a major study of U.S. overseas bases and the authors of the famous "Gaither Report," submitted to Eisenhower on 7 November. Despite its primary concern over reducing the vulnerability of the U.S. strategic deterrent, and the derogatory information on IRBMs it had received, the Gaither group recommended an increase in the number of IRBMs produced from 60 to 240 and the deployment of at least some of them overseas as quickly as possible. The president rejected the report's main recommendations, but to the extent that it otherwise represented alternative, solicited views on national security, the document reflects a broad official consensus behind the IRBM proposal as it took shape.[31]

Within the North Atlantic alliance, however, no such consensus obtained, for while allied governments did fret about the U.S. nuclear guarantee, and while they certainly hoped for a December summit producing real accomplishments, an agreement to base IRBMs on their territory was not what most of them had in mind. After Dulles and Defense Secretary Neil McElroy made the first public mentions of the missile offer on 5 and 15 November, respectively, the allied response was mixed. The dissenting governments were moved by a combination of strategic logic, domestic opposition, and, from the Soviets, alternating offers of disarmament and threats of destruction.[32]

The Europeans' objections assumed several forms. First and most basic, many felt that IRBMs would transform a host country into a prime target in case of war. Second, who would decide to launch the missiles? Would host countries enjoy a real measure of control? As a Herblock cartoon updated the old game, "Button, Button, Who Gets the Button?" Third, many believed other moves such as political consultation, conventional force expansion, or renewed disarmament talks with the Soviets should top the summit agenda rather than an agreement to station IRBMs in Europe. A few governments also complained about the advance publicity given the offer, about having first learned of it from the newspapers, or, particularly in the case of France, about receiving the missiles in the NATO context when the British Thor agreement existed separately.[33]

These objections translated into potential refusal by enough countries to overshadow potential acceptance by any others. A rough tally of potential hosts' attitudes going into the conference would look like this: three countries more or less in favor (France, the Netherlands, and Turkey); six countries doubtful or ambivalent (Belgium, the Federal Republic of Germany, Greece, Italy, Luxembourg, and Portugal); and two countries opposed (Denmark and Norway). This distribution was not disastrous; the United States would need only a few host countries for deployment anyway, and a refusal to base missiles on one's territory would not preclude one's acceptance in principle of missiles for the alliance. But of those favorably inclined, only Turkey was enthusiastic. And most important, the mixed response amounted to neither the reality of support nor the appearance of unity that the Eisenhower administration wanted. A proposal intended to help bind the alliance together had, already before the Paris conference, caused considerable division.[34]

The administration quickly sensed and attempted to accommodate the lukewarm reaction. "It would be quite wrong to assume that Europe wants these missiles, or is ready to receive them," Dulles remarked privately, and candidly, on 26 November. "They are not pressing us to get missiles to them right away." But the Europeans did want to know, he believed, that the United States was "keeping up technically." This was an argument, however, for providing them with information about U.S. progress, not for actually supplying them with missiles. Nevertheless, Dulles still argued that it "would mean something" to the allies if they were to learn "that they could have missiles in 1958" and that U.S. bomber superiority would be quite adequate until 1960. Perhaps he feared, the logic of his assessment of European attitudes notwithstanding, that a mere report on U.S. missile programs would fall short of the alliance-strengthening substance needed for the auspicious NATO meeting.[35]

On 19 November, Dulles publicly tried to deny the existence of opposition in NATO, although in reality he recognized it all too clearly. "Obviously we are not going to force these missiles on anybody that doesn't want them," he noted, adding that "there would be a very considerable measure of allied participation in the handling of these missiles." The administration already found itself trying to walk a fine line on the control issue. It had to assure NATO members that they would enjoy something approximating a veto over the decision to launch, while at the same time promising domestic audiences, especially powerful lawmakers, that NATO members would not have such a veto. The administration solved the problem by doing both.[36]

In the meantime, the administration could not ignore domestic politics. Between 25 and 27 November, McElroy proposed and Eisenhower approved production of both the Thor and the Jupiter, four squadrons of each, despite their virtually identical characteristics. Dual production would, it is true, hedge against one program failing as well as yield more finished missiles at an earlier date. But this "settlement" of the long-standing Thor-Jupiter controversy was a costly surrender to interservice rivalry, public anxiety, and mounting congressional criticism of the administration's overall defense effort. It is no coincidence that the administration committed to dual production just as opposition Democrats launched a series of well-publicized Senate hearings on the impact of *Sputnik*. In private, McElroy stated flatly that the "chief reason" for dual production was psychological: "to stiffen the confidence and allay the concern particularly of our own people. Militarily, the acceleration is not needed." Dulles agreed: "The great excitement over missiles is not in Europe but over here. . . . [Our real concern] is not the Europeans but rather our own people, who feel exposed to attack for the first time."[37]

It is less clear whether this public and congressional pressure affected the offer to *deploy missiles in Europe*. McElroy and Vice President Richard Nixon predicted that Congress would demand early deployment of a squadron in Europe, and McElroy was careful to assure lawmakers, "We are going to do everything we can to get these . . . missiles on bases in Western Europe at the earliest practicable date." Yet there is no evidence that Congress was directly interested in or pushed the administration to secure any particular IRBM deployment. It focused its attention more broadly on the strategic arms race and administration defense policies. Similarly, the American public does not appear to have strongly desired the distribution of missiles. The most relevant question posed by the Gallup poll, two to three weeks before the NATO summit—"Would you favor or oppose a plan to exchange information on H-bombs, rockets, and guided missiles" with the NATO nations?—indicated no consensus: 44 percent in favor, 37 percent opposed, and 19 percent no opinion.[38]

The powerful domestic demands that helped spur dual IRBM production, however, cannot be completely dismissed in explaining the offer to NATO. Policymakers did not always rigidly segregate the production and deployment issues in their thinking, just as it is unclear which constituency motivated them at a given moment: domestic, allied, or both. What had been true in 1955 remained true after *Sputnik*: IRBMs manufactured were useless unless deployed somewhere, so direct domestic pressure to churn out missiles amounted to indirect pressure to deploy them around the Soviet Union.

Suffice it to say that neither the decision to produce sixty Thors and sixty Jupiters nor the post-*Sputnik* domestic climate did anything to impede the progress of the NATO IRBM offer.

Despite the early signs of a mixed reaction in Europe, the administration had to admit, in now–Deputy Defense Secretary Quarles's words, that the IRBM deployments were still "really the crux of the forthcoming NATO meeting." And in any case, policymakers still viewed the IRBMs primarily in political and psychological terms. McElroy spoke of propping up "the morale of [U.S.] Allies," making them "feel" defended, and impressing them with U.S. resolve to match Soviet ICBMs with IRBMs. Dulles, as before, argued that if the U.S. delegation in Paris tabled an IRBM offer, "the effect would be very reassuring." It is almost as if policymakers were unwilling to allow contrary signals, from allies supposedly needing reassurance, to disturb their assumptions about what those allies would find reassuring.[39]

As if these pressures and uncertainties were not enough, U.S. preparations were temporarily dealt another setback when, on 25 November, Eisenhower suffered a stroke. He bounced back with remarkable speed and was able to make it to Paris, but his questionable health only heightened presummit anxiety and publicity on both sides of the Atlantic.

By early December, Dulles's fears for the alliance had become even more acute. Whereas he had at first opposed Eisenhower's attendance of the NATO conference because of his health, he now "urged that the President should take all possible care of himself so as to be able to go." Indeed, the secretary asserted that Ike's presence "should in itself provide a rejuvenation of NATO," that it *was* "the main importance of the meeting." Dulles was no doubt coming to believe that the meeting could not have its bolstering effect with Eisenhower absent. Still more striking is a shift he almost made on the issue of warhead custody. At the time of the Macmillan visit, Dulles had thought it unnecessary to go as far as relinquishing warhead control to allied countries. Yet while in Paris, according to Randolph Burgess, the U.S. ambassador to NATO, Dulles wondered whether the United States was giving its allies enough: "I think we ought to go further in giving them authority with these nuclear weapons." His subordinates allegedly convinced him to abandon such radical thoughts, which certainly would not have survived U.S. domestic opposition in any case. But if Dulles expressed such views, they testify to a truly profound concern on his part about the state of NATO and what it might take to hold it together.[40]

Dulles was skeptical, even cynical, about the value of the summit alone in this regard. While in Paris on the eve of the conference, he met with

Macmillan, who recorded, "[Dulles] seemed rather vague about this NATO meeting, and to be wondering whether we had been wise in 'writing it up' so much. He seemed to think it could be just a sort of 'jamboree.' We would accept the American nuclear rockets, give three cheers for ourselves and one for Uncle Sam and then go home." Although Macmillan added that Dulles was mainly worried about Eisenhower's health, his characterization suggests that Dulles now regretted having given the meeting such a grand form. But now it was too late; Dulles and Eisenhower could only hope for an impressive display of alliance unity and the smoothest possible acceptance of their proposals, chief among them the IRBM offer.[41]

THE SECOND OFFER: THE NATO HEADS OF GOVERNMENT MEETING, DECEMBER 1957

Although historians have given it scant attention, the Paris conference was a major event at the time. There in the Palais de Chaillot, world attention focused on Eisenhower and Dulles. And what they put on display, apart from the IRBM deployment, was the creation of the NATO atomic stockpile discussed earlier; a program for the pooling of scientific research, education, and training; and a plan for the cooperative production of modern weapons systems, including, ultimately, a European IRBM. Dulles also mentioned the possibility, pending U.S. legislative approval, of joint development and production of nuclear-powered submarines. Beyond these proposals, Dulles merely stressed the importance of continued force contributions, liaison among the various alliances, and increased political consultation. The IRBM offer, in short, did not stand alone, but it clearly towered over the rest of the U.S. package in terms of notoriety. It was what drew people's attention—for better or worse.[42]

The IRBM offer had evolved from the specific to the vague. U.S. officials, understandably, had not decided several issues concerning IRBMs for NATO, including their mode (mobile or fixed, exposed or "hardened"), financing, the number to be deployed, and therefore total cost. At no point had they considered negotiating details with potential host countries at the summit. The State and Defense Departments already had their preferences regarding deployment locations, but in light of the opposition in NATO and the resulting uncertainty, State put off compiling its list until after the summit. The offer had originally mentioned dates of deployment and numbers of squadrons; in a mid-November draft, the United States would do its "utmost to make available" one squadron by December 1958 and four more in 1959 and

1960. But with only a crash program of prohibitive cost capable of promising missiles so soon, and with expectations of lengthy negotiations over bases and other details, this specificity quickly eroded. Soon the deployment was described as beginning in "the latter part" of 1959 and comprising "several squadrons." By the time Dulles actually announced the offer—apparently drafted by Norstad—on the opening day of the summit, dates and quantities had disappeared completely, and the offer overall was extremely imprecise:

> If this council so desires, and in order to strengthen NATO's deterrent power, the United States is prepared to make available to other NATO countries intermediate-range ballistic missiles, for deployment in accordance with the plans of SACEUR. Nuclear warheads for these IRBM's will become a part of the NATO atomic stockpile system.
>
> Such IRBM deployment would be subject to agreement between SACEUR and the countries directly concerned and to agreement between each such country and the United States with respect to material, training, and other necessary arrangements.
>
> We expect to be able to deliver intermediate-range missiles as soon as the NATO nations in which they would be deployed are ready to receive them.[43]

For the moment, however, the offer ran into what the administration viewed as the greatest obstacle at the conference: the interest several NATO governments expressed in talks with the Soviet Union. Leading the charge was the Norwegian prime minister, Einar Gerhardsen, who advocated postponing a decision on IRBMs to allow the Soviets "an opportunity to prove their willingness to enter into serious negotiations." Supporting Gerhardsen was his Danish counterpart, Hans Christian Hansen. Others, including West Germany's Konrad Adenauer, Secretary-General Spaak, and indeed Harold Macmillan himself, expressed a general openness to negotiations, although they stopped short of linking the IRBM to them.[44]

These leaders were largely responding to a shrewdly timed series of public letters that each of them, including Eisenhower, had received from Soviet premier Nikolai Bulganin less than a week before the conference. Bulganin (which is to say First Secretary Nikita Khrushchev, for whom Bulganin was by now a mere figurehead) clearly intended the notes to split NATO and derail the IRBM offer. They combined less than subtle threats of devastation with various conciliatory proposals, including a nuclear test moratorium, a superpower summit, and a nuclear weapon–free zone in central Europe, this last initiative an echo of the "Rapacki Plan." Despite the accompanying

A "sort of 'jamboree'"? The NATO heads of government meeting, Paris, December 1957. The allies were lukewarm toward the IRBM offer and unanimously accepted it in principle only after the Americans gave in on the question of negotiations with the Soviets. (G. D'Amato and J. Dear, Supreme Headquarters, Allied Powers Europe; courtesy Dwight D. Eisenhower Library)

threats, the Kremlin's seemingly peaceful gestures had great appeal and appeared to many serious enough to warrant discussion at least.[45]

By contrast, the Eisenhower administration scarcely responded at all. Although Ike in particular did maintain a sporadic interest in pursuing a nuclear test ban, such topics as disarmament and such means as negotiation hardly dominated the administration's thinking during this period—thus its apparent failure to consider using the IRBMs at this stage as a bargaining chip with Khrushchev. Eisenhower and Dulles also regarded a superpower summit as pointless because they felt nothing would come of it, at least not without serious progress achieved by talks at lower levels beforehand. In short, they assumed the Bulganin proposals to be a ploy and displayed little interest in finding out for sure one way or another.[46]

The U.S. delegation realized by the second day of the conference, however, that if it was to secure *unanimous* acceptance of the general IRBM proposal—which would be necessary for its inclusion in the conference communiqué—it was going to have to relent on negotiations. Behind the scenes,

Macmillan said as much to Dulles, who reluctantly agreed. Domestic parliamentary pressures to seek a relaxation of international tensions were too much for several governments to resist. On 18 December, Norway, with Denmark again following its lead, did withdraw its call for postponement and signed on to a general endorsement of the missile proposal (although it remained a virtual certainty that neither country would offer its own territory for basing). Eisenhower and Dulles were greatly relieved, but they could still not avoid giving in on the question of negotiations.[47]

Thus the conference communiqué released on the last day, 19 December, included the negotiation track in which the administration continued to place so little faith. The NAC declared that it would "neglect no possibility of restricting armaments within the limits imposed by security and . . . take all necessary action to this end." Alliance members also expressed their willingness to pursue talks with the USSR if they promised acceptable results, to examine any disarmament proposal from any source, and to meet "at the Foreign Ministers' level," should the Soviets refuse to take part in the recently restructured UN Disarmament Commission, "to resolve the deadlock." The language contained all the obvious escape clauses, so the alliance was hardly tying its hands. But it also paid lip service to the issue of negotiations and thus represented, to the U.S. delegation, a dilution of the defiant message it had wanted the summit to convey.[48]

On the other hand, the communiqué also accused the Soviets of blocking disarmament efforts while arming themselves to the teeth with nuclear weapons and missiles. The NAC declared that, as a result, it had no choice but to counter with such programs as the nuclear stockpile. "In view of the present Soviet policies in the field of new weapons," it continued, "the Council has also decided that intermediate range ballistic missiles will have to be put at the disposal of the Supreme Allied Commander Europe." Alliance military authorities were to submit recommendations on the deployments, and then later, in permanent session, the NAC would "consider the various questions involved."[49]

Dulles, for one, would have liked something more concrete; a week before the summit, with his famous bluntness, he had publicly admitted his distaste for an agreement in principle: "That means that you accept the general idea but you reserve the right to frustrate that idea by a lot of detailed objections." But an agreement in principle is all the United States could get, and all that it could have gotten. Anything more specific would have failed to gain unanimous approval and thus would not have made it into the final communiqué. In retrospect, the lack of specificity was a good thing for both

the United States and its allies, because it shunted some allies' expected refusal to base the missiles to a subsequent meeting, out of the spotlight.[50]

So in the end, the United States compromised with its allies; it made
concessions but got what it came for. The IRBM offer had been the center-
piece of the U.S. presentation, and its rejection would have been a major
embarrassment for Eisenhower. With the unanimous acceptance of IRBMs,
however general, he achieved his main objective. Coupled with the favorable
response of at least a few alliance members, he could expect the commitment
to result eventually in the deployment of some IRBMs. Even the concession on negotiations entailed little real cost; the communiqué wording there
was even less binding than that regarding the missiles. Finally, the administration could claim that the heads of government meeting had matched
Sputnik and shored up a sagging alliance, and the ability to make that *claim*
may have been the most useful result of all.

CONCLUSIONS

It remains, first, to assign relative importance to the various considerations
that went into the Eisenhower administration's decision to offer IRBMs to
NATO, and second, to make a preliminary assessment of that decision. For
the first task, a precise reconstruction of the decision is difficult, because the
evidence is far from complete. It is possible, however, to divide the reasons
for the decision into primary, secondary, and tertiary categories.

Primary, Secondary, and Tertiary Motives

The immediate cause of the IRBM decision was indisputably the Soviet
launch of *Sputnik*. That achievement set the events of late 1957 in motion;
without it, the United States might not have offered IRBMs to NATO at
all, and certainly not as early as it did; later the obsolescence of these first-
generation missiles might have precluded their deployment altogether. The
British Thor deployment had proceeded at a casual pace before 4 October
1957, and without the Soviet satellite, that pace would have persisted and
additional IRBMs might not have gone to NATO. With *Sputnik*, multiple
needs arose for the Eisenhower administration that IRBMs, the most sophisticated, strategic ballistic missiles *in short-term prospect* for the U.S. arsenal,
seemingly promised to help satisfy. As a result, the speed and breadth of the
IRBM deployments suddenly increased.[51]

That having been said, the most important motive behind the offer to
NATO was the need to restore U.S. strategic credibility in post-*Sputnik*

alliance politics. Eisenhower and especially Dulles were deeply alarmed by tension in the alliance stemming from the transatlantic disparity between nuclear haves and have-nots, nuclear decision makers and nuclear hostages, and the resulting loss of allied confidence in the U.S. strategic guarantee. Although these problems had existed for some time, *Sputnik* decisively exacerbated and dramatized them. Eisenhower and Dulles viewed IRBMs for NATO as first and foremost a means of narrowing, if not completely closing, this credibility gap.

Alongside this primary motive exist secondary considerations that, while not decisive, still significantly contributed to the decision. These include:

Intra-alliance equality. Not only did the administration intend IRBMs to buttress NATO by recoupling U.S. and European security; it also saw the missiles as establishing a balance within the alliance between Great Britain and the other European allies. France in particular was making it clear that fissures in the alliance were widening as the Anglo-American special relationship entered the nuclear realm. The Thor deal of March 1957 did not go unnoticed in other European capitals, and with it Eisenhower and Dulles had placed significant pressure on themselves to extend the IRBM offer to all the allies.

Need for substance at the NATO meeting. The October 1957 announcement that the upcoming NAC meeting would assemble the heads of government—a U.S. initiative—created a need for concrete U.S. proposals at that meeting. This seems to be a reason why they failed to consider a simple *declaration* that the United States was making significant progress in the missile field, even though several of their justifications of the NATO offer in fact only justified dispensing information, not missiles. A broad IRBM offer, by contrast, represented a real program, involving real weapons with real costs, commitments, and strategic impact.

At the tertiary level are several elements even less significant but deserving mention nonetheless:

Military utility. As taken as U.S. policymakers were with the political and psychological value of the missiles, the documents clearly suggest that they were unimpressed by their military utility. Most of the enthusiasm on military grounds was confined to the military itself. The administration refused to believe in an emerging "missile gap" and considered strategic bombers a sufficient deterrent until American ICBMs were ready. It was also quite aware of the interim nature of first-generation IRBMs (a characteristic underscored during the Paris summit when the United States successfully flight-tested an Atlas ICBM for the first time). The administration therefore saw IRBMs as stopping a military gap that was either fictitious or short term. It placed little stock in IRBMs as an asset in the arms race or as a counterweight to Soviet ICBMs. Nevertheless, military considerations cannot be dismissed. Most policymakers expected that the IRBMs would work; that despite their many drawbacks, they would increase the power of the U.S. strategic arsenal; that they would help offset the IRBMs that U.S. intelligence expected the Soviets to deploy in Europe in the near future; and that they promised, for at least some period of time, to be the only U.S. strategic missiles—if deployed quickly enough. But military considerations were definitely tertiary.[52]

Domestic politics. Although a direct role for domestic politics cannot be discounted completely, there is little evidence for it. However, the domestic reaction to *Sputnik* did cast a large shadow over almost everything the Eisenhower administration undertook in late 1957. Dual production of IRBMs resulted largely from domestic demands for a more vigorous defense effort; administration officials sometimes blurred the distinction between production and deployment, and perhaps understandably so, since the former only made sense with the latter; and a commitment to deploy IRBMs abroad was another positive, highly visible step the administration could take in response to *Sputnik* that might help restore confidence at home. For these reasons, public and congressional pressure exerted some indirect influence on the decision to make the offer to NATO.

The disposal problem. This piece of the domestic puzzle deserves elaboration. As mentioned at the outset, the decision to manufacture IRBMs had to play some role in any deployment decisions—but not necessarily a major role in any particular one. Settlement on production of both Thor and Jupiter was clearly not decisive, for the administration did not formally do so until 25 November—at least one month after Eisenhower and Dulles had begun discussing the NATO offer. This suggests that they would have made the offer even if only one type of IRBM had existed. Furthermore, the earlier Thor deal with Britain had "consumed," indeed, had determined the size of, the four-squadron force previously programmed. Thus in October 1957, there were no programmed IRBM squadrons still in need of base agreements. All this is not to say that the Jupiters did not create additional pressure to proceed with the NATO deployments after 25 November and after the December summit during the search for hosts; they probably did. But these considerations do tend to minimize, while not entirely ruling out, a role for the disposal problem in the origins of the NATO offer.

U.S. and NATO security strategies. There was nothing in the existing security strategies of the alliance or the Eisenhower administration that required the deployment of IRBMs in Europe. However, the New Look as well as MC 48 and MC 14/2 had declared a heavy reliance on nuclear weapons and thus had fostered an environment in which nuclear sharing in general and the IRBM offer in particular could more easily emerge. Dulles argued in effect that the New Look was transforming nuclear weapons into conventional ones and thus creating pressure for nuclear sharing. This position, coupled with an alliance formally committed to nuclearization, cleared the tracks for innovation of the type represented by the IRBM plan.

The decision, therefore, was propelled by a variety of considerations, direct and indirect, powerful and subtle. The strategic credibility problem in alliance politics that *Sputnik* had greatly sharpened, however, was central. Indeed, Eisenhower's and Dulles's deep, perhaps excessive concern for U.S. credibility in the alliance produced an ill-considered—and ultimately regrettable—decision to distribute strategic nuclear missiles.

The U.S. Decision and U.S. Decision Making
From the standpoint of late 1957, was the U.S. offer to NATO justified? Part of the answer to this difficult question lies in the alliance reaction. Had Eisenhower's proposal met with widespread enthusiasm, then one could argue that even though the IRBMs were at best interim weapons of dubious military value, the offer made sense because of the perceived political and psychological need created by *Sputnik*. But this was not the case. The immediate reaction in NATO was mixed, ranging from politely negative to noncommittal to positive. Only in one case, Turkey, was it enthusiastic, and nowhere did the Europeans' sense of urgency match that present in Washington. It therefore seems that Eisenhower was seeking to satisfy a legitimate need in an illegitimate way, by offering jointly controlled nuclear missiles capable of hitting Soviet territory. The reasons U.S. officials gave for deployment were mostly reasons for doing *something*, not necessarily for doing this in particular. A move intended to enhance alliance solidarity in fact caused disagreement. It is thus difficult to see how the offer was justified in terms of what the United States and the NATO alliance needed in late 1957.

The other part of the answer lies in the availability of options, for it is unfair to criticize policymakers who had no choice. However, even for the moment accepting the predicament in which Eisenhower and Dulles had placed themselves by calling the summit meeting, and the resulting need for a substantive proposal, the IRBM offer is questionable because other options existed. Perhaps the most feasible was suggested to Eisenhower by none other than Norstad, in late October, that is, before the administration announced the IRBM offer: the nuclear stockpile, standing alone and not in the shadow of the IRBM offer as actually occurred. After asserting the insufficiency of a mere communiqué, Norstad said, "In this connection, . . . although the NATO stockpile is no longer new, that could be the announcement the President would make." Here was an arguably viable alternative, a substantive proposal involving nuclear sharing, put forward by someone certainly well positioned to gauge what might do the trick, which nevertheless did not entail deployment of missiles scarcely sought by the allies and yet capable of hitting, and thus provoking, the Soviet Union. Therefore the IRBM proposal was necessary neither to satisfy some allied demand nor for lack of anything else to place on the table.[53]

The decision to offer the IRBMs was flawed at least in part because the administration's decision making on this issue was flawed as well, in three ways:

Inflexibility. First, the administration was not flexible enough to reconsider the offer when European opposition quickly arose. This opposition should have served as a warning that the offer was unnecessary. Dulles's and McElroy's November announcements might have been trial balloons, but they were not. Instead, they amounted to the presentation of an accomplished fact, and there is no evidence of official second thoughts after opposition formed. This, in turn, is partly a result of a second flaw:

Self-imposed limitation of options. Public announcement of the IRBM offer, tied as it was to a high-profile NATO summit, would have made reconsideration difficult even had the administration hesitated; it probably would have found withdrawal of the offer too embarrassing. But the administration helped tie its hands with other decisions as well. The decision to produce an IRBM made friendly countries in Europe prime candidates to host the missiles. Similarly, the resulting decision to deploy IRBMs in Britain in turn created, particularly in Dulles's eyes, a powerful need to extend the IRBM deployment to NATO as a whole.

Insufficient prior evaluation. Such decisions might not have been made when or how they were had the administration thought them through ahead of time. This was the greatest overall weakness in U.S. decision making. It is, of course, difficult to prove that the administration devoted insufficient attention to all aspects of the offer beforehand, and evidence may yet emerge demonstrating otherwise. But the documents now available offer remarkably few signs of prior consideration. The administration had to hurry to have the proposal ready in time for the Paris summit, and the Joint Chiefs understandably expressed concern about the rush. Not until 6 December—long after the administration had committed itself to making the IRBM offer—did the JCS order their Joint Intelligence Committee to estimate the probable Soviet reaction to a NATO IRBM deployment. Similarly, only on 15 December, the eve of the conference, did JCS chair Nathan Twining receive and propose changes in the major Eisenhower-Dulles presentation. Thus Marc Trachtenberg's suggestion, that the decision "did not receive anything like the attention it deserved" before it was made, seems most fitting.[54]

This lack of forethought, in turn, manifested itself in several ways:

Reliance on assumption. Eisenhower and Dulles perceived problems that were real: *Sputnik*'s immediate effects at home and abroad, and NATO's loss of confidence in the U.S. deterrent. The alliance may even have been as fragile as Dulles believed, although this is impossible to determine. The problem was not the diagnosis, though, but the prescription. The administration based it on an assumption that IRBMs in Europe would help cure the malady, but it did not investigate whether the patient was somewhat allergic. This seems to be one of those instances in the Cold War when the United States assumed that what it was doing was best for its allies without bothering first to find out what those allies thought.

Lack of internal debate. Often a good way to produce good policy is to subject it to rigorous debate, but Eisenhower's administration seems to have skipped that step in this case. Rather, a broad consensus on the NATO offer went unchallenged. There is no evidence that any top policymaker played devil's advocate or forced proponents to answer any serious questions about the policy. Low- and mid-level officials may have produced relevant studies, but there is no evidence that they sparked any critical discussion at the top.[55]

Failure to account for interplay of external actors. As is often the case, the administration found itself playing a multilevel game: the United States was interacting with Great Britain, NATO, and the Soviet Union simultaneously; IRBM decisions taken with regard to one of these affected the others in unforeseen ways. The bilateral offer Ike made to Macmillan in Bermuda helped create the perception that a broader IRBM proposal to NATO was needed. That initiative, in turn, helped stimulate a response from the Soviet Union, of which the December 1957 Bulganin notes were merely a first taste. And that Soviet response, finally, fed back into the Paris summit and complicated the allies' acceptance of the U.S. proposal. No policymaker can fully predict the outcomes of a particular policy. But the administration should have been more alert to the interplay of actors as prominent as the other NATO allies and the Soviet Union.

Policy driven by crisis. In the absence of top-level planning, the IRBM decision was driven by political crisis; in fact, there is a broad symmetry between the two 1957 IRBM offers in this regard. Twice in one twelve-month period, political crises intervened decisively, albeit in different ways, to revive what had been dormant or sluggish IRBM deployment efforts. First, the bilateral crisis stemming from Suez in late 1956 led to the bilateral offer in Bermuda. Then, a multilateral crisis caused by *Sputnik* resulted in the multilateral offer in Paris. The United States had been in no particular hurry to arrange for the missiles' deployment; after all, they were still in their development phases. Political crises were therefore critical in forming a sense of urgency, creating needs that nuclear weapons promised to help satisfy in their auxiliary role as political tools. There is nothing inherently wrong with the political use of nuclear weapons, of course, but the Eisenhower administration seems to have allowed external events, rather than a careful examination of the missiles' merits, to determine its basic IRBM deployment policy.

In fairness to Eisenhower and Dulles, the IRBMs did not occupy the center of their policymaking universe. The missiles constituted but one part of the administration's response to *Sputnik*; that response was but one part of its complex foreign policy; foreign policy itself had to contend with domestic events for the president's attention. Eisenhower wrote to a friend on 18 November that he could not "remember a day" since mid-1956 that had not "brought its major or minor crisis." Eisenhower's burdens, however, do not excuse the weaknesses in his IRBM policy, for he did not have to make the NATO summit a major foreign policy event that demanded substantive proposals on short notice. He did not have to include the IRBM offer among those proposals. Judging from the reaction in NATO, he did not have to offer IRBMs as the solution to the undeniable credibility problem. This was a major, unprecedented initiative, and it deserved a closer, less hurried look.[56]

Finally, the curious reality that unfolded in late 1957 bears reemphasizing: Eisenhower was committing the United States to deploying in Europe military systems he considered as having little military value. After leaving office he would, of course, defend the IRBMs and their placement in Europe — on military grounds. Their "military value would, for the time being, be practically equal" to that of ICBMs, he wrote in his memoirs. "While vulnerable to surprise attack," the IRBMs nevertheless "gave the Free World a strong missile capability while the longer-range ICBMs were being devised." He wrote about the Thors that "in later days of concern over Soviet ICBM development," they "would serve as a powerful deterrent to any atomic transgression by the Communists." At the time, however, he privately expressed a different view. He repeatedly stressed the "political and psychological" importance of developing and deploying IRBMs, including the recoupling of U.S. and European security, while questioning their military worth. He recognized not only that they were vulnerable but that they "would be prime targets for an enemy attack." He knew, in short, that the missiles promised at best a limited military dividend, which was unfortunate in view of the political "cost overruns" apparent already at the time of the NATO summit.[57]

Yet a full assessment of the decision to deploy IRBMs in NATO Europe requires a look into what came next: an effort lasting nearly two years to identify and reach agreement with countries that would actually host the missiles. The difficulty Eisenhower and Dulles encountered in making the IRBM offer would pale in comparison.

2

TRYING TO DUMP
THEM ON OUR ALLIES

It is a very elaborate and complicated business . . .
in the case of the British; it has taken us now almost
a year to negotiate that agreement. Of course,
having done it once with the British, it ought to be
easier to do it the second time with the French.
John Foster Dulles, 9 January 1958

The President said one thing . . . bothering him
a great deal . . . is the plan to put IRBMs in Greece.
If Mexico or Cuba had been penetrated by the
Communists, and then began getting arms and
missiles from them, we would . . . look on such
developments with the gravest concern and . . .
it would be imperative for us to take positive action,
even offensive military action. . . . He wondered
if we were not simply being provocative.
Memorandum of conference, 16 June 1959

Whether the NATO conference of December 1957 was a "success" for U.S. diplomacy, as Eisenhower and one historian later claimed, is debatable. The president and his secretary of state probably gained some ground in terms of public relations, but they then quickly managed to lose much of it upon returning to Washington. On 23 December, they briefed the American people about the summit in a joint television appearance, and like many in the age before Hollywood successfully tutored Washington, it was a dismal performance. After Ike's brief introduction, Dulles droned on for twenty minutes as his boss, on camera throughout, fidgeted next to him. Harry S. Truman spoke for many when he quipped the next day that he was "just about as thoroughly bored with Mr. Dulles as the President was." The presentation pointed up Eisenhower's larger failure to use the Paris conference to help lift public and allied confidence from their presummit condition.[1]

This was unfortunate for his administration, because without continued benefits for Western morale, the major legacy of the summit was an IRBM plan still on the drawing board. After all, the December 1957 offer was merely a down payment; as the new year dawned, the United States now had to deliver the balance. Therefore, just as the Anglo-American statement of purpose in Bermuda had led to protracted negotiations on the details of the Thor deployment in the United Kingdom, so did the December 1957 NATO communiqué set in motion a drawn-out search for host countries. This effort, however, was a journey even more prolonged, and even more torturous, than its predecessor.

Speed was an important concern to U.S. policymakers, for two reasons. First, they obviously felt an immediate need to strengthen confidence in their post-*Sputnik* strategic deterrent. This was particularly true of top military officials, who wanted all of the programmed American IRBMs in place as soon as possible, which meant having all the necessary agreements completed as soon as finished IRBMs rolled off the lines at Chrysler and Douglas

Aircraft. The Joint Chiefs believed that "the military risk of locating the initial IRBM units on unhardened bases [was] justified by the political and psychological advantages that accrue[d] from *the early deployments*." Second, officials remained quite aware of the first-generation IRBMs' interim nature. Because of this, for example, Norstad opposed inclusion of a complete IRBM deployment program in NATO's five-year force requirement plans. With the first Atlas ICBMs now scheduled to become operational in June 1959, and the first three Polaris submarines (armed with sixteen SLBMs each) by late 1960, the administration would have to conclude IRBM agreements and get them deployed quickly if the missiles were to fulfill their stopgap role for any significant period.[2]

Speed, however, ran up against the difficulty of actually reaching agreements with individual allies, a situation administration officials anticipated in some measure. To outsiders, they expressed their confidence that, as Dulles told Senator Lyndon Johnson, they would get missiles where they needed them. But all too aware of how long the Thor negotiations had taken with the British—the formal agreement was not signed until 22 February 1958, almost a full year after Bermuda—policymakers knew better than that. Mindful of the presummit opposition among the allies, Dulles even before Paris had acknowledged "there was a real danger" that the quest for missile bases "could become a serious political issue." Although known for his overstatements, he had a gift for understatement as well.[3]

THE SOVIET REACTION

A cartoon in the *London Daily Herald* captured the situation well. Amid crumbling ancient columns on the Mediterranean shore, two men in shirtsleeves pore over "Plans for Rocket Sites in Greece and Italy." One looks over his shoulder to find standing there Nikita Khrushchev, cradling in his arm one of the IRBMs he is threatening to ship to Albania in response. Pointing to the missile, the Soviet premier asks, "Want some more ruins?"[4]

During the search for hosts, the Soviets issued numerous threats against potential NATO IRBM hosts that were scarcely more subtle. In addition to wielding the stick, however, they dangled a few carrots. Soviet leaders did not like the idea of NATO IRBMs pointing at them, and with this blend of bribes and threats they sought to block the deployments or, failing that, to make them as difficult as possible. They thus created an important context in which the search for bases took place: prospective IRBM hosts had to consider the offer and then, if they accepted in principle, negotiate the details, without ever being certain how they might be punished, or what gain might be denied them, by the Kremlin. For the United States, the Soviet response not only hampered the search for hosts but reflected an additional strain the IRBMs had placed on the superpower relationship.

The reaction was predictable. The Soviets had always raised a fuss about NATO's actions; in the spring of 1957, for example, they had sent warnings to several NATO members as they prepared to receive tactical nuclear weapons. By this time, however, Soviet protests had acquired a boy-who-cried-wolf quality. When Admiral Radford argued, "We do not need to worry too much about Soviet blackmailing of our allies in order to render our overseas bases in their territories untenable," Ike apparently agreed, noting that "the Soviets had been writing the same threatening letters to [America's] allies as long as six years ago." When it made the NATO IRBM offer toward the end of that year, his administration was not predisposed to take Soviet complaints too seriously.[5]

After the heads of government meeting, the administration did exhibit some sensitivity to the possible Soviet reaction, at one point even in its official policy. In March 1958, while the NSC reaffirmed the wisdom of IRBM deployments "around the Sino-Soviet periphery" in reviewing U.S. policy on overseas bases, it also resolved that such deployment must be "carefully planned" to avoid having the Soviets interpret U.S. motives as aggressive and thus "feel obliged to react violently." Eisenhower then strongly supported a change in the official policy to the effect that the implications of IRBM deployment were "of such import that a decision to do so should be made through NSC procedures, only in light of the over-all advantages and disadvantages." The president thus disputed the view of some officials "that this was solely a military matter," and the NSC approved the new language. The extent to which the administration would allow this political sensitivity to influence its IRBM policy remained to be seen.[6]

The intelligence community gave little reason for circumspection. In April 1958, the Office of National Estimates issued a Special National Intelligence Estimate (SNIE) on the Soviet reaction to the IRBMs—again, a work most likely commissioned, and definitely submitted, only after the administration had decided to offer IRBMs to NATO. It framed the issue in the manner of the worries expressed in mid-March: Would the Soviets interpret IRBM deployments as portending U.S. aggression? Would they react violently or in such a way as to increase the risk of war? The SNIE's answer to these questions was no. It accurately gauged the Soviets' emerging anti-IRBM propaganda campaign and predicted they would consider the missiles "a substantial addition to western capabilities," but it failed to probe very deeply into how the Soviets might react along the spectrum between propaganda and force.[7]

Thus this SNIE, the most important study of its type, did nothing to change the approach of U.S. policymakers. On the one hand, they were concerned over Soviet reaction in the abstract, and this influenced policy to some extent in individual cases. On the other hand, because the Soviet reaction did not seem likely to include force, overall they were indifferent toward it.

The Soviet reaction sorely tested the limits of this indifference. Its "scope and intensity," as Michael Armacost writes, "were virtually without precedent."[8] For two extended periods, in early 1958 and early 1959, the Soviet government laid down a steady barrage of statements, speeches, and diplomatic notes aimed at snuffing out the NATO IRBM threat before it materialized. Often the Soviet rhetoric seemed indiscriminate, targeting all of NATO's nuclear-tipped missiles or all U.S. overseas bases, but obviously the IRBMs, uniquely capable of reaching Soviet territory, inspired most of it.

Phase one of the campaign, kicked off in grand fashion with the Bulganin letters right before the NATO summit, rested on two classic divisive strategies: split Western European publics from their governments and those governments from the United States. In pursuit of these objectives, the Soviets waged, with varying intensity, a peace offensive in which they repeatedly called for summit meetings, a nuclear test ban, establishment of a Rapacki-type nuclear-free zone, and international harmony in an attempt to appear as reasonable and conciliatory as possible. Against this background, they publicly issued numerous statements about NATO IRBMs. The missiles, they asserted, would have grave consequences for host countries, straining relations with the Soviet Union and neighboring neutral countries in peace and bringing nuclear destruction in war. They might, in West Germany's case, prevent German reunification, although they would present no problem if central Europe were made into a nuclear-free zone. They were so vulnerable to attack that they did not frighten the Soviets. The United States was forcing them upon the Europeans, in order to divert Soviet nuclear strikes toward its "cannon fodder" allies. Countries such as Greece ought to reject them in favor of the "sensible course" adopted by atomophobic Norway and Denmark. They might trigger matching Soviet deployments in Eastern Europe. And finally, they would in reality come under sole control of the Americans, allowing them to start a war from a host country's territory without its knowledge.[9]

After a comparative lull in the latter half of 1958, the Soviets resumed their anti-IRBM effort in the spring of 1959, which saw the first bilateral IRBM agreement (with Italy), nuclear stockpile agreements with West Germany, Greece, Turkey, and the Netherlands, and a foreign ministers conference on Germany. The Soviets repeated their approach of the previous year but with some new emphases and tactics. They directed much of their effort toward West Germany, charging in April that its impending nuclearization was intended to torpedo the foreign ministers conference upcoming in Geneva. Then at the conference, especially during its first half (11 May–20 June), Soviet foreign minister Andrei Gromyko made it clear that the provision of "atomic and rocket weapons" to the "revanchist" government in Bonn was, for his superiors, the main source of alarm and the main motivation for seeking to resolve the broader German issue.[10]

Beyond Geneva, the Soviets focused on the Mediterranean, sending threatening notes to Italy, Turkey, and Greece, urging Greece to become a neutral country, and threatening to deploy their own IRBMs in Albania and Bulgaria. As with Poland and the Rapacki Plan the previous year, they drew their satellite regimes into the campaign, portraying NATO missiles as a threat to them as well. Khrushchev prevailed upon the regimes in Bulgaria and Romania to propose for the Balkans a prime ministers conference, a collective security treaty, and a nuclear-free zone. This tactic had the side benefit of reinforcing the satellites' sense of dependence on Soviet protection while at the same time, by letting them put forward some of the proposals, safely increasing their sense of autonomy.[11]

The Soviets' campaign, however, did not remain in the realm of public diplomacy. In 1959, they also made use of private channels at the highest levels, as did Deputy Premier and close Khrushchev ally Anastas Mikoyan when he visited the United States in January. He told Dulles that he "did not think the United States wanted war now," but its bases around the Soviet Union made him worry about the future. After all, "these bases were not there to play football." Later Mikoyan asked why the United States was arming them with nuclear weapons, a policy about which his country "could not remain tranquil." Dulles replied that he need not fear U.S. aggression from allied countries; with the latest missiles, "it made no practical difference whether a base were nearby or far away"; and countries close to the Soviet Union "naturally" wanted proof of U.S. protection nearby. "This was more of psychological than of great practical significance," Dulles summarized with remarkable candor. When an engine on Mikoyan's homeward plane caught fire, it made an emergency landing in Argentia, Newfoundland, a U.S. outpost. "Maybe [he] won't yell so loud about our overseas bases from now on," Dulles quipped.[12]

Khrushchev himself complained privately about NATO bases when he played host to Averell Harriman and Richard Nixon that summer. "You have surrounded us with bases," he warned Harriman in June, "but our rockets can destroy them. If you want a war, we may die but the rockets will fly automatically." Harriman was impressed with how successfully the official line had permeated Soviet public opinion. He later recalled that all across the Soviet Union during his visit, people asked him, " 'Why do you have your bases threatening to attack us?' "[13]

A month later, Nixon had his turn. Khrushchev told him that Turkey, although "a poor, hungry country of beggars," was extremely vulnerable to Soviet missiles. Why then, he wondered, did the United States maintain bases in such countries? To use them as lightning rods for a Soviet nuclear strike? "If you intend to make war on us, I understand; if not," he asked, "why do you keep them?" The Soviet premier even let the topic spoil diplomatic niceties for his guest, hoisting his glass of American wine and proposing a toast to the "elimination of all military bases in foreign lands."[14]

Had the campaign been limited to propaganda, U.S. officials might have been justified in viewing it as their Soviet counterparts simply going through the motions of the Cold War. But taken together with the intensity and duration of the public campaign, the fact that the Soviets bothered to raise the IRBM issue privately should have suggested to the Americans that, justified or not, Soviet concerns were real, that there was "signal" to be discerned among the usual rhetorical "noise."

The impact of the Soviet campaign is difficult to judge: it had certainly left its mark in Paris in December 1957, increasing the reluctance of many potential hosts and helping to fuel the call for negotiations. It also fed opposition to the IRBMs inside NATO countries, among the public as well as the political parties on the Left, whether acting on orders from Moscow or independently agreeing with its arguments. As we shall see, it thus made the search for hosts more difficult in some countries and had some slight, intermittent effect on official U.S. thinking.

But overall, NATO governments on both sides of the Atlantic either rejected or ignored the Soviet complaints. After July 1959, the Soviet campaign in both its public and private forms tapered off for a substantial period. This could only have reinforced the impression that the anti-IRBM campaign had been nothing more than the standard propaganda, that now the Soviets would grudgingly learn to live with NATO's strategic missiles just as they had with all its other armaments. Based on the visible indicators, that was a reasonable inference for outsiders to draw. Within the Kremlin walls, however, the IRBMs would continue to rankle.

GOING CRAZY ON MILITARY STUFF:
THE IRBM PROGRAM, DECEMBER 1957–APRIL 1958

How many IRBMs would be deployed? How many would there be to deploy? These were two difficult questions made more so by the fact that the answer to one would obviously affect the answer to the other. The plan approved in November 1957 had comprised eight fifteen-missile squadrons, four each of Thors and Jupiters. With all the Thors earmarked for Great Britain, only the four Jupiter squadrons would be available for NATO. Norstad, however, publicly estimated the needs of the alliance to be between six and ten squadrons. A year later, Norstad would admit privately that the number "was a balance of political acceptability and minimum requirements and that it came out to about 6 squadrons."[15]

The two-squadron shortfall between production plans and Norstad's deployment plans did not last long. At an NSC meeting in late April 1958, DOD recommended enlarging the total IRBM force from 120 to 180 missiles (twelve squadrons, nine Thor and three Jupiter). Deputy Defense Secretary Quarles explained that this new figure represented a compromise between the sixteen squadrons recommended by the Gaither Report (and sought by the air force) and the eight squadrons currently planned. In any case, he added, twelve was the "minimal" number necessary to meet NATO's needs (presumably as defined by the Joint Chiefs). The president was skeptical. He commented that before all 180 IRBMs were produced, officials would have a clearer picture of their effectiveness. If that turned out to be low, then the administration might have to junk some of them. He also warned that the United States should not let its defense programs "pyramid" simply because it had once established these programs. The president's attitude seemed so negative that his national security adviser, Robert Cutler, assumed that he had rejected the force expansion. Incredibly, however, Ike said he "was going along" with the DOD recommendation, "even though this did not constitute the austerity program" he would have preferred.[16]

One is at a loss to explain Eisenhower's decision, particularly in light of his dim view of IRBMs and his near obsession with fiscal restraint. The documents offer no clues, and Robert Divine's argument, that Ike's decision "reflected his need to hedge his bets" while proceeding cautiously with second-generation, solid-fuel missiles, may be plausible but lacks substantiation. The expansion decision does seem to be, as Trachtenberg notes, "an extraordinary example of the President as 'kibitzer in chief.'" It is not clear whether the twelve-squadron plan generated additional pressure to locate bases, Quarles's assertion of "NATO's needs" notwithstanding. One can say, however, that especially beginning in April 1958, there would certainly be no shortage of IRBMs as the search for hosts got under way.[17]

PROCEDURE AND PRIORITIZATION

"Norstad," Paul-Henri Spaak would later write, "was fascinated by politics."[18] For the general's sake, it was a good thing, because he was designated point man in the search for hosts, and his was a complex, overwhelmingly political task from the very start. Basically, Norstad was first to canvass potential hosts, by contacting either their representatives at NATO in Paris or their defense ministers, and then to secure a potential host's agreement in principle to deploy IRBMs. He would next oversee bilateral, U.S.–host country negotiations, either diplomatic/political, military/technical, or both concurrently. The goal of these, respectively, was first a formal, government-to-government agreement and then an air force–to–air force technical agreement that would permit base construction, crew training, and deployment. Only after all this could the missiles become operational delivery systems in NATO's nuclear arsenal.

U.S. officials ranked potential hosts—those that had responded at least somewhat favorably before and during the Paris summit—and would approach them in sequence to minimize European and especially Soviet anxieties. Prioritization required a reconciliation of largely incompatible military and political considerations. The U.S. military, initially including Norstad, was most concerned with target coverage, irrespective of any commitment to the allies. This argued for siting IRBMs on NATO's flanks, the points closest to Soviet territory, as well as on U.S.-controlled territory in the Pacific. Thus after the United Kingdom, with which the Thor agreement was finally nearing completion, the JCS and DOD placed Turkey, Alaska, Okinawa, and France at the top of their list, in that order.[19]

Political considerations prevailed, however. The State Department recommended that France be listed ahead of Turkey, for a variety of reasons. France's status as the most powerful NATO ally after Great Britain was important, and this helped ensure that other facts—France's early expression of interest in IRBMs, its obvious jealousy of any preferential treatment the

General Lauris Norstad (USAF), Supreme Allied Commander, Europe, 1956–63. To him fell the politically charged and unenviable task of canvassing potential host countries and reaching deployment agreements with them. It would take almost two years. (National Archives)

British enjoyed, and its serious national nuclear aspirations—could not be ignored. Moreover, if the French were to receive missiles, they wanted to do so at the same time as their colleagues across the Channel, and with the head start the British Thor deal had, this meant talks must start as soon as possible. All these considerations seemed to demand France's placement at the top of the list. Italy would soon occupy the second spot, with Greece eventually joining Turkey in the third (see below).[20]

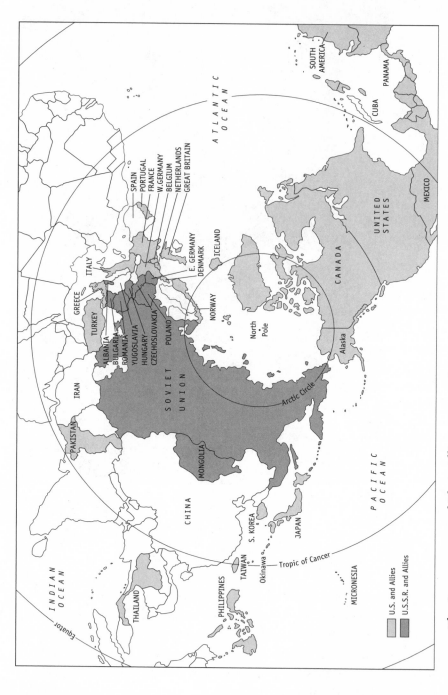

MAP 1. The Superpowers and Their Allies, 1957–1963

There were other reasons to pass up Turkey in the first round. Norstad told Dulles in mid-January that "there would be strong opposition to the installation of IRBMs in Turkey," and in part he meant the Soviet reaction; State Department officials worried that installing IRBMs in a country bordering on the Soviet Union might trigger a fierce response and in turn increase anxiety and tension throughout Europe. Deferring a Turkish deployment, however, would allow the Soviets to become accustomed to less provocative IRBMs first.[21]

More serious, in addition, were suspicions of Turkey inside NATO. Norstad, although sympathetic to strong JCS preference for it on military grounds, reported that if the "Northern Europeans" thought Turkey would receive the missiles, "it would blow the whole thing up. They believe[d] the Turks would be too warlike with them." Were he to submit a plan for Turkey now, he felt "it would be held up in the NATO Council for 2 years." Some Americans subscribed to this national stereotype; a year later, Robert Murphy would also voice concern over the alleged "Turkish temperament" and the related risk of an "irresponsible" missile launch. Such attitudes were complex, at times appearing as admiration of the Turks' "toughness," but especially when it came to responsibility for nuclear weapons, these easily turned negative. At work may even have been some simple bigotry, of the type Harold Macmillan would reveal a few years later when he objected to the multinational crews of the proposed Multilateral Force: "You don't expect our chaps to share their grog with Turks, do you?" For the moment, whatever the underlying attitudes, it was enough for Norstad that some NATO allies objected strongly to the Turks as missile hosts.[22]

Thus in late March 1958, Norstad stated that "in three to six months," after the procedure had become "normalized" through the conclusion of agreements with France and Italy, talks could begin with Turkey. The Eisenhower administration had decided, unsurprisingly, that major allies would come before minor allies in receiving IRBMs, France and Italy before Turkey. But concern over possible reactions among NATO allies and the Soviet adversary, stemming from the Turks' presumed character and geographical proximity, also bumped Turkey further down the list.[23]

FRANCE

The number one candidate for IRBMs, France, was alone among alliance members in having expressed interest before the December 1957 offer. But along with this early interest appeared early hints of the difficulties to come.

First, the French had their own ideas on the issue of launch control, at times indicating that they would accept the purely bilateral arrangement set for the British Thors, at other times, such as during the Paris summit, stating that "French control" was a "political necessity." Neither alternative conformed to the apparatus of SACEUR authority established by the conference communiqué. The French National Assembly sent one ominous signal regarding control in December, when it unanimously passed a resolution requiring its approval before deployment of "any military equipment not controlled by the French government." Second, before the summit the French informed U.S. officials of their commitment to produce their own IRBMs and warheads, which the Americans interpreted in part as pressure to achieve an IRBM offer most congenial to France. And third, U.S. officials detected French efforts to link a missile deployment to other issues, especially the sharing of general nuclear and IRBM design information, something of crucial importance to prenuclear France. With all these signs, General Norstad's confidence that he could get an agreement was unwarranted.[24]

Right away, Norstad spoke bluntly with the French. He rejected any "linkage" and lectured them that they were in no position to seek concessions because they were more interested in an IRBM deal than was the United States, which was "not necessarily inclined to accord to France the highest priority in this regard." The French government agreed to begin formal talks and examined a draft IRBM agreement. But it continued to express interest in a bilateral, extra-NATO agreement, something that Norstad, true to U.S. policy, refused to consider. Thus already in mid-February, for "several reasons including French procrastinations," Norstad decided that he must now approach the Italians as well. In late March, he claimed that "Italy had been useful as a spur to progress with the French."[25]

But how much progress? Multiple minor delays on the French side, as U.S. officials saw it, amounted to one major delay. These included the temporary absence of Foreign Minister Christian Pineau; a French request for cost figures; and the inability (or unwillingness) of top French officials, including Prime Minister Felix Gaillard, to devote attention to the issue. In the eyes of the U.S. ambassador in Paris, Amory Houghton, the French government remained in a state of "suspended animation" on the IRBM issue.[26]

By mid-May, moreover, the rapid disintegration of the Fourth Republic and the increasing political chaos that resulted had upset French IRBM policy. In the military realm, the focus of efforts at this stage, French air force officials had seemed eager to get moving. While they did express their desire to place the IRBMs under French bomber command, they apparently made some headway in technical discussions with their USAF counterparts. These talks ended indefinitely, however, when in the political turmoil, the last government of the Fourth Republic forced the generals responsible for the IRBMs into retirement. General Ely resigned in protest, making the disruption on the military side complete. On the civilian side, the government in Paris was consumed with its own domestic political survival and seems to have had little time to devote to the IRBM question.[27]

It would be wrong, though, to view the collapse of the Fourth Republic and the advent of the Fifth under Charles de Gaulle as a major turning point in this regard. It was Fourth Republic leaders who first wanted national control of the IRBMs and their warheads, and failing that, a bilateral arrangement identical to what the British had, outside NATO and free of SACEUR's involvement. It was they who first sought to use NATO IRBMs as a lever with which to extract substantial U.S. assistance for their national nuclear program (indeed, it was one of them, Felix Gaillard, who in April 1958 set a date for the detonation of France's first nuclear weapon). The Eisenhower administration, by contrast, would have had great difficulty permitting national control of the warheads, and it opposed narrow bilateral control, which constituted a violation of the 1957 communiqué. Indeed, it objected to any quid pro quo involving what it saw as unrelated issues. Virtually irreconcilable differences thus separated the U.S. and French positions on IRBMs before de Gaulle came to power.

Nevertheless, if the handwriting had already been on the wall during the Fourth Republic, de Gaulle replaced it with an enormous neon sign. Successive Fourth Republic governments had lent halting, uneven support to the independent French nuclear program; de Gaulle's fiercely nationalistic regime made a steady, unequivocal commitment. Similarly, sole or predominant control of nuclear weapons on French territory now became an unquestioned imperative in French policy. Any hopes that France would host NATO IRBMs evaporated definitively once de Gaulle established his nuclear policy soon after becoming premier on 1 June 1958.[28]

The Americans did not wait for de Gaulle before they shifted U.S. policy. They would now avoid asking for a clear yes-or-no answer, fearing that this might provoke him into raising the issue of equality with Britain under a revised McMahon Act and thus "generate serious friction" in U.S.-French relations. More generally, de Gaulle might "react vigorously" to what he would interpret as U.S. pressure. Therefore, the State Department directed Norstad not to raise the IRBM issue but rather to place the ball in de Gaulle's court. The likely alternative to a "showdown"—the replacement of France at the top of Norstad's list by other potential hosts—also had its disadvantages, but State considered it the lesser evil. If the French failed to raise the issue and contribute to "satisfactory progress" by 1 July, a deadline of which the Americans reminded them repeatedly over the next few weeks, Norstad would immediately begin talks with the Italians and Turks.[29]

The deadline passed without such a French move, although nuclear issues were on the agenda when Dulles met with the new French leader for the first time on 5 July. De Gaulle told his visitor that he had "little interest" in weapons under command of SACEUR and that they could be kept in France "according to a general NATO plan" only if France had "control over [their] custody and disposition," with the United States being "associated with such control." How such an arrangement of primary but not exclusive French control would work is hard to imagine. But it was unacceptable to the United States in any case, in view of U.S. law and the December 1957 communiqué, and in retrospect the meeting demonstrated that the control issue alone would preclude an IRBM agreement.[30]

Thereafter, the French continued to demonstrate interest in an IRBM deal but did not, from the U.S. standpoint, do anything that constituted taking the initiative. U.S. officials extended the 1 July deadline and leaked accounts of French "stalling" to the press, but with no effect. The French sought to switch the negotiations to a direct political channel and expressed optimism that the two sides could reach a compromise on warhead custody, but U.S. officials considered such moves mere "probing actions" designed to test U.S. adherence to the NATO deployment structure. Related developments, especially de Gaulle's remarkable proposal in September for a Franco-Anglo-American directorate apparently to have joint control over all the members' nuclear weapons, undoubtedly did little to prop up the sagging U.S. hopes for an agreement.[31]

By October, although French officials promised to present new proposals, the Americans had unequivocally given up. Norstad first informed the French that they "would be hearing nothing more" from him on the subject, that it was up to them if they wanted to proceed, and then in November he told them he was "definitely" uninterested in putting IRBMs in France. Privately he grumbled that the United States could "forget the French entirely." Dulles must have come to the same conclusion when in December he again saw de Gaulle, who "made it clear that France was not interested in cooperating with NATO" on IRBMs and other issues "when in effect the whole show was being run by the US."[32]

All along, the French had been interested in American IRBMs primarily as a means by which to maximize their control over some nuclear weapons and delivery systems and to facilitate, one way or another, their acquisition. They wanted a strictly bilateral missile control arrangement such as that enjoyed by the British, concessions in the form of assistance for their national nuclear program, and then, under de Gaulle, primary, if not complete, control over any warheads on French soil. On none of these points was the United States prepared to yield. An agreement on IRBM deployment under the terms of the NATO communiqué was highly unlikely under the Fourth Republic, and impossible under the Fifth. The Eisenhower administration learned the hard way that its early optimism had been misplaced, but considering the importance of France in the alliance, it would have had to try in any case. Thus the Americans spent the first half of 1958 devoting their main effort to France—and all for naught. Now they would have to look elsewhere for the necessary nuclear hospitality.

ITALY

Norstad next turned to the Italians, whom he had first contacted in February 1958, partly to goad the French into action. Again he was optimistic, not only about concluding an agreement but about the time required as well. According to the head of the U.S. military team involved in the technical discussions, General Gabriel Disosway, Norstad assured him, "You can go down there and make a deal with the Italians in about 30 days." Yet in the end, Disosway recalled with only slight exaggeration, "It took me a year and a half."[33]

The Italians' motives for hosting NATO IRBMs differed from those of the French, most importantly because they never considered embarking on an independent nuclear program. True, the Italian rationale was to some extent strategic; Italy's defense minister through early 1958, Paolo Taviani, claims that he welcomed an IRBM deal because of the missiles' alleged ability to "recouple" U.S. and European security. Such an arrangement would also provide Italy with some degree of control over strategic nuclear weapons for the first time. But one has to agree with Leopoldo Nuti, the closest student of the Italian IRBMs, that the primary motivation of successive Italian governments was political: policymakers wanted, first, to elevate their country's status within NATO, and second, to improve its relationship with the United States.[34]

From the outset, domestic politics constrained Italian leaders. In early 1958, the government of Christian Democrat Adone Zoli did win votes by

big margins in the Chamber of Deputies that cleared the way for acceptance of IRBMs, but the Italian public was divided on the issue. Polls from
March 1958 showed 22–30 percent of respondents in favor, 39–48 percent
opposed, and 29–30 percent having no opinion. The opposition Communist
party (PCI) and its allies quickly made the IRBMs one of their major campaign issues heading into the general elections scheduled for 25 May. Under
these circumstances, the Italians told U.S. officials they wanted to avoid
being the only Europeans to host the missiles. More important, although
they were ready to go ahead with technical discussions, they wanted to do
so only under conditions of maximum secrecy. Appreciating these concerns,
the Americans agreed in late March to wait three weeks for a NATO defense ministers' meeting, at which Norstad could consult with the Italians
discreetly. In short, when it came to dealing with IRBMs in the middle of a
political campaign, the Christian Democrats' main slogan—"Progress without Adventures"—was appropriate in more ways than they knew.[35]

After the May elections, further delays resulted when Taviani told the
Americans that as a lame duck defense minister, he felt unable to commit his
government to accepting IRBMs, "even in principle." A new ruling coalition
did not emerge until July, under Christian Democrat Amintore Fanfani, who
assumed the portfolios of both prime minister and foreign minister. Fanfani
visited Washington at the end of the month and reaffirmed his country's
interest in having IRBMs, but he still wanted to avoid publicity, informing
Eisenhower personally that he preferred that it remain "purely a matter for
the military" and not become "a highly charged political issue." Ike promised the prime minister U.S. cooperation in meeting this need.[36]

Another stumbling block arose that summer. In mid-June, the PCI introduced a bill in the Chamber prohibiting the establishment of any nuclear
missile installations on Italian soil. It never had any chance of passing, but
the government still preferred to put off the acceptance in principle and bilateral political negotiations until it could dispose of the bill—which caused
another delay of at least six weeks. Only in the first week of August did
Fanfani's government formally agree in principle to receive two squadrons
of IRBMs.[37]

With substantive political talks finally under way, the Italian government
nevertheless tried to tack on more conditions, thus causing even more delays.
The first condition related to financing. Italian representatives first declared
impossible the provision of land, support facilities, and utilities without U.S.
financial assistance, and they then went so far as to claim their inability to
spend a single lira on the deployment in view of their country's defense bud-

get deficit (it hardly helped that the chief of the Italian defense staff, General Giuseppe Mancinelli, had earlier sold Italian civilian leaders on the IRBMs in part by claiming that the United States would pick up the tab). Next they asked to choose the sites for the missiles, a minor matter that posed no problem, except for the additional two weeks' delay because the selection had to await President Giovanni Gronchi's return from abroad. Far more serious, they also demanded additional U.S. assistance for their conventional forces, arguing that they needed augmentation because the IRBMs would make Italy more vulnerable to enemy attack. And finally, they sought a "most favored nation clause," by which Italy would receive any additional benefits enjoyed by any subsequent IRBM host country. Thus even as Fanfani agreed to a timetable by which the first squadron was to become operational by February 1959, he was seeking concessions that, while perfectly understandable from his government's standpoint, nevertheless rendered that date increasingly unrealistic.[38]

U.S. negotiators managed to evade the conventional-force compensation and most-favored-nation issues with relative ease, but the question of funding took more than two months to resolve. The Americans conceded a fair amount here, no doubt in part because both Norstad and the U.S. ambassador in Rome, James Zellerbach, sympathized with the Italian position. For operation of the two squadrons, Fanfani ultimately agreed to pay up to $8.8 million annually, a figure surprisingly high and thus acceptable to U.S. officials.[39]

On 11 January 1959, Norstad reported that an agreement was "practically ready for signature," but such optimism collapsed along with the Fanfani government on the 26th. There would have been some additional delay regardless, because the State Department repeatedly sought last-minute textual changes, leading a distressed Ambassador Zellerbach to accuse it of having lost interest in obtaining an agreement. A caretaker government took more than two weeks to emerge under Antonio Segni, a conservative Christian Democrat, who was certain to follow through on the IRBM deal. But his government first had to familiarize itself with all the relevant documents, wait for a final vote of confidence in the Italian Senate, and secure approval of the Council of Ministers.[40]

The only thing that happened with any speed was the new government's own attempt to win additional concessions and to parlay the agreement into additional political gain. First, the new foreign minister, Giuseppe Pella, and his colleagues tried to resurrect the most-favored-nation issue. Moreover, because the IRBMs increased Italy's contribution relative to other NATO members, its value as a military target, and its government's political vulnerability, they also sought participation on equal terms with Britain and France in any foreign ministers or East-West summit meetings. Most-favored-nationism would soon evaporate, but Italy's summit aspirations had a fairly long life ahead of them. In a meeting with Ike in late September 1959, for example, Segni would again cite Italy's acceptance of IRBMs as one of the reasons it deserved a seat at the major summit then planned for spring 1960. But the difference in March compared with seven months earlier was that when met with U.S. reticence on such issues, the Italians were unwilling to let them hold up the agreement now so close to completion. And so finally, after thirteen months of negotiations, in the last eight of which Italy was the focal point of the IRBM deployment effort, the two sides formally exchanged notes on 26 March 1959.[41]

The Eisenhower administration could derive some satisfaction from the way the negotiations with Italy had gone. The Italians had proceeded despite the numerous protests and threats issued by Albania, Yugoslavia, and the Soviet Union; they rejected all such communications in no uncertain terms. Dulles said on one occasion that Italy deserved the larger role in allied consultations that it wanted, citing its acceptance of IRBMs as proof that it was a staunch NATO ally unfazed by Soviet intimidation. Successive governments in Rome had likewise forged ahead, however timidly, in the face of strong opposition from the domestic Left. The administration was both pleased and relieved by the outcome. Although Dulles acknowledged that the Italians had been "annoyed" with his department over the missiles, he hoped the signing would restore their goodwill.[42]

Above all, however, the story of the Italo-American negotiations is one of almost farcical delay. This resulted partly from Italian domestic politics, which featured unstable coalition governments that fell twice during the negotiation period; each new government then had to form, get settled, and familiarize itself with the IRBM issue before proceeding. Domestic opposition also produced a cautious, secretive approach on the part of the government in Rome. All told, these domestic realities added at least four months to the talks, and one can see why they stood out in the mind of one U.S. diplomat who recalled the episode.[43]

It was also the case, though, that despite being moderate conservatives committed to the Western alliance (and keen on demonstrating that commitment), Italy's leaders nevertheless governed a sovereign state and had their own conception of national interests. Naturally they sought concessions and conditions in return for their acceptance of the IRBMs, which after all did represent a major cost and responsibility, a source of diplomatic conflict and military danger that other NATO allies had not yet taken on. However justified they may have been, these demands further delayed the agreement on deployment.

Finally, U.S. actions probably contributed to the delay; some U.S. officials themselves certainly thought so. Without access to Italian internal documents, one must rely almost exclusively on U.S. sources with their U.S. bias, and a complete, balanced assessment is thus impossible. But we do know that the by-products of Italian domestic politics and Italian national interests—as well as the Eisenhower administration's attempts to deal with them—largely explain the long road to the first IRBM agreement.

THE IRBM PROGRAM, MARCH 1958–APRIL 1959: THE BREAKDOWN OF CONSENSUS

While the Eisenhower administration engaged the French and Italians, the American IRBM production program continued to evolve. Even before President Eisenhower approved the expansion of the IRBM force from eight to twelve squadrons in April 1958, doubts about these missiles had begun to arise within his administration, and they only multiplied as the deployment effort stalled.

The first strong doubts emanated in late March from the Policy Planning Staff of the Department of State (PPS). Its director, Gerard Smith, argued that the IRBMs were vulnerable, obsolescent, and insignificant, effectively whetting the allies' appetites for their own national nuclear forces, undermining arms control efforts, and provoking domestic opposition inside potential host countries that threatened alliance unity. Smith acknowledged the risks of an abrupt reversal of policy, and so he suggested slowing the pace of deployment to allow for possible advances in arms control or missile technology. By the end of spring, he and his staff were suggesting that the IRBMs "be viewed as a bargaining counter" to help achieve the ban on production and deployment of missiles under consideration during this period. Nothing came of these notions, but they underscore the gravity of these first misgivings about the IRBMs, mere months after NATO had agreed to deploy them.[44]

By August, doubts were emerging inside the Pentagon as well. Its Weapons System Evaluation Group (WSEG) came close to excluding European-based IRBMs from its comprehensive comparison of missiles and aircraft because of their higher vulnerability and the "complications" inherent in dual control. The study allowed that the missiles made Soviet strategic calculations more difficult, but it ascribed to them only "limited utility" for counterforce attacks because of their relative inaccuracy and declared them "supplementary" to U.S. land- and sea-based weapons systems. Rear Admiral John Sides, WSEG director, elaborated on this critique in a presentation before the NSC in October. Not only would the planned IRBM emplacements be "highly vulnerable," Sides argued, but hardening them would not be worth the financial cost. He concluded that "little benefit would accrue by the additional deployment of IRBM's in a configuration similar to those already planned." Rather, the United States should move on to the more advanced, mobile or hardened systems then in prospect, either land or sea based.[45]

This WSEG critique helped spark reconsiderations but also confused debate more widely within the administration. In October, citing shortages of funds and willing host countries, and without consulting Norstad, the JCS recommended cutting back to eight squadrons: four to the United Kingdom and one each to Turkey, Okinawa, Alaska, and some unknown NATO ally. At the NSC meeting on 30 October, Secretary Dulles voiced concerns about the missiles, including their cost-effectiveness and likelihood of provoking the Soviets if deployed in Greece and Turkey. Defense officials disagreed and defended the missiles. The extent of the disarray over IRBMs became clear two weeks later, when the two sides traded positions publicly. "The further you go down the road toward an operational capability of the ICBM," a date that was "coming closer," Secretary McElroy remarked at a press conference, "the less interesting it is for us to deploy additional . . . IRBM's." The State Department, worried that NATO partners might view the comment as indicating a reversal of U.S. policy, hastily "interpreted" it by announcing that there was "no lessening" of its "intention to proceed" with the NATO deployments, which were "best suited to strengthening that part of the free world's defenses which [lay] in Europe." The earlier consensus on IRBMs had eroded so badly that individual departments, even individual policymakers, were now of two minds on the issue.[46]

Such was certainly the case with Dulles and the State Department. The Bureau of European Affairs, headed by Livingston Merchant, understandably fretted about a backlash in the alliance and continued to support the deployment program despite its drawbacks. Gerard Smith's Policy Planning Staff pressed its serious questions on military, political, and economic grounds. Between them, Smith and Merchant at least agreed to urge Dulles to propose a joint State-Defense review of the IRBM deployments in an effort to clarify matters. Whether Dulles did so is unclear; he himself was torn, his doubts about the missiles coexisting with his desire to "avoid the appearance of weakness, or an appearance of reacting to Soviet pressure" that a shift in policy would create.[47]

Smith continued to object to the IRBMs well into 1959, especially on military grounds. He pressed for a "technical evaluation" conducted jointly by State, Defense, and now also the President's Science Advisory Commission (PSAC), a composition likely to produce a defeat for DOD by a vote of 2–1. McElroy, seeing no reason to review the deployment program, complained to the State Department about Smith's proposal and succeeded in blocking it. Undeterred, Smith would soon add the issue of unauthorized launch to his case against a Turkish deployment. Amid this bureaucratic struggle, the deployment policy managed to escape intact.[48]

The IRBM production program did change, however, even if the basic deployment policy did not. On 28 November 1958, top defense officials joined the president at his retreat in Augusta, Georgia, to discuss the FY 1960 defense budget. In accordance with the views of the Joint Chiefs, McElroy proposed reducing the IRBM force from twelve to eight squadrons. When the defense secretary discussed deployment prospects, admitting that the administration must consider the allies' willingness to receive IRBMs, Eisenhower reacted with palpable irritation. Why do we spend "billions on these systems," he asked, "and then and only then" determine whether our allies want them? "The real question, is whether we are doing our homework ahead of time." This was a flash of insight. Almost three years after approving the manufacture of IRBMs, more than one year after deciding to offer them to NATO, the president for the first time was asking hard questions about the entire enterprise. The moment of introspection came too late and vanished as suddenly as it had appeared, but it would not be the last such episode for Eisenhower in the IRBM story.[49]

Ike approved the recommended reduction to eight squadrons, five Thor and three Jupiter, in mid-December. His struggle to contain a defense budget that had threatened to mushroom ever since *Sputnik*, the increasingly evident obsolescence of the IRBMs, the weak allied demand, and the arbitrariness of the earlier force expansion all help to explain the curtailment. The total planned IRBM force reverted to the 120 missiles approved a year earlier, and with four squadrons going to Britain and two to Italy, the administration now had only two more to place.[50]

Meanwhile, the administration was finding it more and more difficult to rationalize the IRBM deployment. Air force strategists no doubt had found a place for the missiles in their war plans, but they failed either to inform or to impress those at the top, civilians in particular. Thus when members of a congressional committee asked about the missiles' vulnerability to attack, especially in light of the minimal warning time they could expect, Secretary McElroy and JCS chair Twining quickly conceded the point: the IRBMs' only military virtue was the increased number of targets the Soviets would have to destroy. If the missiles helped little in defending the nation, however, at least they could help defend the administration: General Twining did invoke the IRBMs to help ward off questions about the alleged "missile gap" by administration critics such as Senator John Kennedy (D-Mass.).[51]

On 2 January 1959, with the Italian agreement far enough along for him to expand the search in earnest, Norstad informed Greek and Turkish representatives at NATO of his readiness to begin formal discussions on IRBM deployments. Because of the long-standing Greco-Turkish rivalry, he assumed that IRBMs should not go to one country without also going to the other. The next day, however, the State Department instructed him not to initiate talks with either Athens or Ankara, because of persistent political doubts within the department on the one hand and new funding problems on the other.[52]

The political reservations found a new voice inside the State Department as the Bureau of Near Eastern Affairs (NEA) weighed in, focusing on the projected Greek and Turkish deployments in particular. The bureau argued that although deployment promised some benefits and a withdrawal of the IRBM offer would harm relations with the eager Turks, to go ahead would fuel neutralist sentiment and divert valuable resources in both countries. It would also lead the Soviet Union to exert greater pressure on its neighbor Turkey and cause shortages of funds for needed conventional weapons. The political and economic costs far outweighed any military utility, NEA concluded, recommending that the administration consider placing the IRBMs on U.S.-controlled territory instead. Yet despite obvious sympathy for these arguments elsewhere in the State Department, they too resulted in nothing more than slight additional delay in negotiations with the Greeks and Turks.[53]

The funding issue, however, could not be ignored and had a much greater impact. At one level it was simple—a prospective shortage of funding for the Mutual Security Program (MSP), responsible for footing the U.S. share of the IRBM deployment bill. At another it was extraordinarily complex, involving rising but largely inestimable costs, the search for other sources of funding, the size and timing of disbursements, and the extent to which other MSP programs would have to be sacrificed. Compounding the complexity were sharp differences between State and Defense over how grave the shortfall was and what would be necessary to make it up. The ensuing memo storm within and between the two bureaucracies lasted well into spring. Only toward the end of April 1959 did Norstad receive authorization to engage the Greeks and Turks—and this, incredibly, based on still further deferral of the funding issue.[54]

This time, U.S. officials had no one to blame but themselves. Their failure to anticipate funding needs lengthened the deployment process by another four months. Of course, for them to approach Greece and Turkey without having settled the question of financing would have been irresponsible. Certain realities, moreover, lay beyond the Americans' immediate control: the overlapping jurisdictions of the State and Defense departments; a Mutual Security Program both vast and intricate; and an IRBM deployment program featuring multiple, variable costs. Nevertheless, throughout 1958, these officials had at any given point a fair idea of how many IRBM squadrons were slated for Europe, and the protracted negotiations with France and Italy provided ample time in which either to secure sufficient funds or to scale back the NATO deployment plan. But State and Defense officials squandered those months, and when Norstad was ready to move ahead, they were not.

As for the internal debate over the missiles that began in the fall of 1958, what is most striking is that the opposition to the IRBMs—despite its increasingly powerful arguments and the feeble case put forth in favor of deployment—had virtually no effect. To be sure, criticism helped trigger the production cutback of December, which in the long term meant fewer IRBMs in need of bases. But neither the dying hopes for a French agreement, nor the slowly emerging Italian deal, nor the prospective talks with Greece and Turkey were seriously threatened in this period. As U.S. officials marked its first anniversary, the IRBM deployment effort had taken on a life of its own. It was sustained against all comers and all criticisms by two prior commitments: to manufacture IRBMs, and to give them to the NATO allies. Strategic and political logic, significant dollar costs, national interest—none of these could overcome the perceived need to dispose of missiles being produced and to make good on a major promise to allies. Thus even though by now many officials wished to sell the thirty unassigned missiles for scrap, the search for hosts had to continue.

WEST GERMANY

A "new" willing recipient had appeared in late 1958: the Federal Republic of Germany (FRG). The question of IRBMs for West Germany is bound up in the broader question playing itself out at the same time, that of the Federal

Republic's acquisition of nuclear weapons generally. Throughout the 1950s, it was one of the major controversies in Cold War Europe, affecting both Germanys as well as the opposing blocs of which they were members. It was not an issue that Chancellor Adenauer could take lightly, certainly not in late 1957. Despite his Christian Democrats' electoral victory in September, he was operating by late fall in a domestic political arena strewn with nuclear land mines. One of these was IRBMs: a December poll showed 74 percent of West Germans opposed to having such missiles on their territory. Under these circumstances, a cautious approach made eminent sense, at least for the time being.[55]

Considering some of the signals his government sent, one can see how observers then and since could conclude that Adenauer unequivocally opposed stationing IRBMs in his country. But it now seems clear that the chancellor was more open to the idea than he appeared at the time. He was not enthusiastic; however, he accepted what he saw as the necessity of reconnecting U.S. and West German security after *Sputnik*.[56]

The Bonn government was not only extremely sensitive to domestic politics but also aware of the international political and military drawbacks of German IRBMs. Friends and enemies alike might charge it was developing an offensive or first-strike capability, and there was no telling how the Kremlin might react. Militarily, echoing conclusions drawn by the Armed Forces Command Staff, Adenauer and his ministers had doubts about the IRBMs' utility. To them, the missiles were primary targets vulnerable to both air and ground attack because they would sit immobile, close to the Iron Curtain, and thus enjoy little warning time. Moreover, NATO partners might use them as an excuse for withdrawing ground troops from the Federal Republic. Such pitfalls were enough to give the Bonn government serious pause, but not to sour it on IRBMs completely.[57]

In short, the West German government wanted IRBMs; yet it faced, indeed needed to appease, a domestic public and parliament not yet ready for them, and it had a strong military critique close at hand. So it chose to play up the military criticisms to suggest to domestic audiences that it was uninterested in IRBMs, while in the meantime preserving its ability to accept the missiles in the long run.

Specifically, Adenauer secretly assured the Americans that the FRG would ultimately accept IRBMs. To Dulles, he "indicated he would be willing" to have missiles and "was confident" he would win parliamentary approval (although only after debate); but until then, German IRBMs would remain wishful thinking. To some like Harold Macmillan, on the other hand, he said simply that he did not want them. Publicly, while being careful to avoid rejecting the missiles outright, his government dwelled on the missiles' military drawbacks, thus leaving the impression that it would decline the U.S. offer. "It would be foolish," Defense Minister Franz Josef Strauss announced, "to put heavy artillery in the front lines." Such argumentation still left the door open to a German deployment on the west bank of the Rhine. And finally, as his biographer puts it, Adenauer "played the peace harp for German ears" at the Paris conference, joining the call for exploring the possibility of negotiations with the Soviets. With this intricate approach, Adenauer if nothing else preserved maximum flexibility for himself once he had sufficiently contained the domestic opposition.[58]

This he managed in March 1958, when, after the most bitter debate in the history of the Bundestag, his government won broad approval for equipping the Bundeswehr with nuclear weapons. And yet it did not raise the IRBM issue within NATO until the latter half of November. What caused this seven-month lag is unclear; the opposition's potent grassroots *Kampf dem Atomtod* ("Campaign against Atomic Death"), persistent nuclear fears among the wider German public, and important provincial elections in July, in which the nuclear issue figured prominently, all no doubt promoted caution. Even though the press reported as late as 7 November that Bonn still would "prefer not" to host IRBMs, on 22 November Defense Minister Strauss suddenly sent word to Norstad that he "would like to have two squadrons of THORS in Germany." Perhaps Khrushchev's speech and actions beginning on 10 November, which foreshadowed the crisis over Berlin he would formally precipitate on the 27th, removed whatever restraints had kept Strauss from requesting IRBMs earlier.[59]

Strauss dropped in on Norstad shortly thereafter. "Germany would be delighted to be the first country to have the IRBMs," declared Strauss in Norstad's perhaps somewhat sarcastic retelling. "I have not offered them to Germany," the general recalled answering, "and I do not have that in mind at the moment." The United States was stopping production, he explained to his now "furious" applicant, so not enough IRBMs would be available. Ineptly failing to see this as the pretext for refusal that it was, Secretary McElroy proceeded in mid-December to tell Strauss the truth: missile production would not be a problem should additional demand materialize before 1 April 1959. He did also, however, inform his German counterpart that the decision whether to offer him IRBMs rested with NATO, that is, SACEUR.[60]

Norstad was against the idea of German IRBMs on military grounds, but he was also aware that the political considerations were "probably of greater import" and thus sought State Department guidance in the first week of 1959. State replied that no contrary political needs overrode Norstad's military reservations; indeed, it believed that "on balance political factors would argue against such deployment at present." In fending off Strauss's request, however, Norstad did the same thing the Germans had earlier: he stressed military motives to conceal political considerations. On 17 January, he informed the German military representative at NATO that "he did not have any military requirement at this time" for placing IRBMs in Germany, although he tried to soften the blow by holding out, whether sincerely or not, the prospect of second-generation IRBMs somewhere down the road. There the German subplot ended. Strauss stopped raising the issue, and in early February Norstad declared the matter "dead."[61]

While Norstad would have liked more potential hosts from which to choose, at no point was he so desperate that he seriously considered the FRG. The military and political reasons against basing IRBMs there were simply too powerful. Deployment behind the Rhine might solve the military problems, but enormous political pitfalls would remain. Not only had the Soviets made clear their deep concern over German nuclearization, which they would go to great lengths to prevent, but in their view IRBMs would give Bonn the ability to visit nuclear destruction directly upon Soviet soil. Policymakers at Supreme Headquarters, Allied Powers Europe (SHAPE) and in Washington had to reckon with what might be a violent Soviet reaction. Finally, no deployment would be as controversial within NATO as one in the country that had propelled the continent into total war not twenty years before. Thus when Strauss came knocking in November 1958 — with the IRBM program being scaled back, with other basing options still available, with a major crisis over Berlin brewing — Norstad and his U.S. superiors did not hesitate to say no.

GREECE

Greece, on the other hand, remained a real prospect in early 1959. As mentioned earlier, the Greek government had seemed a "doubtful" candidate for IRBMs on the eve of the Paris conference. The conservative government of Constantine Karamanlis sent mixed signals, informing the Americans of its willingness to accept IRBM bases so long as other NATO allies did, but then waffling at the Paris summit. There, Karamanlis and his ministers stated that the need for IRBMs had not been established; if it were, then all the allies should host them. Yet Greece reserved the right to decide later whether it would accept the missiles.[62]

As with France, Germany, and Italy, domestic politics and other unrelated matters explain the attitude of the Greek government. The controversial nature of nuclear weapons played a familiar role in Greece too, as did the government's resentment of a reduction of U.S. military assistance. But more important was a public opinion increasingly hostile toward NATO because of the role other members, especially Britain and Turkey, were playing in the worsening dispute over Cyprus. Few Greeks were in a mood to cooperate with an alliance they felt was letting them down on such a vital issue. Their representatives in parliament, who shared this sentiment, felt compelled to follow suit, particularly in the general election campaign of February–May 1958. Thus while the parties of the Left predictably advocated a neutralist course and a flat refusal of IRBMs, which they said would only place Greece in the nuclear bull's-eye and further under U.S. domination, those in the Center were scarcely more receptive. They sought major concessions before accepting, such as a satisfactory resolution of the Cyprus imbroglio or, as in Italy, equal status within the alliance. Similarly, the conservatives grouped around the Karamanlis government, on most occasions openly pro-American and pro-alliance, scrupulously avoided taking a clear stand—other than to state that they would decide whenever NATO actually offered missiles to Greece. This was something Norstad was certain to defer in the touchy preelection atmosphere.[63]

The conservatives were vindicated at the polls in May, but while this was obviously the best possible result for those in favor of an IRBM deployment, Karamanlis did not feel any freer to approach Norstad. After SACEUR contacted the Greeks and Turks on 2 January 1959, the Greeks said they were "not opposed in principle" to stationing IRBMs on their territory. But the Karamanlis government wanted to put off talks indefinitely, in part because of municipal elections in March; even after that it felt compelled to deny publicly that deployment was yet an issue. Then, in late spring, Soviet bloc propaganda worked its chilling effect. While the Greek government remained interested in principle and discussed deployment with Norstad, as summer neared, it had still not agreed to accept the missiles. It continued to view the missiles, in the words of one unhappy U.S. official, "with something of the immobile fascination of a bird hypnotized by a snake." Even though the Americans had finally gotten their own act together and finessed the funding problem, the Greeks were still prisoners of domestic politics and the Cyprus dispute.[64]

NOT QUITE AN AGONIZING REAPPRAISAL: EISENHOWER'S DOUBTS, JUNE 1959

On 3 June 1959, Ellis Briggs, the ambassador designate to Greece, made the customary stop at the White House before departing for his new post. Although his audience with the president lasted only ten minutes, it was long enough for Briggs to point out, as he later recalled, that the placement of "certain military gadgets" in Greece "could hardly be soothing to Moscow," even with a U.S. veto over launch. He mentioned the missiles' obsolescence and suggested that deployment farther from Soviet soil would deter equally yet provoke far less. Eisenhower perked up when Briggs introduced the topic, "asked some sharp questions and scribbled notes on a pad: he would raise the matter with the Joint Chiefs." Without knowing it, Briggs had steered Ike as close as he would ever come to a reconsideration of the IRBM deployment.[65]

Eisenhower sent a memo to McElroy that same day. Invoking news reports about Soviet objections to the proposed Greek IRBMs, the earlier decision against trying to induce allies to take the missiles, and the need to deploy them only where they would be "useful," he peppered the defense secretary with questions. Was there a firm plan to put IRBMs in Greece? Had the Greeks "initiated a firm request" for them? How many more U.S. military personnel would have to be stationed in Greece? How much would the deployment cost? What was the virtue of deployment in Greece, a country "both small and exposed"?[66]

McElroy's point-by-point reply, citing the Joint Chiefs' recommendation, defended the Greek deployment. The administration had firm plans for Greece, he wrote, but was waiting for Athens to agree in principle. The Greeks had not "initiated a firm request" but had said they would "give favorable consideration" to a recommendation by SACEUR. American forces in Greece would grow by eleven hundred to fifteen hundred men, and the total cost to the United States for FY 1960–63 for one squadron would be just over $110 million. Finally, Greece promised target coverage impossible from Britain, while it was plenty big and no more vulnerable than the other hosts. Alternative NATO hosts for the Greek squadron did not exist; doubling up on Turkey was neither "politically feasible" nor logistically sound.

And the State Department, McElroy reported, although seeing no particular advantage to placement in Greece, nevertheless supported the plan.[67]

Still, Eisenhower was not convinced, and now U.S.-Soviet relations intruded upon his thinking. He was preoccupied with the Geneva foreign ministers conference, which had begun 11 May, and by early June, despite the low expectations he had for these sluggish talks, he nonetheless did not want to jeopardize them by presenting "a threatening appearance to the Soviets." Indeed, he was seeking a way to break the diplomatic logjam, and this desire became intermingled with his reservations about the Greek IRBMs. Meeting with his staff secretary Andrew Goodpaster and Undersecretary of State Douglas Dillon on 15 June, the president lamented that "he had racked his head" trying to come up with new possibilities for negotiation and "was at his 'wits end.'" The only thing that came to mind, in light of Khrushchev's objections to their presence "in nearby countries," was the IRBMs. Were the United States to achieve "a break-through in more advanced missiles," he suggested, "it might be possible to give up these IRBM plans."[68]

Eisenhower raised this point again before Dillon and Goodpaster the following day, but this time with a remarkable introduction:

> The President said one thing is bothering him a great deal in the present situation, and that is the plan to put IRBMs in Greece. If Mexico or Cuba had been penetrated by the Communists, and then began getting arms and missiles from them, we would . . . look on such developments with the gravest concern and . . . it would be imperative for us to take positive action, even offensive military action. He could see the reason for Redstone, Corporal, or Honest John missiles, which are short-range, but not IRBMs. He wondered if we were not simply being provocative, since Eastern Europe is an area of dispute in a political sense.

And the day after that, the president called another meeting, this one specifically devoted to the question of foreign bases and IRBMs, with McElroy and national security adviser Gordon Gray on hand as well. He made several points: again, the Cuba-Mexico analogy should give pause; the United States should not pressure Greece, and lower-level officials should understand this; deployment might be reasonable in such countries as Britain but was "very questionable" in "advanced areas such as Greece"; nor would it "serve to reduce tensions" with the Soviets. Together with the long-term political costs of the U.S. foreign base system, the IRBM deployment should undergo thorough analysis by State and the JCS.[69]

Ike's lieutenants disagreed. McElroy replied that the question should be considered in the context of Soviet threats and the resulting uncertainty in Western Europe, which had led to the IRBM offer in the first place. Goodpaster disputed the president's Western Hemisphere analogy. Dillon remarked that State would accept a swap of Greek IRBMs for comparable Soviet concessions, perhaps as part of a broader disarmament deal, but then suggested prodding the Kremlin in that direction by going ahead and deploying the missiles in forward areas. He also worried that treating Greece and Turkey differently than the other allies would create problems, especially with the Turks. Finally, as Dulles had the previous December, both McElroy and Dillon warned against the appearance of having reversed policy in response to Khrushchev's complaints. Eisenhower tried to square the circle, approving an unspecified delay in deployment but agreeing that it should bear no link to Soviet threats.[70]

There, after three days of intense discussion, the reconsideration fizzled. No fortuitous "breakthrough in more advanced missiles" materialized, State and Defense did not restudy the deployment, and Eisenhower abandoned the bargaining-chip idea; neither Herter at the Geneva talks (concluded on 5 August) nor the president himself at the Camp David summit with Khrushchev used it. Ike had duplicated for himself the process his subordinates had gone through months earlier: a solid case against the IRBMs came easily, but when presented with the costs of reversal—the appearance of giving in to Soviet threats, the wrath of allies double-crossed, the accumulation of expensive missiles—he too found it easier to step aside and let the IRBM deployment proceed at its torpid pace.

The only element of the reconsideration that survived was Ike's no-pressure approach. This became enshrined in the Basic National Security Policy (BNSP) paper for that year, NSC 5906/1, which stated that IRBMs would go only to those countries "which demonstrate[d] a desire to have them and officially request[ed] them." With the Greek government, the president went so far as to direct that it be allowed to decide "at a time of its own choosing" whether to accept. Through the end of July, U.S. officials sought to execute this wish, but in such an extreme form, it yielded Athens the power to tie up deployment indefinitely. Both State and Defense soon felt they had either to secure Greek acceptance or to send the squadron in question to another country. State Department officials argued that seeking the "latest Greek thinking" or informing the Greeks that the United States now planned to deploy the squadron elsewhere unless they wished "to have it themselves in the reasonably near future" did not constitute applying pressure "in the sense meant by the President."[71]

By the end of August, this view had become policy. Norstad, who as early as 5 August had proposed dropping the Greeks from consideration, finally forced a showdown with them. He warned that he would recommend deployment elsewhere and gave them two weeks to decide definitively. While still professing their general interest, the Greeks regretfully explained to Norstad on 14 September their inability to accept "within the time limits set"; they could not assume another domestic political liability until after the successful launch of an independent Cyprus Republic, an event not due until February 1960.[72]

Once again, unrelated issues and the internal politics of a potential host country had interfered with the search for bases, only this time they prevented deployment. The interplay of the Cyprus dispute with Greek domestic politics had turned a conservative government that otherwise would have welcomed IRBMs into one reluctant from the outset. Caught between its desire to be a reliable ally abroad and its need to survive at home, the Karamanlis government sent mixed signals at first and procrastinated thereafter until U.S. and NATO officials demanded a clear yes or no. The latter, given the circumstances, was the Greeks' only possible answer.

TURKEY AND THE END OF THE SEARCH

The superficiality of Eisenhower's second thoughts in June is demonstrated most starkly by his omission of Turkey, a candidate for IRBMs that in June 1959 held far more promise than Greece.[73]

From the very beginning, Turkey was unique in its enthusiasm for the IRBMs. In Paris, where most of the heads of government avoided any specific reference to the missile offer in their opening statements, Prime Minister Adnan Menderes went out of his way to say that IRBMs and other nuclear weapons should be stationed "in as great numbers as possible in all NATO countries which [could] use them in an effective and satisfactory manner." Turkish officials were well aware of the IRBMs' weaknesses, but as many of their alliance counterparts did, they thought the missiles would bring them greater international prestige, counteract Soviet ICBMs, not render Turkey any more a military target than it already was, and increase Turkey's security. As Foreign Minister Fatin Rustu Zorlu argued, "The only way to defend oneself is to arm to the best of one's ability."[74]

At the regular NAC meeting in December 1958, as Norstad later put it, he "practically announced" that the Turks were to get IRBMs. Along with the 2 January 1959 signal of his readiness to begin talks with them, this put him in a tight spot when Washington instructed him to back off. Turkish representatives at NATO were understandably irked and anxious about the delay and "telephoned almost daily" about getting the talks under way. They worried that the postponement was tied to Mikoyan's U.S. visit that same month. Norstad tried to allay this fear and frankly informed the Turks of the funding difficulties that were causing the delay.[75]

When Norstad restarted the process in late April, the Turks displayed a responsiveness commensurate with their enthusiasm. Indeed, the familiar roles were now reversed, with the impatient Turks prodding the entangled Americans to move more quickly. Within days of Norstad's formal offer, the Turks agreed in principle to accept IRBMs, but the Americans took months working out the preparatory details on their side. Again, their biggest problem was funding, but there were others: they had to choose a missile site, which would in turn affect construction costs; State sought clarification of the physical control arrangements from Defense; and the two departments took several weeks to arrange a meeting on the subject. Conferring in mid-July with Herter, Foreign Minister Zorlu "expressed some surprise" that his government had not yet received an IRBM agreement for signature. Only on 10 September did the document change hands; the Turks accepted it without change in less than a week and signed it on 19 September.[76]

Unresolved were when and how to exchange notes and announce the agreement, usually trivial matters now made significant by the approach of Khrushchev's U.S. tour. An accord announced just before or during the visit might appear as a deliberate attempt to intimidate the Soviets or otherwise spoil the atmosphere. State Department officials also suspected that the Soviet premier might raise the broader IRBM issue anyway. Thus the briefing papers they prepared tried to anticipate and rebut such complaints. Herter, citing the U.S. refusal up to this point to allow Soviet actions to delay the deployments and the possibility that circumstances would be no better afterward, recommended no postponement of the agreement process on account of Khrushchev's presence. Eisenhower approved this suggestion, although State did instruct the Ankara embassy to make only a "low-key" announcement after the exchange of notes and keep related publicity minimal.[77]

In the end, however, none of this preparation was necessary. During his memorable U.S. trip Khrushchev did decry U.S. military bases, at one point asking Victor Reuther, "How would you feel if there were Soviet military bases in Mexico and Canada?" ("Who is keeping you from having them?" Reuther answered. "Set them up.") He also sarcastically griped about the secret missile installations preventing him from visiting Disneyland. But neither on the road nor in his private conferences with Eisenhower at Camp David (25–27 September) did he broach the IRBM issue. One can only speculate, but with divisive issues such as Berlin already on the table, with the reduction of East-West tensions and arrangement of a great power summit topping his immediate agenda, Khrushchev had reason to avoid repeating objections that promised to have little effect anyway. Moreover, the IRBM deal with Turkey was not completed until well after Khrushchev had returned to Moscow. Having eagerly signed its copy of the agreement, the Turkish government wanted to put off any announcement until it could present the document to the Grand National Assembly, the Turkish parliament. This it did only on 26 October, the same day it exchanged notes with the Americans, who publicly acknowledged the agreement only in response to press inquiries.[78]

The Americans must have been chagrined to encounter the most attractive IRBM host only at the end of their frustrating quest. Not only did Turkey offer the best coverage of Soviet targets from a military standpoint, but it also combined unmatched enthusiasm for the IRBMs with a minimum of conflicting national objectives and domestic impediments. The Turks wanted the latest weaponry for their armed forces as soon as possible and were willing to forgo modifications or concessions that might get in the way. They had neither illusions nor qualms about the U.S.-proposed control arrangements. That the United States would shoulder most of the financial burden helped, as did the relatively authoritarian political system in Turkey: the ruling party had no coalition partners or powerful opposition to worry about and could accept IRBMs with relative impunity. All this made for an IRBM deployment deal that, once the negotiations began, was completed with relative swiftness. The snags that occurred were almost entirely caused by the Americans. This was the last phase of the search—and the first to go off with few hitches.

The only loose end was the fifth Thor squadron, which had been earmarked for Greece. The Greeks had said they had no objections to its placement in Turkey along with the third Jupiter squadron, but U.S. officials lost interest in it altogether. When asked for his view, Norstad, despite claiming to remain a "strong advocate" of the IRBM deployments, could not justify the $110 million of scarce Military Assistance Program (MAP) funds— equal to one-fourth the annual total for Europe—that the additional squad-

MAP 2. IRBM Deployments in NATO, 1959–1963

ron would consume; this would seriously hamper his effort to meet NATO's overall force goals. Thus he, along with the air force leadership and the man soon to succeed McElroy at Defense, Thomas Gates, recommended that the squadron be scrapped even though it was 90 percent manufactured. Ike gave his approval on 21 October.[79]

CONCLUSIONS

In this way the search for hosts finally drew to a close, twenty-two months after it had begun. The scope of the IRBM deployment was now settled: in addition to the sixty Thors being readied in Great Britain, there would be a NATO IRBM force of forty-five Jupiters, thirty in Italy and fifteen in Turkey. The necessary intergovernmental agreements were complete, and the way was now open for intermilitary agreements and base construction. How the Eisenhower administration found two host allies (apart from Britain), how it cleared what turned out to be the highest of hurdles, is a multifaceted story that raises many questions.

Why did the search take so long? This is no trivial matter, because the most important military rationale for IRBMs had been the role they would play as *interim* strategic missiles, weapons that would largely, if not completely, erase the period in which Soviet ICBMs stood unchallenged.

The overarching reason why the search was so drawn out is quite simple: the 1957 NATO offer necessitated bilateral agreements between independent, sovereign states. Obviously, this was more complicated than deployment on U.S.-controlled territory (which is why USAF chiefs promoted Alaskan or Okinawan basing with increasing vigor). That said, several specific phenomena caused delay, on the U.S. as well as on the European side. In Europe, these included:

Domestic politics. Especially in Italy, but also in Greece, West Germany, and France, domestic politics seriously disrupted the search for hosts. Governments faced vigorous opposition, lengthy election campaigns, or their own sudden collapse and difficult reconstitution. They responded with timidity, secrecy, and hesitancy on the IRBM issue. If one of them fell, its successor needed time to get up to speed. Moreover, issues in domestic politics not otherwise relevant to deployment came to disrupt the search. Such was the case in Greece, where the Cyprus issue played a key role in the government's hesitation and, ultimately, reluctant rejection of the missile offer.

Pursuit of self-interest. Interested governments understandably sought to obtain the missiles on the best terms possible; hosting IRBMs was a serious matter, fraught with significant risks, and to settle for less would have been to shirk their responsibilities. So officials in Paris and Rome sought to gain concessions—the former, sole or primary control over the missiles and aid to their own nuclear program, and the latter, increased conventional military aid, a "most-favored nation" clause, a larger role in great-power diplomacy, and a reduction of its share of the costs. Only Turkey accepted U.S. terms without modifications. Satisfying, fending off, or finessing these demands took time, and in the case of France, still did not end with an agreement.

Delay stemmed from U.S. sources as well:

Sequence, not simultaneity. There were reasons for ranking potential hosts and approaching them sequentially. Policymakers wanted to minimize Soviet antagonism and thought holding off on Turkey might help, and in any case the effort involved in approaching just one country suggests that approaching four or more at the same time might have proven an overwhelming task. Still, a simultaneous pursuit of all prospective hosts would have meant the search could absorb failures, such as France, without requiring additional months for other candidates to be contacted for the first time.

Multidepartmental involvement. Two departments, State and Defense, each comprising several bureaus, shared responsibility for the search, and this compounded U.S. difficulties. Because the IRBM deployment blurred the lines between foreign and defense policies, perhaps this was unavoidable. But the two bodies lacked coordination, disputes between and within each sometimes broke out, the number of meetings and memoranda multiplied, and the resulting obstacles the search encountered required that much more time to clear.

Funding difficulties. The organizational drag is most clear in the case of funding. The administration simply failed to secure sufficient MSP funds for the IRBM deployment ahead of time. But beyond that, rising costs and interdepartmental disagreement over the nature of the problem and the measures required to solve it added still more months to the search. There was no point in scouring Europe for bases if there would be no money to pay for them, and thus the search for hosts had to wait for the search for funds, frustrating in its own right.

In sum, by offering IRBMs to the NATO allies, the Eisenhower administration exposed their deployment to the interests of and circumstances surrounding allied governments. These combined with the administration's own failures to transform a process that it originally estimated would take one year—from offer to operational status for the first IRBMs—into one that took almost two years merely to sign two basing agreements. At the time of the December 1957 offer, U.S. officials reckoned that the first NATO IRBMs would become operational by December 1958, whereas the first Atlas ICBMs would do so only by June 1959. They could thus claim that the NATO IRBMs, even if lagging behind the British Thors, would substitute for their intercontinental and submarine-launched counterparts for at least six months. By October 1959, when the last agreement was signed, officials had been forced to move the operational dates for the first Jupiters in Italy and Turkey back to April 1960 and June 1961, respectively. This adjustment made all the difference, because now they were scheduled to become functional after the first few Atlases (and shortly the first Polaris SLBMs) were already on-line.[80]

Did the United States "force" IRBMs on its NATO allies? Eisenhower holdover Douglas Dillon remarked during the 1962 Cuban missile crisis, according to notes jotted down by President Kennedy, that the Jupiters had been deployed because "they were flops—they couldn't have been fired if they had to." In Theodore Sorensen's account, Dillon said the Jupiters "had practically been forced on Italy and Turkey by an administration unable to find any worthwhile use for them." But neither the available evidence nor Dillon himself supports this claim. American officials did attempt, he writes, "to convince the Italians and the Turks that in our mutual interest they should take the Jupiters." But his 1962 comment was merely his way of saying that the Eisenhower administration knew that the Jupiters were a "clumsy and not very useful weapon." American officials at lower levels may have played rough with the Europeans, and if so, perhaps they acted on their own initiative, had no explicit directive forbidding such tactics, or misunderstood Eisenhower's wishes—as did Ambassador Zellerbach, who told Ike he had been instructed to "twist the arms of the Italians." The administration did apply pressure to countries that were seeking to extract concessions or dragging their feet; nor were they above playing one ally off against another, as Norstad did with Italy and France in early 1958. But these were countries that had already freely expressed interest in having IRBMs. There is no evidence that the administration tried to coerce unwilling allies to take them, and France, Italy, Greece, and Turkey were all, to at least some degree, willing candidates.[81]

Why did the deployment policy survive, even as U.S. doubts about the missiles deepened? This is a far more difficult question because the available evidence is sketchy, but the most plausible answer has three parts:

Credibility and the Soviet reaction. American policy embodied a paradox. On the one hand, administration officials demonstrated a vague sensitivity to Soviet apprehensions that could, on occasion, influence IRBM policy. This sensitivity shaped the ranking of potential hosts, bumped Turkey off the top of the list, and largely kept West Germany off it entirely; it also helped trigger Ike's second thoughts in June 1959.

But this awareness of Soviet concerns was eclipsed by an unwillingness to modify the basic policy—or to appear to do so—in response to Soviet threats and complaints. Shackled like other Cold War presidents by the chains of "credibility," Eisenhower worried about the effects of accommodation: if he withdrew the IRBM offer in response to the Soviets' opposition, what would they do next? Would appeasing them not merely spur them toward more ambitious undertakings? For both Eisenhower and Dulles, the fear of giving in or appearing to give in to Soviet pressure prevented them from acting on the increasingly serious doubts they had about the IRBMs. Ironically, had the Soviets kept quiet about the missiles, the Americans might have felt less bound to carry out the deployment.[82]

Credibility and the NATO allies. American officials seem to have feared the impact on NATO of withdrawing the IRBM offer. Regardless of the generally cool response to the 1957 U.S. initiative, those few countries that were interested might feel betrayed, with unpredictable consequences. Similarly, even if going ahead with deployment did nothing to enhance U.S. "credibility" in NATO, pulling the offer once it had been made might actually damage that credibility. Working from such assumptions about how best to promote allied cohesion, U.S. officials preferred IRBMs deployed and unproductive to IRBMs undeployed and counterproductive.

In any case, moreover, the search for hosts resulted from the unanimously approved Paris communiqué, which was not the United States' to revoke unilaterally. Withdrawal of the offer might require a protracted and highly visible struggle to achieve unanimous approval, as well as embarrassing public explanation. Broadcasting that it had made an error, that it had not allocated sufficient funds to deploy the missiles, that they were obsolescent and provocative, that only a few alliance partners were willing to provide bases for them—all of this would have been difficult for an administration concerned with demonstrating its international reliability in the midst of a perilous Berlin crisis (not to mention proving domestically its efficacy in safeguarding U.S. national security). The U.S. government's well-established view of its own credibility made reversing a policy, particularly a high-profile security measure within NATO, more onerous than seeing it through, no matter how questionable it was.

The disposal problem revisited. The accomplished fact of IRBM production, the "disposal problem," also played some role in sustaining the search. It had had little to do with the U.S. decision to offer missiles to NATO in 1957, but thereafter it probably did influence pursuit of the deployment even as the rationales for it withered. By mid-1959, IRBMs were coming off the production lines at a rate of between three and nine per month and were slowly piling up in U.S. warehouses. The pressure on policymakers to deploy the missiles solely because of their existence can only have increased as a result. The documents, not surprisingly, contain few explicit references to this disposal problem. And yet some administration officials cite it, at least in broad terms, in their later reflections on the IRBM deployment.[83]

These three motives for continuing the policy could work in tandem. For example, the administration could have solved the disposal problem with the deployment on U.S.-controlled territory increasingly favored by air force leaders, but its aversion to reneging on the 1957 offer dictated disposal in Europe. Addressing one problem and avoiding the creation of others together made perpetuation of the IRBM policy irresistible despite the troubling questions it raised. By committing itself to producing IRBMs, and, by committing itself to their deployment in Europe, thereby placing U.S. credibility on the line with allies and archrivals alike, the Eisenhower administration had created a policy version of the Frankenstein monster: ill conceived, fundamentally defective, yet assuming a life of its own and lurching forth with great resilience, impervious to its inventors' reconsiderations.

Eisenhower, Dulles, and the IRBMs

Finally, what about the monster's creators? Because the IRBM deployment would no longer require the involvement of top policymakers after October 1959, this is an appropriate point at which to step back and assess Eisenhower's and Dulles's handling of the IRBM issue, even though the administration would continue to oversee the deployment for another fifteen months. Such an evaluation is useful in light of "Eisenhower revisionism," which views Ike as an intelligent, forceful, even subtle leader, as well as more recent similar treatment of Dulles.[84]

The IRBM deployment episode at least confirms the suggestion of revisionists that Eisenhower was no idiot. He recognized, in 1959, that IRBMs represented a new development in strategic weapons, in that NATO could now hit the Soviet Union while giving its forces little warning and no hope of defense. That awareness is reflected in his sensitivity to the Soviet reaction. He knew what IRBMs could mean for host countries; as he would note in December 1959, "[The Italian deployment] has changed Italy's situation because it is now possible to strike from her territory both for defense and retaliation." And he certainly sensed the multiple problems that had cropped up around the missiles. "It would have been better to dump them in the ocean," he muttered at one point, "instead of trying to dump them on our allies." Thus did he express his regrets—that the search had been so troublesome and that the objects of that trouble were scarcely worth it. Clearly the president was capable of understanding the ramifications of his IRBM policy.[85]

Beyond mere competence, moreover, Eisenhower at times exhibited superior leadership qualities. He could ask uncomfortable questions about his own policy, like the one in November 1958 about first spending so much on IRBMs and only then determining allied interest in the systems. In raising questions about the Greek deployment in June 1959, he showed his respect for the NATO allies by insisting that they not be forced to take IRBMs. His use of the Cuba-Mexico analogy and sensitivity to Soviet concerns at that same moment combined stunning prescience with admirable empathy. His speculation—only six months after Fidel Castro's seizure of power—about "communist" missiles pointing north from Cuba is amazing in retrospect. More impressive still is the president's attempt to put himself in the Soviets' shoes, a relatively rare event in the early Cold War.

But this is only part, and not the most important part, of the picture. Eisenhower's awareness and insights were fleeting, narrow, and tardy. While he could recognize that his administration had not "done its homework ahead of time," that should not obscure the fact that indeed it had not done its homework ahead of time. It decided to offer IRBMs to NATO and only then bothered to learn how the Europeans and the Soviets might feel about the matter, or whether the necessary funds were available. The obstacles preventing withdrawal of the IRBM offer on the one hand and its swift fulfillment on the other lay to a large extent beyond Eisenhower's control. But this only made adequate consideration and preparation beforehand that much more crucial, and he had insisted on neither.

Consider Eisenhower's second thoughts about the Greek IRBMs in June 1959. He strangely failed to apply his understanding of this deployment to the Italian agreement reached in March or to the Turkish deal then nearing completion; there is no evidence that he reconsidered these other deployments or viewed them as provocations or potential bargaining chips. Thus the questions he posed to McElroy, far from illustrating "his insistence on personally controlling and monitoring policy making and execution," as Fred Greenstein writes, in reality suggest the opposite: the president was not in control of the IRBM policy. He conceived of hard, detailed questions too narrowly, asked them when it was too late, and abandoned them too quickly. In the IRBM episode, Eisenhower thus conforms to the less flattering assessments of scholars such as John Gaddis, who notes Ike's "persistent failure to follow through on his usually quite sound initial instincts," and Marc Trachtenberg, who sees in Ike the "kibitzer in chief": it is as if the president "were criticizing someone else's administration." That he indirectly acknowledged his earlier failure does not exonerate him for the earlier failure.[86]

A similar point holds true for Eisenhower's trusted secretary of state, John Foster Dulles. Although his resignation in April 1959 and death shortly thereafter prevented his involvement in the near reappraisal of June or the completion of the search for hosts that followed, Dulles had played a key role in American IRBM deployment policy up to that point. Although certainly undeserving of his reputation as a rigid, militant "international prosecuting attorney," he too emerges from the IRBM deployment confirming some of the criticisms scholars have made in their recent reassessments.[87]

Dulles understood the danger in distributing nuclear weapons to some allies and not others, and yet he helped to do just that, thereby creating a need to balance the intra-alliance equation. He clearly—perhaps too clearly —sensed allied unease about the post-*Sputnik* U.S. strategic guarantee, and yet to address it he pushed for an IRBM offer that Washington examined with little care and NATO received with little enthusiasm. He knew the missiles were at best interim weapons and promised to require a lengthy effort to deploy, and yet he went ahead. To his credit he worried, like Eisenhower, about provoking the Soviet Union with missiles close to its borders, but still he allowed such deployments to proceed. Even accounting for the immediate and long-term Cold War constraints that might have led others to act similarly, one must join John Gaddis in asking, "What good was Dulles's sophistication if conceptualization did not lead to implementation?" The IRBMs constitute one of those policies, in Ronald Pruessen's words, "not sufficiently aligned with the insights that preceded them," one that "spawned other, even more troubling problems." More broadly, far from being one of the policies "Dulles arranged" to create a "viable NATO" out of what had been a virtual "paper tiger," as Frederick Marks claims, the IRBM deployment would prove at best a mixed bag for the alliance and thus for the secretary's record of achievement.[88]

"We have taken . . . decisions of major import," Dulles had announced in a speech just after the 1957 NATO summit, "the full significance of which may not be apparent for some months or even years to come." As often is the case, insight comes unintended. By October 1959, part of the significance was clear: the Eisenhower administration had to struggle for almost two years to secure bases for forty-five Jupiter IRBMs that were, by the tacit admission of most top officials, politically provocative and militarily unnecessary. The other part of the "significance" lay in the future—awaiting Eisenhower's successor.[89]

3

FARCE & STATECRAFT

Don't get me wrong. A lot of good things have
come out of this missile program. My crew, you
know, was one of the first to go to America to
be trained. Lots of action there. And what a trip
it was. We went over by ship, and with all those
young ladies on that liner I didn't get to sleep
in my own bed one night.

RAF sergeant, Thor Squadron, ca. 1960

After October 1959, the Eisenhower administration continued to preside over the Jupiter deployment, but with the intergovernmental agreements with Italy and Turkey now signed, the policy no longer required the direct involvement of top civilian officials in the way that the search for hosts had. Rather, the IRBM program now entered a phase in which three other groups figure more prominently. First is the air forces of the United States, Italy, and Turkey, which now had to negotiate formal military agreements and execute the deployments. Second is a group excluded from the discussion thus far for the sake of clarity but one that had helped shape the IRBM policy environment from the start: the "strategic community" of defense journalists and nuclear analysts that had grown markedly in size and influence during the Eisenhower years. And third is the U.S. Congress, in the form of its Joint Committee on Atomic Energy, which toward the end of the Eisenhower administration entered the picture by investigating NATO's nuclear deployments, including the Jupiters. A look at the involvement of these three groups will carry the story to early 1961, when Eisenhower passed on the increasingly dubious—and still incomplete—Jupiter deployment to John F. Kennedy.

SOLDIERS: THE AIR FORCES TAKE OVER

With the intergovernmental agreements signed, primary responsibility for executing the Jupiter deployments now fell to the United States Air Force. It had to negotiate detailed technical agreements with the Italian and Turkish air forces to complement the political agreements reached by the diplomats. Then it had to oversee base construction, Turkish and Italian crew training, and actual missile deployment. All these tasks entailed additional effort and difficulties—as well as more delay, with the result that the NATO IRBMs did not take their place in the Western strategic deterrent before Eisenhower left office.

Italy

Evidence on the military implementation of the U.S.-Italian IRBM agreement is relatively sparse, although the rough outline and a few details are clear. Military talks began soon after the March 1959 exchange of notes between governments. The two sides had to settle such questions as whether Italians could supply some of the common support equipment, whether they would receive reimbursement for it, and if so, how much. Italian air force (IAF) representatives insisted on solving this and all other outstanding funding issues before signing. In addition, the two sides had to agree on a site for the second squadron; they decided in the end to place both squadrons in the Apulia region, south of Bari in southeastern Italy. Although the main base was to be located in the town of Gioia del Colle ("Joy of the Hill"), the ten three-missile launch positions were dispersed over an area of roughly eight hundred square miles. The IAF did not raise any control or launch issues; its main concerns were to keep the talks quiet and wring as much additional money from the Americans as possible. Only on 10 August 1959, months behind the more optimistic schedules, did the two air forces sign the technical agreement. Equipment began to arrive from the United States in October, and base construction made enough headway to allow erection of the first on-site training missile in mid-January 1960.[1]

The Jupiters were installed, inspected, and declared operational, in accordance with their deployment configuration, in three-missile increments (launch positions). The delays in concluding the intergovernmental and technical agreements allowed enough time to train IAF personnel so that they could tend the IRBMs from the outset, with no interim period of U.S. control as originally envisioned (under U.S. law, USAF personnel were to retain constant control of the nuclear warheads, of course, only releasing them to be matched to the missiles in case of war, but as we shall see, the actual custody arrangements assumed a different form). American forces transferred the launch positions to their Italian crews between July 1960 and June 1961, roughly within the schedule foreseen when the deployment began. But construction crews and technicians hit numerous snags along the way. These included supply bottlenecks and parts shortages, circuitry glitches, severe corrosion, spontaneous detonations of electric batteries and explosive bolts, and foul weather, including heavy rains and a spell of high winds—which, at one launch position ready for final inspection, tilted two Jupiters and toppled the third, which had to be returned to the United States for salvage. As a result of these problems, although the two Italian squadrons became operational in their entirety by the end of the scheduled period, the individual

TABLE 1

Achievement of Operational Status, Jupiter Launch Positions, Italy

LAUNCH POSITION/ SQUADRON	PLANNED	ACTUAL	DAYS BEHIND (−) OR AHEAD (+) OF SCHEDULE
1/1	1 June 1960	Feb. 1961?	−250?
5/1	1 Oct. 1960	13 Feb. 1961	−123
7/1	15 Mar. 1961	3 Mar. 1961	+12
4/1	1 Nov. 1960	24 Mar. 1961	−144
3/1	1 Dec. 1960	14 Apr. 1961	−134
2/2	1 Sept. 1960	26 Apr. 1961	−236
9/2	29 Apr. 1961	29 Apr. 1961	0
6/2	1 June 1961	7 June 1961	−6
8/2	30 June 1961	13 June 1961	+17
10/2	July 1961	July 1961	?

Source: Compiled from Brassell, "Jupiter," 18–21; Strother to AFCCS, 10 February 1961, attachment; Neufeld, *Ballistic Missiles*, 225–27; James M. Grimwood and Frances Strowd, "History of the Jupiter Missile System," History and Reports Control Branch, Management Services Office, U.S. Army Ordnance Missile Command, 27 July 1962, #252, *CMC*, 103.

Note: Most dates given are those on which the launch positions were transferred to the IAF, and actual operational status undoubtedly was achieved a bit later in most cases. Launch positions 1/1 and 2/2 had been transferred to the IAF in July and October 1960, respectively, but did not become operational until the dates shown, at the earliest. The planned operational date for 1/1 as of 10 August 1959 had been 1 April 1960, but the date given for it and all other launch positions represents a revision, made sometime in the latter half of 1959.

launch positions did so only beginning in February 1961 (see table 1). Thus the first Italian Jupiters had become operational some eight months behind schedule, and none had before Eisenhower stepped down.[2]

Turkey

Six weeks after the Americans and Turks sealed their intergovernmental IRBM agreement, Eisenhower, having stopped in Ankara on a goodwill tour, heard firsthand that the Turkish government remained enthusiastic about the missiles promised them. Foreign Minister Zorlu told the president he was "glad to have the IRBMs" and wanted "to get them set up as soon as possible." Whether the U.S. or Turkish air forces then worked as quickly as he would have liked is open to question.[3]

Technical discussions between the USAF and the Turkish air force (TAF) began on 17 November 1959, and the two sides quickly agreed on the air base at Çigli, just north of Izmir on the Aegean coast, as the main base for the Turkish Jupiter squadron. A shortage of TAF personnel led to an agreement in April 1960 under which USAF personnel would tend the missiles (when operational) until the Turks completed their training. The two sides signed the technical agreement only on 1 June 1960, the process having taken three months longer than in the Italian program. As the talks with the TAF drew to a close, however, DOD reported to President Eisenhower that it was satisfied with their progress.[4]

The USAF issued construction contracts between July and September 1960, but when Eisenhower left office on 20 January 1961, the deployment had made little additional headway. The first surface shipment of Jupiter equipment did not leave for Turkey until 23 January (arriving 11 February), and on 10 February the USAF reported that the deployment was "in the preliminary construction phase." Thus while the Italian Jupiters were almost operational when Ike left office, for the Turkish Jupiters—now thirteen months after conclusion of the deployment agreement—base construction had scarcely begun, if it had at all. Unlike its Italian counterpart, the Turkish Jupiter program was not behind its established schedule. But it was taking a long time. Perhaps the timetable in its case was merely more realistic.[5]

EXPERTS: THE VIEWS OF THE STRATEGIC COMMUNITY, 1957–1961

While the IRBMs in general did not become a major public issue during the late Eisenhower years, they did not escape the attention of the "strategic community" outside government. This amorphous group, consisting of nuclear strategists, defense correspondents, and other commentators, saw its influence grow as the superpower arms race accelerated, particularly in the wake of *Sputnik*. Scholars have rightly devoted a great deal of attention to this community in recent years but virtually none to its views on the IRBM issue. An exploration of those views will reconstruct a key context in which the Eisenhower administration's IRBM deployment decisions and efforts took place.[6]

From early on, most public observers of the IRBM deployments were critics, such as the intellectual architect of containment, George Kennan. A private citizen in 1957, Kennan caused a considerable stir with his six Reith Lectures, delivered over BBC Radio in late fall of that year. Best known for exploring the possibility of superpower "disengagement" from central Europe, the lectures also took strong exception to NATO's heavy reliance on nuclear weapons and efforts to distribute them among its members. In the final talk, which he gave on the eve of the Paris summit, Kennan argued that NATO IRBMs and other nuclear weapons would not increase Soviet willingness to accept Western disarmament proposals (unless, perhaps, their withdrawal were part of an agreement). Rather, Kennan continued with uncanny prescience, "Elaborate military arrangements of this nature, once put in hand, have consequences. They produce countermeasures on the other side. People come to depend on them as essential elements of their security. In the end it becomes difficult to consider their withdrawal or to make them the subject of negotiation." Kennan remained critical of NATO missiles thereafter, testifying before a Senate subcommittee in early 1959 that their deployment increased "Soviet nervousness" about the German problem and thus complicated its solution. Washington's assurances that the warheads would remain under U.S. control meant little: "[The Soviets] sort of smile when they hear us say that; they think that is a thing which is easily evaded or changed at the last minute."[7]

Kennan's analysis was general and political; other early critiques were more specific and military. Perhaps the best example is an article Robert Albrook published in the *Reporter* in February 1958. Analyzing the IRBMs and first-generation ICBMs as a group, Albrook noted that not only were these missiles fixed, unprotected, and thus vulnerable, but because they were liquid-fueled, their preparation time was unavoidably longer than the warning time before a Soviet strike against them (a particular problem for IRBMs, which sat that much closer to Soviet bases). Therefore these missiles would, like the U.S. Pacific Fleet at Pearl Harbor, invite rather than deter an enemy attack, a situation that might encourage the United States to strike first. And because they could not deter Soviet retaliation at the strategic nuclear level, they would indirectly discourage U.S. resistance to limited Soviet advances. With U.S. plans dependent on "a vulnerable missile system" that seemed "ill suited to keep the peace," Albrook concluded, "These plans must be altered now."[8]

Nor could one find much pro-IRBM sentiment in the two most influential books of this period by dissident retired generals. In *War and Peace in the Space Age* (1958), which claimed the United States was entering a period of a "missile-lag" vis-à-vis the Soviet Union, General James Gavin did imply that IRBMs would serve as stopgap retaliatory weapons. He recommended deployment of these "Model T's of the missile age" in southeastern Europe, however, only if they were "completely mobile." Similarly, in his critique of massive retaliation, *The Uncertain Trumpet* (1959), General Maxwell Taylor recommended that as a "quick fix" the IRBMs should be made mobile; otherwise, they constituted a cost-ineffective, "sterile asset" that invited nuclear attack.[9]

To be sure, the IRBMs received some favorable commentary, but most of it was qualified, fleeting, or both. One could find the most enthusiastic support in mass circulation magazines, in particular *Time* and *Fortune*. At least in part owing to the efforts of air force reserve officer and defense correspondent Charles Murphy, who was affiliated with both magazines, they echoed the Eisenhower administration's public position on the IRBMs. This they did as late as April 1959 when, after conclusion of the Italo-American IRBM agreement, *Time* printed a map of Europe depicting the missiles' range arcs. Across its top, readers found the equation "IRBM + NATO = ICBM." By November of that year, however, even Murphy cited the missiles as "one example of the unprecedentedly swift onset of obsolescence."[10]

Additional tempered support came from Hanson Baldwin, chief military correspondent for the *New York Times*, who in the summer of 1958 fueled the public debate over U.S. strategic vulnerability with his book *The Great Arms Race*. Baldwin wrote that IRBMs would "greatly strengthen . . . [U.S.] deterrent power against any massive enemy aggression." But he also assumed their deployment would begin at the end of that year, doubted their accuracy and reliability, and noted their contribution only together with that of ICBMs.[11]

Like that within the Eisenhower administration, the enthusiasm of other supporters waned over time. Such was the case of another major contributor to the strategic debate, the Rockefeller Panel, a blue-ribbon study group commissioned by the Rockefeller Brothers Fund and directed by Harvard academic Henry Kissinger. The first report of the panel, released in January 1958, advocated "the most rapid development and procurement" of both IRBMs and ICBMs. By the end of 1959, however, another panel report argued only that the European IRBM deployments had been "a necessary answer" to *Sputnik* and admitted that the importance of these bases might "diminish in the future."[12]

Henry Kissinger's own views underwent a more stark transformation. He

Three-missile Jupiter launch position, Turkey, 1963. Trailers and structures for personnel, launch control, fuel and power, and other purposes dot the site. Experts argued and investigating congressmen discovered that, because the Jupiters sat above ground and immobile, they were provocative, obsolescent, and vulnerable to air attack, sabotage, and even the weather. (National Archives)

had first defended the IRBMs in the summer of 1957 with his famous brief for a strategy of limited nuclear war, *Nuclear Weapons and Foreign Policy*, which he had distilled from the work of a Council on Foreign Relations study group. "[The] 1,500-mile missile would add substantially to our strategic capabilities," Kissinger had written, and it might enhance the allies' ability "to withstand Soviet atomic blackmail." The March 1957 Bermuda agreement was "a hopeful step" that "could become a model for all of NATO." His own major statement in favor of IRBM deployments, however, appeared in *Foreign Affairs* in spring 1958. Here, Kissinger rejected arguments that the missiles rendered the Western alliance "offensive" or any more vulnerable than it already was. Rather, they represented "the only means by which Europe [could] gain a degree of influence over its future." This idea rested on his implication that the missiles would be completely European-controlled; he was thus claiming to support *the* IRBM deployment while in fact supporting *an* IRBM deployment not in prospect. Before long, however, such distinctions mattered little. In 1960, as he did on the issue of limited nuclear war, Kissinger flip-flopped. In *The Necessity for Choice*, he now viewed IRBMs as vulnerable, hampered by two-key control, lacking any purpose as interim weapons, and ineffective against Soviet blackmail. Well before their deployment was complete, the IRBMs had thus lost one of their few scholarly proponents.[13]

Indeed, apart from Kissinger, leading nuclear strategists were united in their opposition to the missiles. Some of them expressed doubts about the IRBMs even before the U.S. offer to NATO of December 1957. Albert Wohlstetter, a leading RAND Corporation analyst, worried when he learned earlier that year that the Gaither Committee was going to recommend a larger IRBM force. Wohlstetter reasoned that the IRBMs, so close to the Soviet Union and thus so vulnerable, would undermine deterrence by encouraging a preemptive Soviet strike against them. He and RAND colleague William Kaufmann thus urged the committee to scrap the IRBM proposal. The committee, set on deploying some strategic system as quickly as possible, ignored them.[14]

Wohlstetter presented the most formidable case for the prosecution in January 1959 with "The Delicate Balance of Terror," which Marc Trachtenberg has called "perhaps the single most important article in the history of American strategic thought." Here he argued, first, that IRBMs based in Europe would not increase Soviet difficulties in case of war and indeed, owing to their close proximity, would actually lessen those difficulties compared with forces based in the United States. Second, IRBMs were inferior retaliatory weapons, because their reaction time, contrary to popular notions of "rapid, 'push-button' response," was rather poor. This resulted from the high standard for evidence of enemy attack required for the launch of IRBMs and all other missiles (stemming from their "unrecallability"), the greater complexity of launch decisions inherent in dual control, the clumsiness of liquid-oxygen fueling, (again) the close proximity of Soviet forces, and the lack of any protection afforded the missiles against a Soviet first strike. Third, any hopes that IRBMs could deter all-out attack against the European host countries were irrelevant, Wohlstetter argued with elegant simplicity, because the missiles "would not be able to deter an attack which they could not survive." Fourth, being useless for purposes of "limited war" and even liable to increase dependence on the massive retaliation strategy, IRBMs failed utterly to broaden the range of options available to NATO in case of war. And finally, they were provocative because their inappropriateness for retaliation might suggest to the Soviets an intention to strike first.[15]

In the wake of Wohlstetter's broadside, the commentary of other leading nuclear strategists was an anticlimax. In *Strategy in the Missile Age* (1959), Bernard Brodie seconded Wohlstetter's arguments, concluding that the IRBMs "could have no dependable retaliatory value." Not only were they unsuited to limited war, but they "could well make much more difficult the maintenance of limitations on whatever local conflict [broke] out." Herman Kahn, in his massive *On Thermonuclear War* (1960), similarly minimized the deterrent value of IRBMs because of the Soviets' ability reliably to wipe them out in a first strike. When one considers the views of Wohlstetter, Brodie, and Kahn together with those of less famous nuclear analysts and academics, it becomes clear that an impressive majority either raised serious questions about the IRBM deployments or opposed them outright.[16]

This opposition, in turn, blends with the views of journalists, former generals, and other commentators discussed above to form an equally striking majority within the strategic community as a whole. Widespread, thoughtful, both political and military, the criticism was seldom rebutted, and small wonder. Support for the missiles often faded over time or came saddled with reservations. Had the debate been a contest, it would have been no contest.

The predominance of anti-IRBM sentiment is important for two reasons. First, it meant that policy making inside the Eisenhower administration took place while serious, learned criticism swirled around on the outside. Throughout the search for host countries, sound arguments against deployment continually surfaced that could only have encouraged detractors and discouraged enthusiasts within government. They may even have helped fracture the official consensus in 1958–59.

Second, several public IRBM opponents in the 1957–61 period would go on to influence national security policy in the next administration. Although a handful of IRBM advocates would do so as well, including a few who had sat on the Gaither and Rockefeller Panels, these individuals never demonstrated any specific attachment to the missiles. The critics, by contrast, developed sophisticated, sustained arguments about national security strategy in general—and corresponding arguments about the IRBMs in particular—that they would bring with them to Washington. After all, their criticisms of the IRBMs' vulnerability, poor response and warning times, low second-strike utility, high first-strike utility, and resulting propensity to provoke were born of compelling strategic logic unlikely to be quickly forgotten. Indeed, the logic was so obvious that members of Congress hit upon it as well—although they would do so based on firsthand experience.

LAWMAKERS: THE JOINT COMMITTEE ON
ATOMIC ENERGY INTERVENES, 1960–1961

The Joint Committee on Atomic Energy of the U.S. Congress (JCAE) cast a final shadow on the IRBMs as Eisenhower prepared to leave office. Established to monitor compliance with the McMahon Act and enjoying wide statutory latitude—wide enough for Ike to deem it "unconstitutional in its functions"—the JCAE considered the preservation of both U.S. and civilian control over nuclear weapons among its most vital responsibilities. By the late 1950s, it was becoming increasingly alarmed by the state of custody and control arrangements in NATO, and in the summer of 1960 it formed an ad hoc subcommittee to undertake a comprehensive review of the subject. The review culminated in a European inspection tour at year's end that exposed the committee to the practical details of the administration's IRBM policy.[17]

The delegation, made up of five JCAE members, representatives of the Atomic Energy Commission (AEC) including its chair, John McCone, and various staffers, visited nuclear installations in eight countries from 26 November to 15 December 1960, and by all accounts it was appalled by what it saw. Weapons-control horror stories were nothing new to the JCAE; one member had inspected U.K. Thor installations in 1959 and discovered that one British officer had in his possession both firing keys—his and that of his U.S. counterpart—while he went about demonstrating how accident-proof the launch system was. But the ad hoc subcommittee was prepared for neither the number nor the potential gravity of the inadequacies it encountered. One of the more serious was the Quick Reaction Alert (QRA) aircraft, which were nuclear-armed and ready for their European pilots at a moment's notice; at one airfield, the delegation learned that the only U.S. hope of preventing an unauthorized takeoff—and thus, conceivably, World War III—was a solitary, eighteen-year-old U.S. sentry at the end of the runway who had been issued a carbine but no specific instructions. When asked what he would do in case of such an incident, he replied that he would try to shoot the renegade pilot.[18]

The subcommittee also found major flaws in another weapon system: the Jupiter IRBM. Members noted four main problem areas:

Control. "We were scared stiff by what we saw," recalled JCAE executive director John Ramey, referring to the two-key system already suspect among committee members. Again they wondered what would happen if at a missile position the European launch control officer, in Ramey's words, "decided to overpower our man and take away his key? Why, [he] would

have himself quite a modern weapon, that's what." They considered this particularly likely amid political upheaval and had in mind the military revolt
that had failed in France a few months before.[19]

Custody. Apart from the question of control, the original procedure for
custody as understood by the JCAE entailed location of W-49 thermonuclear
warheads in U.S.-controlled "igloos" hundreds of yards away. They would
be released and "matched" to their missiles only in case a war had broken
out and the United States decided to use nuclear weapons. The delegation
was reminded, however, that the USAF had persisted in establishing "Alert
Procedures" in which the warheads sat atop the Jupiters *at all times*, raising
serious questions, to say the least, about the real extent of U.S. custody.[20]

Communications. The ad hoc subcommittee identified some still-classified
deficiencies in communications. Subcommittee chair Chet Holifield (D-
Calif.) later claimed that the only way the Jupiter crews could communicate
with SHAPE in Paris was by telephone—over wires, above ground. Thus,
Holifield remembered, any saboteur with lineman's spurs and a "two-bit"
pair of pliers could sever this link. No backup system existed, so in case of
a cut neither launch nor any other orders could get through. This version
should be viewed with caution; it is clear, for example, that as of September
1961 (although conceivably because of the JCAE's criticism), the Jupiter sites
had secure, redundant communications with outside authority. Clarification
of this point awaits full declassification of the subcommittee report.[21]

Vulnerability. This was the weakness that impressed the delegation most.
Members visited a launch position in Italy that was situated on flat terrain
with scrub brush, a public highway, and private residences all easily within
rifle range. They noted that the Jupiters, with extremely thin skins, thus
represented attractive targets to saboteurs, who, particularly if they acted
during fueling, could easily put the missiles out of commission with a few
bullets. The surrounding area, moreover, in which the Communist party had
received 22.8 percent of the vote in 1958, seemed likely to produce saboteurs. "In periods of . . . incipient hostilities," the subcommittee wrote in its
report, "the vulnerability of these missiles to such sabotage would appear
especially acute."[22]

Some of the subcommittee's views on the as yet uninstalled Turkish Jupiters remain classified, but it did argue that the liquid-fueled, fixed Jupiters
were "obsolete" compared with the solid-fueled, mobile Polaris SLBMs or
with second-generation medium-range ballistic missiles (MRBMs, technically of shorter range than IRBMs, although officials often conflated the
two terms). Echoing the nuclear strategists, the subcommittee argued that

the unhardened, immobile IRBMs were of "highly questionable" retaliatory value. "In the event of hostilities, assuming NATO will not strike the first blow," it continued, "the USSR with its ballistic missile capabilities could be expected to take out these missiles [with what] would undoubtedly be a surprise attack."[23]

In its February 1961 report, "The Study of United States and NATO Nuclear Weapons Arrangements," the subcommittee urged a fundamental reevaluation of NATO's nuclear weapons systems and military posture. And, while acknowledging the readiness-versus-safety dilemma inherent in the Alert Procedures, it pointed the way toward the placement of electronic locks, or Permissive Action Links (PALs), on U.S. nuclear weapons. Specifically on the IRBMs, the report recommended that the thirty Italian Jupiters, already installed and almost operational, be protected by enlarging their base perimeters beyond rifle range or fashioning for each of them a vertical bulletproof housing removable for launch. As for the fifteen Jupiters in Turkey, however, it concluded that construction should not be permitted to begin. "Instead of placing 15 obsolete liquid-fueled JUPITERS in Turkey, an alternative system such as a POLARIS submarine with 16 IRBM's operated and controlled by U.S. personnel could be assigned to NATO in lieu [thereof]. Such an assignment could be made before 1962 when the JUPITER system would be coming into operation. The POLARIS submarine system would be mobile and thus a much better retaliatory force." The subcommittee handed the report to President John F. Kennedy on 15 February 1961, three weeks after his inauguration, and drew his attention to, among others, the Jupiter recommendations. It was Kennedy's first encounter with the IRBMs as president, and it undoubtedly seemed routine enough at the time.[24]

TORCH PASSERS: EISENHOWER'S BEQUEST, JANUARY 1961

In January 1961, as President Eisenhower looked back on his two terms in office, he could have proudly noted several positive accomplishments in the realms of foreign and national security policy. Unfortunately, the IRBM deployments were not among them, and he knew it. Of course, neither he nor his subordinates would admit as much publicly. Indeed, in its final year, the administration continued to proclaim the missiles' value. Just days before leaving office, Eisenhower stated in his last budget message that the Thors and Jupiters added "still another important element of strength to the strategic forces."[25]

At the same time, however, his administration in reality took an increasingly dim view of the IRBMs. This is evident in its tacit recognition that the missiles had fulfilled neither their intended military nor political purpose. As we have seen, Eisenhower had ascribed little military value to the IRBMs from the outset but offered them to NATO mainly with the political objective of alliance cohesion in the nuclear realm. Yet by 1960 his administration was acting as if the IRBMs had accomplished nothing even toward this end. At the North Atlantic Council meeting in December of that year, Secretary of State Herter tentatively proposed establishment of a multilateral, seaborne MRBM force (this marked the beginning of the effort to create the Multilateral Force [MLF]). With this, U.S. officials pursued several goals—internal bureaucratic advantage, nuclear nonproliferation, and European integration—but also the reduction of tension within the Atlantic alliance over nuclear weapons, a need that the IRBMs had clearly done little to satisfy.[26]

The administration's low regard for the missiles is even more evident from a conference held on 13 January 1961, one week before Eisenhower left office. The president met with Defense Secretary Gates, JCS chair Lyman Lemnitzer, AEC chair McCone, and a few other officials to discuss the control and dispersal of nuclear weapons. Every bit as disturbed as other participants in the European tour, McCone raised the IRBM issue, citing the Italian Jupiters' location among Communist voters, vulnerability to small arms fire, and obsolescence compared with the Polaris missiles now entering service. He thus urged a reconsideration of deployment plans. Secretary Gates agreed, adding that the Jupiter deployments were "actually more symbolic than useful." But he also accurately sensed the corner into which U.S. policymakers had painted themselves. "To reverse our agreements regarding JUPITER," he warned, "would cause political difficulties which would exceed the difficulty of maintaining the missiles on site." For the president, it was enough to claim to those present that he had opposed "the decision to urge these missiles on Italy in the first place." General Lemnitzer sought the cloud's silver lining by raising the possibility of better protecting the Turkish Jupiters, presumably by hardening the launch positions. And, because the Italian missiles were "already in place, he recommended allowing the deployments to stay for a while." Ike approved the suggestion.[27]

The 13 January discussion was a fitting conclusion to three years of U.S.

policy making on the IRBMs. Top civilian officials were painfully aware of the Jupiters' flaws, hard pressed to name their virtues, and yet convinced there was no turning back. And Eisenhower, as before, was not at his best. Rather than assume ultimate responsibility for the predicament, as would have been proper, he could only revert to his role as kibitzer in chief, this time adding a petty and somewhat perverse I-told-you-so. Again, he acted as if he were criticizing someone else's administration.

More important, however, the policy did not go away, blending in with the routine of numerous other NATO and U.S. defense measures. Rather, Eisenhower now handed over to his successor a program that had been neither completed by the military nor forgotten by the Soviets.

Eisenhower's legacy lay surrounded by doubts that had proliferated and grown stronger between 1959 and 1961. American and host-country air forces encountered more difficulties in deploying IRBMs, quite apart from those surmounted in the search for hosts. This consumed more time, which in turn further diminished the missiles' military value, bringing ever closer the point at which the obsolescent would become the obsolete. Expert opinion outside the administration, moreover, decidedly negative during the search for hosts, only grew more negative thereafter. And finally, lawmakers responsible for nuclear matters discovered some of the IRBMs' drawbacks firsthand and sought to move the incoming administration to stop that portion of the deployment that could be stopped.

Thus a formidable array of doubts accompanied the presidential transition of 20 January 1961—in the form of a troubled military deployment effort still far from finished, a powerful, multifaceted critique shared by many who would influence the new administration's national security policies, and a congressional report that called for the Turkish deployment's cancellation. The question now, as John Kennedy took the reins of power, was whether these latest doubts would succeed in affecting the IRBM deployments where the earlier doubts had failed.

4

THE OLD FRONTIER

We should bear in mind a few impressive lines of advice from [Liddell] Hart's book: . . . "Never corner an opponent, and always assist him to save face. Put yourself in his shoes—so as to see things through his eyes. Avoid self-righteousness like the devil—nothing is so self-blinding."
John F. Kennedy, Saturday Review,
3 September 1960

It is conceivable that [the Soviets] might be prepared to offer something in return for the liquidation of such forward bases (e.g., the SAC overseas bases and IRBM bases in England, Italy, and Turkey) since there is some evidence that such bases, in their eyes, appear to have utility primarily if used in a first strike capacity.
Weapons System Evaluation Group study,
5 September 1961

It has been an axiom of American politics that when one party has wrested control of the White House from the other, the new president has accentuated whatever distinguished him from the old. This was particularly true of the image-conscious John Kennedy, who went so far as to dodge photographers while golfing for fear of comparison to Dwight Eisenhower. To be sure, the sharply contrasting perceptions most people still have of the two leaders are largely justified; real and important differences existed, in foreign and national security policy as well as in other spheres. Nevertheless, significant elements of continuity are often overlooked, and one of these was IRBM policy. Like Eisenhower, Kennedy developed serious doubts about the Jupiter missiles, and like Eisenhower, Kennedy decided to proceed with the policy anyway—and for essentially the same reasons.[1]

In December 1957, John Kennedy was not president and Cuba was not a nuclear powder keg. Rather, he was still a relatively obscure first-term senator, and the island, which he first visited that same month, was to him a mere bawdy amusement park. But by this point Kennedy was seeking to leave his mark in the realms of foreign policy and national defense and thus did have occasion to take a stance on the IRBM issue.[2]

His views traveled a familiar trajectory. On the eve of the NATO heads of government meeting, Kennedy expressed his support for the emerging IRBM offer. "Our allies must possess intermediate range missiles," he wrote in the *New York Times*, "until we develop an intercontinental ballistic missile capable of reaching Moscow from our own shores." Like members of the Eisenhower administration, however, Kennedy began to have doubts about the missiles the following year. In his first major speech warning of a "missile gap," he cautioned that during the approaching years of strategic inferiority, the United States would have no missiles with which to answer a Soviet nuclear strike, "particularly after [the] few exposed IRBM bases in Europe and the Mediterranean [were] attacked." In late 1959, he worried that the security NATO IRBMs afforded the United States rested on host-country consent, which might not be forthcoming in the case of a Soviet attack only on East Asia or the United States, especially if coupled with Soviet threats of retaliation against Western Europe. Thus, he said that although these missiles were "important in contributing to the sense of security of the countries involved," the United States could only obtain genuine security from Polaris SLBMs based at sea and ICBMs based at home. And in 1960, after formally declaring his presidential candidacy, Kennedy stepped up his criticism. He did so indirectly, by demanding that Americans "critically reexamine the far-flung overseas base structure" on which so much of the U.S. retaliatory capability was then based, and directly, by declaring that the IRBMs—" 'soft,' immobile, and undispersed—invite surprise attack."[3]

Kennedy's doubts about the IRBMs stemmed from his broader ideas about the U.S. nuclear force. As a senator, he had criticized Massive Retaliation and promoted its main rival strategy, what Maxwell Taylor would dub "Flexible Response": "a capability to react across the entire spectrum of possible challenge, for coping with anything from general atomic war to infiltrations and aggression such as threaten Laos and Berlin." While Kennedy advocated less reliance on nuclear weapons, however, he did not neglect them—far from it. He consistently stressed the importance of strategic might, as his leading role in the missile gap controversy would suggest.[4]

But JFK, influenced by Albert Wohlstetter and other RAND analysts, wanted to close the alleged gap in such a way as to reduce the vulnerability of U.S. forces. He thus proposed two measures: an increase in the portion of the U.S. bomber force on airborne alert, and an acceleration of the development and production of the Minuteman ICBM and Polaris SLBM. With more bombers aloft, or aloft more quickly, and with strategic missiles protected by either concrete silos or the world's vast oceans, the U.S. nuclear deterrent would be less vulnerable and more credible. During the first months of his presidency, Kennedy carried out these proposals as well as others, such as cancellation of the primitive Snark cruise missile, largely with a view to reducing the vulnerability of the U.S. strategic arsenal.[5]

A POLICY REVIEW, FEBRUARY–MAY 1961

Considering his defense preferences and policies, one could reasonably expect President Kennedy to have stopped the deployment of the vulnerable Jupiters in its tracks, if not also to have begun removing those already installed in Italy. This is particularly so because the Jupiters on their own quickly attracted Kennedy's attention. Even though he had to contend with other, more pressing foreign policy problems of early 1961, especially Laos and Cuba, the missiles became a live issue within the new administration.

To begin with, the Soviets refused to let the United States forget about their recurrent Jupiter anxiety. After mid-1959, their campaign against the NATO IRBMs lost its intensity but persisted. Throughout 1960 and into the spring of 1961, Soviet leaders and analysts periodically blasted the deployments, sometimes all of them—applying such labels as "NATO's Mediterranean Nuclear-Rocket Axis"—sometimes just those in Italy, but mostly those (pending) in Turkey. Nor did Moscow give up using diplomatic channels. In February 1961, it warned the Turks about IRBM base construction on their territory; Ankara responded with its usual defiance, along with the extraordinary claim that its defense measures were "not aimed at the Soviet Union."[6]

Top Soviet officials, moreover, again lodged their protests personally. In late March, Foreign Minister Gromyko complained privately to Kennedy's disarmament adviser John McCloy about U.S. overseas bases and nuclear weapons in NATO; McCloy assured him that the weapons were only for defense and that "NATO could not and would not start a nuclear war." More important, Khrushchev raised the issue in a public letter duel with Kennedy triggered by the failed Bay of Pigs invasion, the U.S.-organized effort in April 1961 to topple the Soviet-backed Cuban government of Fidel Castro. An irate Khrushchev charged that, in contrast with the benign Castro regime, governments in "some countries bordering on the Soviet Union [had] made their territory available for the establishment of American military bases" openly "spearheaded" against his country. In light of the Bay of Pigs, the Soviet premier insisted that the Soviet Union had "no lesser grounds for acting in the same way" toward hostile neighbors as the United States had toward Cuba. There is no doubt that he was referring, first and foremost, to Turkey. Kennedy let the letter go unanswered, thus ending the exchange. What he thought about the Soviet argument remains secret, but as Michael Beschloss has argued, the president undoubtedly missed what in retrospect was an important signal: Khrushchev was not merely lodging another complaint about Turkey and the Jupiters, but he was also, perhaps for the first time, broadly equating Cuba and Turkey.[7]

Influential Americans joined Khrushchev in drawing the administration's attention to the Cuba-Turkey analogy. As we have seen, Eisenhower had made the connection in June 1959. But by early 1961, with U.S.-Cuban relations having broken down completely and with Fidel Castro now cultivating increasingly strong ties with the Soviet Union, a scenario of the type Ike had imagined suddenly seemed less outlandish. In February, at an executive session of the Senate Foreign Relations Committee, Senator Albert Gore (D-Tenn.) described the Jupiter deployment to Secretary of State Dean Rusk as "the kind of provocation" that needed to be "considered very carefully." He continued, "I wonder what our attitude would be if warheads should be attached to missiles in Cuba." In a memo passed on to JFK in May, Senator Claiborne Pell (D-R.I.) pointed out the "inconsistency" in such a case of declaring allied missiles in Turkey acceptable yet Soviet missiles near the United States unacceptable. And that same month, journalist Arthur Krock asked the president in person if he saw the weakness in U.S. statements that the United States, which had "ringed Russia around with military bases, could not accept a pro-Communist base" in Cuba. Kennedy said yes, but at this moment the analogy did not trouble him terribly. He merely expressed his intention thereafter to emphasize the different purposes of U.S. and Soviet overseas bases.[8]

At least a few administration officials, however, hit upon the analogy themselves. After the Bay of Pigs, John McCloy wrote to JFK's special counsel, Ted Sorensen, and wondered whether the United States had the right to demand Castro's ouster. "Even if the Soviet Union had missile bases in Cuba—which it hasn't," he asked, "—why would we have any more right to invade Cuba than Khrushchev has to invade Turkey, where we do have [sic] missile bases?" Similarly, in a memo to the president he ultimately did not send, Undersecretary of State Chester Bowles registered his concern that the United States might fail to understand the Soviet reaction to U.S. defense programs. "A double standard which allows us to react angrily at the slightest rumor of a Soviet missile base in Cuba, while we introduce thirty [sic] missile set ups into Turkey . . . is dangerously self-defeating." The Kennedy administration therefore operated amidst several reminders, from within and without, about the deployment in Turkey and the related Cuba-Turkey analogy.[9]

These reminders could only have strengthened the impact of actual recommendations to cancel the Turkish program, beginning with the JCAE ad hoc subcommittee report delivered to the administration in mid-February. Evidence regarding the report's direct impact is sparse and contradictory, but it is clear that Kennedy, Rusk, and other top officials either read the report, discussed it at length with subcommittee chair Holifield, or both. In addition, they were sufficiently impressed by the general command and control problems it raised to begin an effort to install electronic locks, or "Permissive Action Links" (PALs), on U.S. nuclear weapons. Kennedy's immediate reaction to the report's Jupiter sections is unknown.[10]

Regardless, voices inside the administration soon joined those represented in the JCAE report. In February, JFK had recruited former secretary of state Dean Acheson to chair a major task force on NATO. Acheson presented his report, "A Review of North Atlantic Problems for the Future," soon known as the "Green Book," to Kennedy in late March. It recommended most importantly the adoption of a posture and capability along the lines of Flexible Response, but it also discussed nuclear forces at length. The report called upon the president to "state that nuclear weapons now in the European area would be retained there, and would not be withdrawn without [the] allies' consent or adequate replacement," so it did not recommend immediate efforts to remove the Italian Jupiters. But the authors, undoubtedly influenced by the JCAE report and by the RAND analysts among them (including Albert Wohlstetter), argued that the United States "should consider suggesting to the Turks that their resources would be better used and their interests . . . better served by the projected deployment and commitment of Polaris submarines in place of the first generation IRBM squadron now scheduled for Turkey." Further, "If the Turks feel otherwise, or if the British or Italians object because of the implications for their IRBMs, we should not press the point." Cancellation, they explained, "would free the Turkish and MAP resources involved for other purposes, and it would avoid the deployment of 'strike first' weapons in a politically volatile country on the Soviet border." As compensation, the Turks should be offered other equipment worth the same amount in MAP funds. Despite the important caveat about Turkish, Italian, or British opposition, the Acheson task force had gone out of its way to join the JCAE in urging cancellation of the Turkish deployment.[11]

Robert S. McNamara, Kennedy's energetic secretary of defense, did likewise. The Jupiter deployment did not figure prominently in the sweeping strategic review McNamara launched as his first order of business. The ninety-six projects he unloaded on his subordinates in early March "covered damn near everything," as one military officer put it, but not the IRBMs. Nevertheless, undoubtedly influenced in turn by the Green Book and the several RAND "Whiz Kids" who had come to work for him, and perhaps by the JCAE report, McNamara, too, recommended cancellation of the deployment in Turkey.[12]

With three interrelated yet discrete recommendations—from influential sources—to cancel the deployment hitting his desk, long convinced of the need to modernize the nuclear deterrent, Kennedy nevertheless did not order an effort to cancel. During discussion and revision of the Acheson report in the National Security Council on 29 March, the president asked the head of the State Department's Policy Planning Staff, George McGhee, whether he thought the Turks would allow cancellation. McGhee, who had served as ambassador to Turkey several years earlier, replied that he doubted they would, but the issue could be investigated in depth. Kennedy thus directed that the original passage in the Green Book be deleted and "that a group representing the Departments of State (Chairman) and Defense and the Central Intelligence Agency should review the question of deployment of IRBM's to Turkey and make recommendations" to him. McGhee would chair the group. As it performed its task, construction work on the Turkish Jupiter bases continued.[13]

The McGhee review group began its work in April 1961, soliciting the views of interested agencies and embassies, and many expressed their opposition to cancellation. The Joint Chiefs were clearly against it, as was the Bureau of European Affairs at the State Department. The embassies in London and Rome reported their view that cancellation would cause serious domestic political problems for the British and Italian governments, considering the commitments each had made to their IRBMs already deployed. The Rome embassy added that any effort to obtain the Italians' agreement to give up their Jupiters should entail only eventual removal and be made independently, not as a means of applying pressure on the Turks. Yet neither embassy flatly opposed a Jupiter removal effort in either Italy or Turkey.[14]

General Norstad, SACEUR, submitted the most detailed defense of continuing the deployment. He argued that the Jupiters retained military and especially political and psychological value; that all fixed installations were vulnerable; that command and control problems could be eliminated by making the temporary U.S. control of the missiles permanent; and that with 80 percent of the necessary funds through FY 1963 unrecoverable, savings from cancellation would be insignificant. He ended with what amounted to an assertion that more nuclear weapons meant more security, regardless of their particular characteristics: "This is the time to create strength, not reduce it." And yet this came only after a notable concession. "It is an admission against interest to say so," he wrote, "but I must express my belief that it may be possible to mold [the] Turkish attitude [to allow cancellation]."[15]

Based on available information, the bureaucratic lines were thus drawn something like this: in favor of canceling the Turkish deployment were the Acheson task force (again, with its caveat about allied objections); Secretary McNamara; the JCAE (which continued to pressure the administration through late April); Undersecretary of State Bowles; and the AEC. Advocating continuation were the Joint Chiefs, General Norstad, and the State Department's European bureau. The stances of other interested parties are unknown, but obviously the government was divided, with significant forces on both sides. Another constituency, however, had not yet weighed in—the Turks.[16]

In April, Kennedy instructed Secretary Rusk to sound out the Turks, which he did at a meeting in Ankara of the Central Treaty Organization (CENTO). During an after-dinner stroll, Rusk recalled, he raised the issue with Turkish foreign minister Selim Sarper, offering to station U.S. Polaris submarines in the eastern Mediterranean as a substitute. Sarper, however, objected vigorously on two grounds. First, he explained that his government had just secured the Grand National Assembly's approval for the Turkish share of the deployment funding, and for it immediately to turn around and cancel the project would be deeply embarrassing. Second, he said that cancellation before Polaris submarines were available would seriously undermine Turkish morale. Indeed, the Turks considered Polaris submarines insufficient even if available; on this or some subsequent occasion, they made it clear to Rusk that Jupiters based on Turkish soil represented firm proof of the U.S. commitment to Turkey's security—submarines cruising the Mediterranean did not. The Turks, in Rusk's words, "were very upset." He claims he then returned to Washington and discussed the matter with Kennedy, who "disliked" going ahead "but understood the Turkish point of view." By early May, therefore, the administration was probably leaning toward recommending continuation of the deployment on account of Turkish resistance. The McGhee group had not yet finished its review by early June, however, when Kennedy and Khrushchev met face to face, for the first and only time.[17]

THE VIENNA SUMMIT AND KENNEDY'S DECISION TO PROCEED, JUNE 1961

Both Kennedy and Khrushchev had sought an opportunity to take measure of the other in person, and they agreed to hold a summit in Vienna on 3–4 June 1961. In the briefing papers it prepared and Kennedy read beforehand, the State Department understandably made no direct reference to the IRBMs; the closest it came to doing so was in its discussion of Soviet stances on disarmament issues, which noted continued, low-key promotion of a Balkan nuclear-free zone and a hint the previous year of interest in "a possible mutual withdrawal of forces from both sides of [the Soviet Union's] frontiers with *Turkey* and *Iran*." The State Department considered far more pressing issues such as Berlin and Laos as likely to dominate the proceedings in Vienna, and it directed its preparatory efforts accordingly.[18]

The prediction proved accurate, but Khrushchev nevertheless demonstrated that the issue of the Turkish missiles, now under construction, still stuck in his craw. During lunch on 3 June, Khrushchev spoke of an American engineer who had told him he was building houses in Turkey. The Soviets knew "that in fact he was building military bases there." Khrushchev concluded, "But that is a matter for his own conscience." Later, during the three o'clock meeting, Khrushchev became more specific. The subject was Cuba, and Khrushchev referred to Kennedy's claim that the United States had staged the Bay of Pigs invasion because Cuba posed a threat to U.S. security. "Can six million people really be a threat to the mighty US?" he asked, according to the minutes. "The United States has stated that it is free to act," he continued, "but what about Turkey and Iran? . . . They march in its wake, and they have U.S. bases and rockets. If the U.S. believes that it is free to act, then what should the USSR do?" With the Bay of Pigs, the United States had "set a precedent" for intervention in the internal affairs of other countries. "The USSR is stronger than Turkey and Iran, just as the U.S. is stronger than Cuba. This situation may cause miscalculation," he warned, repeating a term Kennedy had used earlier. "Both sides should agree to rule out miscalculation." In reply, JFK acknowledged the presence of U.S. bases in Iran and Turkey. "However," he added somewhat lamely, "these two countries are so weak that they could be no threat to the USSR, no more than Cuba [is] to the US." Logically, this would appear to have justified a Soviet version of the Bay of Pigs launched across the Black Sea, not to mention the fact that by declaring Turkey "weak," Kennedy was ignoring the construction of IRBM bases on its soil that had provoked Khrushchev's complaint in the first place.[19]

Although the Soviet premier did not exploit this rhetorical opportunity, he was not finished. Some time later in the exchange, he mentioned the 1960 coup d'état that had changed governments in Ankara. The Soviet Union, he claimed, "had remained neutral because it regarded the change as an internal affair of that country." And then, once more he criticized the maintenance of U.S. bases surrounding the Soviet Union, which was "very unwise and aggravate[d] the relations" between the two countries. "We must be reasonable and keep our forces within our national boundaries." Khrushchev couched the plea in a strained argument about how U.S. bases militarized and thus internally polarized the host countries, resulting in unrest which

President John F. Kennedy and Soviet premier Nikita S. Khrushchev in Vienna, June 1961. For reasons of credibility partly stemming from this meeting, Kennedy neither canceled the Turkish deployment nor "ordered" the missiles removed before October 1962. Khrushchev, long irked by the NATO IRBMs, would vow to give the Americans "a little of their own medicine." At left is Soviet foreign minister Andrei Gromyko. (Stanley Tretick, Look; courtesy John F. Kennedy Library)

that United States would then blame on the Soviets. But on the issue of Turkey, he was really using the Vienna opportunity to convey to Kennedy two of his attitudes. One was his fundamental irritation over hostile missiles near his country's borders that had persisted, with varying intensity, for years. And the other was his attachment to the analogy between Cuba and Turkey, which he had now demonstrated to be far more powerful in his mind than a mere public debating point scored after the Bay of Pigs episode.[20]

We have no evidence as to what extent Khrushchev's protests about Turkey impressed Kennedy; they certainly did not affect him as much as Khrushchev's overall bellicosity or his demand, issued on the second day at Vienna, for a settlement of the Berlin question within six months. With this ultimatum, the Kremlin had reopened the Berlin crisis, which would dominate U.S. foreign policy making throughout the summer and into the fall.

Indeed, the Vienna experience and the reemerging Berlin crisis unavoidably created a new context in which the administration would make its final decision on the Turkish IRBMs. A few days after the summit, Rusk asked his various bureaus "to review [the] Turkish IRBM project and to reappraise

[U.S.] policy in light of the Vienna talks," and on 13 June Rusk met with Norstad and Assistant Secretary of Defense Paul Nitze to discuss the issue. All three agreed that the Vienna talks had transformed the policy environment; Nitze felt they had "reinforced the undesirability of asking [Foreign Minister] Sarper again to consider cancellation," and Norstad added that again it was time to demonstrate "increased allied nuclear power" as NATO had done by agreeing to deploy IRBMs in 1957. Rusk raised the command and control problem, but Norstad assured him that U.S. personnel could take the precautions necessary to prevent an unauthorized launch. The secretary ended the meeting by concluding that "there was a consensus that the IRBM program should not be held up or cancelled." As a result, George McGhee submitted a one-page memo to the White House on 22 June in which he cited Foreign Minister Sarper's "strongly adverse" reaction at the CENTO meeting, Norstad's having stressed the Jupiters' military importance to the Turks (which would now make persuading the Turkish military to accept cancellation difficult), and Norstad's own preference for going ahead. Most important, he argued in his memo, "in the aftermath of Khrushchev's hard posture at Vienna, cancellation of the IRBM deployment might seem a sign of weakness." Therefore, he recommended that "action should not be taken to cancel projected deployment of IRBM's to Turkey." Before Vienna, fear of antagonizing the Turks lay behind this view, but after Vienna, fear of encouraging the Soviets came to the fore.[21]

No relevant documents are available, but Kennedy probably agreed with the analysis of Rusk, Norstad, Nitze, and the McGhee group. Dean Rusk has said this was the case, adding that the president hoped that such resolute action would serve to restrain Khrushchev over Berlin. Or, as McNamara's deputy, Roswell Gilpatric, has put it, the administration could not cancel the deployment quickly without making it appear that the United States was "knuckling under" in the face of Khrushchev's demands. In any case, the Turkish deployment proceeded as before.[22]

"In 1961 and 1962 [Kennedy] faced a series of judgments on major systems," his National Security adviser McGeorge Bundy later wrote, and "he always preferred the system which could survive an attack, against the system which might provoke one." Similarly, "he preferred the system which was on the high seas or at home to that which required a base abroad and evoked a real or pretended charge of encirclement from Moscow." Such, to be sure, were his preferences. Kennedy's actions, however, could reflect other priorities. He in fact shares responsibility with his predecessor for the deployment of the Turkish Jupiters, which by mid-1961 were vulnerable and provocative weapons to a degree at least as great as—and, relative to newer systems entering service, even greater than—they had ever been. Kennedy at least theoretically had an opportunity to cancel the deployment, since construction had not yet begun when he entered office. He seriously considered doing so and yet deliberately decided to go ahead. To suggest, as some authors later would, that Kennedy phased out the Jupiters in order to improve the invulnerability of the U.S. strategic arsenal is therefore misleading in the extreme. As we shall see, it would not be until late 1962 that the administration would decide to do what was necessary to overcome Turkish resistance and its own fears and achieve withdrawal of the Jupiters—and under circumstances decidedly different from a systematic weapons system review. In short, the 1961 decision to proceed with the Jupiter deployment is a case in which, for Kennedy, alliance and superpower politics overrode the strategic logic that propelled many of his other national security initiatives.[23]

IBRAHIM II: THE TURKISH DEPLOYMENT, 1961–1962

The Turkish IRBM deployment had a code name, IBRAHIM II, and it was an interesting choice. Ibrahim may have been selected because it was a name from Turkey's past that contained the letters I-R-B-M, but it was not just any name. The seventeenth-century Ottoman sultan Ibrahim was a debauchee, corrupt, neurotic, perhaps even psychotic, who was dethroned and executed before he could completely run his empire into the ground. With him, Lord Kinross writes, "the dynasty plumbed depths of human inadequacy lower than ever before." He had no namesake, and by naming the Jupiters after him the authors may have been signaling their misgivings about them.[24]

For the moment, at least, IBRAHIM II did not weigh quite so heavily on the realm. As occurred in Italy, the deployment in Turkey did have some problems: one missile's electric battery detonated spontaneously, contaminating the instrument compartment, and in a bizarre validation of the JCAE subcommittee's fears, a stray bullet pierced another Jupiter and wrecked its engine. In addition, the language barrier drove the number of dollars, and presumably the number of months, needed to train the Turkish crews well above that for British Thor crews. Turkish personnel did not first attempt a Jupiter training launch at Cape Canaveral until 18 April 1962 (it was successful). But the USAF and Chrysler civilian teams had learned from their Italian experiences; construction problems were fewer, and solutions came more easily. As a result, the deployment proceeded on or slightly ahead of schedule. As shown in table 2, the five launch positions became operational

TABLE 2

Achievement of Operational Status, Jupiter Launch Positions, Turkey

LAUNCH POSITION	PLANNED	ACTUAL	DAYS BEHIND (−) OR AHEAD (+) OF SCHEDULE
2	6 Nov. 1961	6 Nov. 1961	0
3	Dec. 1961	Dec. 1961	?
4	31 Dec. 1961?	21 Dec. 1961	+10?
1	?	23 Jan. 1962	?
5	May 1962	5 Mar. 1962	+55?

Source: Compiled from Brassell, "Jupiter," 23–24; Strother to AFCCS, 10 February 1961, attachment; Neufeld, *Ballistic Missiles*, 225–27.

Note: Some dates given are those on which the launch positions were transferred to the USAF, and actual achievement of operational status undoubtedly occurred a bit later in some cases. The planned operational date for the first (unnumbered) launch position had been 1 June 1961 as of 28 October 1959, but the planned date given for all positions represents a revision made sometime shortly thereafter.

with U.S. crews between early November 1961 and early March 1962. In the end, moreover, the training program made satisfactory progress; the first launch position was transferred to the Turks on 22 October 1962—in the middle of the Cuban missile crisis.[25]

THE ITALIAN JUPITERS, 1961–1962

The thirty Italian Jupiters, in the meantime, had completely achieved operational status by July 1961. Thereafter they sat at their bases in relative obscurity, although at times they could still resurface as a public issue. One such instance involved a Bulgarian pilot who, in January 1962, provided a reminder of Soviet bloc concern about the Jupiters (as well as of the missiles' vulnerability) by reconnoitering the base area and then accidentally plunging his MiG-17 into an olive grove only one mile from one of the Italian launch positions.[26]

Kinks in the Italian program could be discouraging but in the end were not serious. These included shortfalls in liquid oxygen production, housing for Italian and U.S. personnel, and above all, trained Italian personnel. This last problem stemmed in part from the Jupiters' location; the rural Apulia region was widely seen as unbearably backward, "like Africa," and a post there as akin to exile. Many in the IAF thus avoided the assignment if they could, and if they could not, their morale suffered accordingly. In addition, the ranking U.S. officer estimated in September 1961 that only 60 percent of the Italian Jupiters could be launched within the fifteen-minute countdown, 20 percent within the next fifteen minutes, and the remainder some time thereafter. Safety remained an issue as well, most obviously in April 1962, when the in-flight warhead separation explosive spontaneously detonated on one missile and, in the U.S. embassy's calm words, "momentarily lifted warhead from socket." The Italian Jupiter commander, Brigadier General Giulio Graziani, remembers the nose cone, containing the warhead, perched precariously in sixty-mile-per-hour winds as technicians reattached it. At the time, the Italians were apparently kept in the dark as to the presence of the warheads on the missiles, but now they were understandably most interested in knowing. They requested and received a nuclear safety briefing from the Americans. And finally, Graziani also recalls Prime Minister Fanfani's astonishing ignorance about the two-key launch system well into August 1961: he had not realized that his government enjoyed a veto over launch. Yet none of these snags, however alarming, affected the basic ability of the Italian Jupiters to fulfill their mission, however marginal.[27]

In March 1962, a pro-alliance politician alleged that Prime Minister Fanfani, now leading a center-left coalition government, was taking steps to remove the Jupiters as part of a new, more neutralist foreign policy. Although Fanfani denied the charge (with Kennedy personally assuring him of their "similarity of views"), it is clear that behind the scenes, Italian officials had their doubts about keeping the missiles. To be sure, they still relied on their missiles to try to convince the Americans of Italy's importance within NATO, and in any missile replacement scheme they sought to preserve the nuclear status they shared only with Turkey, both of which Fanfani did in a June 1961 visit to Washington. But the Italians also asked Norstad—likewise in mid-1961, just as their IRBMs were becoming operational—whether the missiles were still needed. The U.S. ambassador in Rome, Frederick Reinhardt, reported in March 1962 that the Italians felt strongly that they were "hooked on a poor weapon" and some were considering their replacement with Polaris. A bit later, they were quick to interpret U.S. public criticism of vulnerable nuclear forces as meaning they should remove the IRBMs.[28]

Then, on 19 September 1962—just weeks before the Cuban missile crisis

KENNEDY AND THE JUPITERS 105

—Secretary McNamara met with Italian defense minister Giulio Andreotti, who "agreed readily" to McNamara's suggestions for an "annual reappraisal" of the missiles' value and their "disestablishment when no longer needed." The Italians would require solution of their resulting domestic political problems and would prefer that removal be covered by U.S. public acknowl-edgment of Italy's key role in the alliance, but withdrawal seemed highly feasible. For the time being, however, neither Rome nor Washington consid-ered replacement of the Italian Jupiters a matter of high priority, especially if Italian political problems would stand in the way.[29]

A LITTLE OF THEIR OWN MEDICINE: KHRUSHCHEV RECIPROCATES, SPRING 1962

After Vienna and through the summer of 1962, the public Soviet campaign against the Jupiters reappeared on occasion. The commander in chief of the Soviet navy, for instance, made a threat against Turkey in February 1962, and Khrushchev issued another call that June for a ban on nuclear weap-ons and missiles from the Balkans and Adriatic region, specifically urging Greece and Turkey to renounce nuclear weapons. Soviet propaganda per-formed its usual contortions in the process. Attempting to woo the post-1960 coup regime in Ankara, for instance, it strained to pin the Jupiter deployment on the pre-1960 regime, ignoring the obvious fact that the new government was equally committed to the program; then it reverted to the old attack mode when this fact registered in Moscow. It flip-flopped on the IRBMs' dual-control provisions as well, first dismissing them as a fig leaf concealing sole U.S. control, then taking them seriously when doing so served the purpose of attacking emerging weapons that were indeed entirely under U.S. control, namely, Polaris submarines.[30]

Yet for Khrushchev—who, ironically, had formally abandoned the time-honored concept of "capitalist encirclement" in 1959—the missiles still sus-tained a particular but very real siege mentality, thus transcending the level of throwaway propaganda and intruding upon his personal diplomacy and private thoughts. In August 1961, the Soviet premier warned Italian prime minister Fanfani that the first two countries to be destroyed in a war would be Italy and Britain because of their missiles pointed at the Soviet Union, and he complained about Turkey, along with Iran and Greece, during an interview with Cyrus Sulzberger in September. In a meeting the following March with the new ambassador he was sending to Washington, Anatoly Dobrynin, Khrushchev cited the Turkish Jupiters as an example of the

Americans' quest for strategic superiority. "It's high time," he added without explanation, "their long arms were cut shorter."[31]

It was during visits to the Black Sea, however, when Khrushchev became most obsessive about Turkey. Hosting the journalist Drew Pearson and his wife Luvie in August 1961 at Sochi, one of his oceanside retreats, Khrushchev attributed a booming sound in the distance to the U.S. base to the south. "Maybe they are going to blow us up," he mused (although he added, "There isn't going to be a war"). Such incidents apparently recurred. According to his son-in-law, Khrushchev would ask guests to look through binoculars across the water. Unable to see anything, they would then ask Khrushchev what he saw when he then took his turn. "US missiles in Turkey," he would say, "aimed at my *dacha*."[32]

Khrushchev spent some especially fateful moments on the Black Sea shore in April or May 1962. During a visit to either the Crimea or Bulgaria, according to Khrushchev adviser Fyodor Burlatsky, Minister of Defense Rodion Malinovsky reminded the premier about the bases in Turkey, "which could in a short time destroy" all cities in the southern USSR. Predictably, Khrushchev became angry and asked, "Why do the Americans have such a possibility? They have surrounded us with bases on all sides, and we have no such possibility and right to do the same." This time, however, it occurred to him to respond in kind: he would send missiles to Cuba to "get even" with the United States for its "intolerable provocation." The closest he came to a public hint of his decision was in a speech he gave while in Bulgaria. "Would it not be better," he asked his audience in the city of Varna, "if the shores on which are located NATO's military bases and the launching sites for nuclear-armed rockets were converted into areas of peaceful labor and prosperity?" He obviously thought so, but failing that, the next best thing was to even the score.[33]

To be sure, in explaining Khrushchev's motives for deploying missiles in Cuba, it would be erroneous to assign greatest importance to the Turkish Jupiters. Although the necessary Soviet sources are not yet available, the best accounts agree that Khrushchev's decision stemmed from both his understandable fears for the survival of Castro's Cuba and his equally understandable anxiety over Soviet strategic inferiority, which U.S. officials had repeatedly publicized since the previous fall. The Jupiters in Turkey did, however, serve as a secondary motive and as an important, if not decisive, catalyst for Khrushchev's decision.

A similar point seems valid, incidentally, for Fidel Castro. Although he, too, had other more important reasons for agreeing to the Soviet missile deployment in his country, he also drew on the Turkish precedent for justification. He even urged Khrushchev to deploy the missiles openly. "We had every sovereign right to accept missiles," he insisted in 1992. "We were not violating international law. Why do it secretly—as if we had no right to do it?"[34]

As for Khrushchev, it is possible (although unverifiable) that he would not have sent missiles to Cuba, or would not have done so when he did, without NATO IRBMs arrayed against his country. Yet two points are certain. First, in Khrushchev's eyes, NATO had set precedent, and this justified his acting similarly. "We were not inventing anything new," Khrushchev recalled in retirement. "We were just copying the methods used against us by our adversaries when they encircled us with bases." Or, as he more famously argued, "[The Americans] would learn just what it feels like to have enemy missiles pointing at you; we'd be doing nothing more than giving them a little of their own medicine." Second, the Jupiter precedent was, as Richard Ned Lebow and Janice Gross Stein observe, one reason why Khrushchev thought he could get away with his Cuban move. According to Sergo Mikoyan, whose father was the first Soviet leader to learn of the scheme, Khrushchev intended to inform Kennedy about the deployment only after the U.S. midterm elections in November and "expected it would be received in the United States as the Turkish missiles [had been] received in the Soviet Union." And so by May 1962, in large part to erase an imbalance that had nagged at him for some time, with a powerful sense of justice and an expectation of success that partly grew from it, Khrushchev had secretly committed his country to deploying his own medium- and intermediate-range missiles in Cuba. Unfortunately for him, his adversary did not exactly share his passion for equality.[35]

A DECISION TO REMOVE THE THORS, 1961–1962

During this same period, the other IRBMs, the British Thors, reemerged as a Western defense issue, one with potential implications for the Jupiters. This almost happened already in early 1961, when the U.S. Government Accounting Office drafted a report that raised doubts about the Thors and sharply contradicted U.S. and British claims as to when they had become operational. But alarmed officials at State and Defense, fearful of upsetting London and, true to form, of undermining the credibility of the deterrent in Moscow, quashed the report. Yet again, the government found that in public it was just easier to pretend the IRBMs constituted a first-rate, essential part of the Western arsenal.[36]

That the underlying doubts would affect policy, however, was only a matter of time. The U.S.-U.K. Thor deployment agreement of February 1958 was to have lasted for not less than five years, after which either party could withdraw upon six months' notice. It had also obligated the United States to provide logistical support for the four Thor squadrons, and as the end of the five-year period approached, U.S. officials had to decide whether to do so thereafter. Discerning the British attitude might help, although this was difficult at first. In early 1962, the Macmillan government publicly claimed it had made no decision about the Thors and remained convinced of their utility, but the press reported a shift in British strategy away from land-based missiles toward air-launched missiles, especially the Skybolt.[37]

The Americans disagreed over what to do. The Joint Chiefs considered the Thors worth keeping beyond 1964, until an adequate NATO MRBM force could take their place, with the bill footed by the British if possible, the Americans if necessary. While joining in what was now a public ritual of declaring the missiles still "worthwhile," McNamara did not hesitate to label the Thors a "relatively obsolete system" and was open to ending U.S. support for it. Some in the State Department firmly urged a cutoff, although "in order to minimize the effect" on the Jupiters in Italy and Turkey, they added, "the initiative for this phasing out should be clearly attributed to the UK." Norstad, predictably, was opposed: the annual U.S. cost, he argued, although roughly $20 million at present, would decline to $6 million by late 1964; despite the Thors' drawbacks, no replacement was in prospect for the next few years (a highly questionable assertion, considering the existence of Polaris, Skybolt, and other systems); and to "allow them to be eliminated would detract from [the alliance's] overall strength."[38]

But this time, Norstad did not get his way. On 1 May, Secretary McNamara informed the British that the United States would discontinue logistical support for the four Thor squadrons after 31 October 1964. The British decided the missiles were not worth keeping unaided, and on 1 August Minister of Defense Peter Thorneycroft announced in Parliament, "The arrangements under which Thor missiles are stationed in this country should be brought to an end during the course of next year." Kennedy commented publicly, "Our ability to meet our commitments to the defense of Western Europe remains unchanged."[39]

Understandably, observers concluded that the brief era of the first-generation IRBM was drawing to a close. Neither London nor Washington felt that Thor maintenance warranted even relatively minimal expenditures. Both governments believed that without the Thors, existing and prospective weapons would more than suffice. And yet when rumors sprouted, coinciding with the British Thor announcement, to the effect that the United States was moving to withdraw all the IRBMs from Europe, U.S. officials denied them vigorously. Why U.S. reactions differed so sharply is clear: the Thors' hosts had arranged (for now at least) to secure a replacement weapons system acceptable to them, the Skybolt, and had consented to their dismantlement. By contrast, the Jupiters' hosts—the Turks in particular—had not.[40]

THE ISSUE THAT WOULDN'T GO AWAY, APRIL–OCTOBER 1962

Indeed, the Turks continued to cling as tenaciously to their new Jupiters as they had in the spring of 1961. The available evidence—interviews with policymakers and secondary accounts based on them—is weak, but it suggests that U.S. officials resumed contacts with the Turks regarding removal in the summer of 1962. Exactly why the administration tried again after having decided in 1961 to go ahead with deployment is unclear; opposition to the Jupiters may have been increasing in Congress, and perhaps within the administration itself, which appears in early 1962 to have confirmed the conclusions of the JCAE ad hoc study with one of its own. The administration's misgivings certainly did not diminish during this period. "Those Turkish missiles aren't worth very much," Kennedy remarked to his UN ambassador, Adlai Stevenson. "What the Turks want and need is the American payrolls those bases represent." Most certain is that the Turks rebuffed the later U.S. approaches just as forcefully as they had the previous year.[41]

On 21 August, top officials met to discuss the mounting Soviet military buildup in Cuba—at this point, so far as they knew, consisting only of conventional forces—and Bundy and Rusk saw "a very definite interrelationship between Cuba and other trouble spots, such as Berlin." They expected any U.S. military action against Cuba to trigger a Soviet response against U.S. "bases and numerous missile sites, particularly Turkey and southern Italy," and this reduced the appeal of such action. Two days later, in a meeting with the president, his advisers again drew the link between Cuba and U.S. allies. Eisenhower administration and JCAE inspection tour veteran John McCone, whom Kennedy had appointed Director of Central Intelligence (DCI) the previous fall, took this opportunity to voice his long-held doubts about the Jupiters. Secretary McNamara "agreed they were useless" but declared them "difficult politically to remove."[42]

Nevertheless, the missiles still concerned Kennedy enough for him to include them in the major document that stemmed from the meeting, National Security Action Memorandum (NSAM) 181, dated 23 August 1962. Although it focused on Cuba, even raising the possibility that the Soviets would deploy surface-to-surface missiles on the island, it began,

> The President has directed that the following actions and studies be undertaken in light of new [Soviet] bloc activity in Cuba.
>
> 1. What action can be taken to get Jupiter missiles out of Turkey?
> (Action: Department of Defense)

Some authors identify August as the month in which JFK ordered that the Jupiters be removed; some refer explicitly to this NSAM. Its first point, however, cannot be construed as an "order." Rather, it asked only what could be done, thus constituting a "study" as described in the opening sentence. In addition, had Kennedy issued an explicit removal order before 23 August, one would expect reference to it in this document.[43]

The memorandum scheduled "a further meeting with the President about September 1 to review progress" on its items, but when it was held, the Jupiters were apparently not on the agenda. Paul Nitze or other officials may have contacted the Turks yet again as a result of the NSAM, but even if they did, again nothing came of it. The Jupiters were still sitting on their launch-pads, as Herbert York would later put it, "nestled in the left armpits of the Russians," in mid-October.[44]

Between late August and that point, however, the Jupiter issue lingered inside the administration, and the Cuba-Turkey analogy even made ominous appearances on the public stage. The Soviet buildup in Cuba was "less a matter of the Monroe Doctrine than one of elemental national security," Bundy argued in a memo to JFK, and was "not the same as missiles in Turkey." Similarly, McGhee's successor at PPS, Walt Rostow, did not give the president any additional reason to press the Jupiter matter with Turkey. Advocating the drawing of a line beyond which the United States would not allow the Soviet buildup in Cuba, he anticipated Soviet claims of tit for tat. To these, the U.S. reply must be that under the regional security provisions of the United Nations Charter, "this Hemisphere operates under a different set of rules than the Eurasian land mass." In this connection, Rostow argued, "We would be playing into Moscow's hands to use the occasion of pressure on us in Cuba to withdraw THORS [sic] from Turkey."[45]

After Kennedy issued his first public warning on 4 September against the establishment of an "offensive capability" in Cuba, the Soviet news agency TASS responded a week later with a statement that included further blasts against the hypocrisy and recklessness of the United States installing "rockets, for instance, in Turkey, Italy, and Japan." This provoked Secretary Rusk, in September and October, to tell senators behind closed doors and then a small group of reporters that the United States had neither formally demanded a halt to the military buildup in Cuba nor proposed negotiations on the subject because the Soviets "would attempt to link it with [U.S.] allies, with the situation in Turkey, for example." And at the end of September ABC reporter John Scali asked Rusk whether the United States might "soon be approached with a deal to shut down some of [its] bases overseas in return for which Russia would close down her base in Cuba." Rusk replied, "This is not a negotiable point. . . . We cannot connect in negotiations or in trades the problem of Cuba with the defense of freedom in other places. No. This is not on." Thus in September 1962, as yet eyeing Cuba as a conventional military threat only, the Kennedy administration was already sensitive to the Cuba-Turkey analogy and found itself having to refute it publicly.[46]

CONCLUSIONS

In surveying the first twenty months of Kennedy's stewardship of American IRBM policy, several points deserve emphasis and elaboration.

First, the Jupiters played important catalytic and motivational roles in the origins of the Cuban missile crisis. Although the need to redress the strategic balance and to defend Cuba were the biggest reasons behind Khrushchev's spring 1962 decision to send MRBMs and IRBMs to Cuba, the latest evidence suggests that the presence of Jupiters in Turkey led him to this particular solution, constituted a secondary yet nevertheless significant motivation in its own right, and helped convince him he would get away with it.

In addition, Kennedy neither issued an "order" to remove the Jupiters nor decided to remove them before October 1962. Technically speaking, of course, the missiles were not the United States' to order removed; they belonged to Turkey. And although Kennedy could have ordered the U.S.-owned and -controlled warheads home, thus disarming the IRBMs, that too might have constituted a violation of the formal bilateral deployment agreement and was in any case politically infeasible. More accurately, then, Kennedy did not instruct his subordinates to do whatever was necessary to overcome Turkish resistance and secure an agreement to remove the Jupiters. He certainly would have liked to remove them, for he believed that keeping them deployed entailed serious risks—but risks less serious than those he associated with removal. He thus issued no order, and made no decision, to remove the Jupiters before October 1962, despite the many works that have continued to make this claim.[47]

In a related sense, moreover, Kennedy did not assume the Jupiters would be removed and then dismiss "the Jupiters from his mind," as Robert Kennedy and Elie Abel later wrote. The president and his top advisers remained well aware of the status of the Jupiter deployment throughout the 1961–62 period.[48]

Lastly, the analogy between Cuba and Turkey—broadly as high-profile client states in close proximity to the adversary's territory, as well as more narrowly as potentially similar hosts for the adversary's nuclear missiles—was widely acknowledged and discussed well before October 1962. Beginning already in early 1961, Soviets and Americans developed a ritual whereby the former would invoke the analogy and the latter would reject it. This makes the analogy's immediate appearance when the missile crisis erupted more understandable.

What about Kennedy's handling of the Jupiter question? To assess it fairly one must, as with Eisenhower and Dulles, place it in its context.

Kennedy's domestic and international environments—in part his own making, certainly—seemed to encourage continuation of the Jupiter policy. Kennedy was a Democrat who had won the White House in large part by promising to wage the Cold War more vigorously; with a wafer-thin mandate, mindful like all Democrats of the party's fate when last in power, he understandably fretted over his right flank. The Soviet Union, most Americans agreed, seemed to be entering a particularly aggressive phase in its policies around the globe. Kennedy thus had compelling domestic and international incentives to pursue a tough foreign policy, to avoid needless tensions with allies that might weaken it, and to augment—not to reduce—the Western arsenal in order to bolster it.

The Jupiter policy was, furthermore, like the preparation of the Bay of Pigs invasion, one inherited from the Eisenhower administration. Changing course in midstream is always more difficult than avoiding a particular course at the outset, even if someone else began the journey and even if it seems increasingly dubious. After all, the policy might turn out all right. If it does not, it has the advantage of being partly attributable to others—not that this necessarily occurred to the Kennedy administration—in this case, so much the better, to the other political party and its erstwhile leader.

In addition, even with the many reminders and warning signals, the policy did not and could not occupy the top of Kennedy's agenda. Considering the crises facing Kennedy—Cuba, Berlin, Laos, the Congo—at the key juncture

Jupiter missile in Turkey, 1963. Note the engine "skirt," which was opened like a flower before launch, and the circle in the insignia, which contains a mushroom cloud (not visible here). Local Turkish civilians, neither allowed near the missiles nor told what these strange objects were, came to believe they were minarets. (National Archives)

for the Turkish deployment, the spring of 1961, one can understand why Kennedy or his top advisers did not stay up more nights worrying about the Jupiters than they did.

And finally, the problem of Turkish opposition was real, and Kennedy could not dismiss it. Turkey was a key NATO ally, the Jupiters were obviously important to it, and who could tell how serious a rift in U.S.-Turkish relations a big push on this issue might produce? Turkey was not without leverage, despite its junior status in the alliance. It could easily have responded to U.S. pressure by complaining loudly within NATO or making a few "neutralist" gestures. On at least one occasion, on which the IRBMs were also discussed, the Turks demonstrated their willingness to exploit the Americans' fears about credibility. Such moves would have caused major headaches for the Kennedy administration and might have led it to back down, even if mere private resistance did not.[49]

Nevertheless, Kennedy's policymaking environment did not preclude a cancellation of the Jupiter deployment. He was no mere captive of past policy; his administration did consider a reversal; despite strong opposition from some subordinates, support at least as strong was also expressed; and the question whether the administration explored all avenues with the Turks, including various forms of compensation, remains open. Other policies set in train in early 1961 provided space in which to maneuver: the administration could have cited the defense buildup it launched in March to cover cancellation, especially considering the formidable logic of strategic invulnerability upon which it based the expansion.

Similarly, Rusk's explanation that Turkish morale would not survive cancellation without the substitution of Polaris submarines deserves close scrutiny. As of April–May 1961, the State Department expected Polaris submarines to become available for assignment to NATO "beginning in 1962 or 1963," and the first Jupiters in Turkey to become operational no earlier than September 1961 (and probably closer to December). Thus the lag between a realistic operational date for the first Jupiters in Turkey and the earliest point at which Polaris submarines for NATO could plausibly be expected to appear was not terribly long, certainly less than one year. This gap narrows drastically, or disappears completely, when the comparison is made with the earliest date expected for turnover of the first launch position to the Turkish air force, doubtless one of great importance to the Turks for the purpose of fulfilling their interest in having the missiles: October 1962, and subsequent positions not until 1963–64. When one couples this with the fact that, in May 1961, Kennedy did indeed publicly announce his intention to commit five Polaris submarines to NATO, the question arises: If he could do this, could he not also have used part of that same commitment, and made a strong case for the insignificance of any Jupiter-Polaris lag, to help secure Turkish acquiescence in cancellation?[50]

Finally, on the domestic front, Kennedy enjoyed an impressive diffusion of responsibility. Key members of Congress, a top adviser on NATO with solid hard-line credentials, an assertive secretary of defense, and others all recommended cancellation of the Turkish deployment. Kennedy would not have waged any ensuing struggle alone, and domestic opposition would not have posed a serious problem.

It is therefore difficult to maintain that Kennedy's hands were tied. He ordered a full-scale, unhurried, interdepartmental review of the issue to explore his options, and then he chose one: carry out the deployments. And like his predecessor, he knew it was a choice replete with pitfalls.

Why, then, did he choose as he did? Although no prisoner of inherited policies, Kennedy did share a cell with Eisenhower and Dulles built from particular assumptions about credibility, toward both NATO and the Soviet Union. These assumptions dictated pursuit of even the most questionable policy because under their terms, any reversal would signal weakness. Would cancellation or removal have seriously affected U.S.-Turkish relations, especially if Washington had made a strong presentation to Ankara? Would the withdrawal of forty-five obsolete missiles really have emboldened the Soviets? Would not other U.S. and NATO defense measures under way have maintained the same levels of deterrence, and could not the administration have made this argument persuasively? Could not the administration have *enhanced* U.S. credibility by discontinuing a bad policy and emphasizing the resulting improvement—which is what it would do ultimately? Available evidence suggests that top administration officials did not seriously explore such questions, and they did not because their assumptions about credibility stood in the way. More to the point, they failed to challenge these assumptions, just as they failed to display their famous empathy for the adversary's concerns, or to adhere to their own effort to reduce U.S. strategic vulnerability. They showed some interest in reversing policy, but not enough to overcome the same fears for U.S. credibility that had led Eisenhower to initiate and then continue the Jupiter deployments. Now, under Kennedy, the military benefits of the missiles had dwindled further while their political costs had only increased—the decisive concern over credibility, however, had remained constant and kept the deployments moving ahead.

"What's all the excitement about?" Khrushchev asked Foy Kohler, the new U.S. ambassador in Moscow. "Just because I am building a fishing port in Cuba, you want to go to war. After all, I'm not doing anything you haven't done to me in Turkey and Iran." It was 16 October 1962, and the Soviet premier had finally granted Kohler an audience in the Kremlin. Their three-hour chat was fairly pleasant, Kohler cabled Washington, "cordial and frank with no tirades." But Khrushchev did remind his guest that the United States had "bases in countries neighboring [the] USSR, such as Turkey" and others. "[If the United States] thinks it has the right to do as it likes about Cuba," he asked, "why hasn't [the] USSR [the] right to do as it likes about these countries?" It was the same argument he had made before. This time, however, his indignation could not have had the same edge to it, for the secret policy with which he hoped to redress the inequality was well under way. The only problem was that on that same day, 16 October, the secret policy became known to John Kennedy. Both leaders, along with hundreds of millions of ordinary citizens, would soon learn the true meaning of "excitement." [51]

THE CUBAN MISSILE CRISIS OCTOBER 1962

5
GODDAMN DANGEROUS

The Russians like parallel situations.
Llewellyn Thompson, 19 October 1962

Sure, we'd go for that.
A leader of Young Americans for Freedom, who were picketing the White House with placards reading INVADE! and APPEASEMENT IS FOR COWARDS, when asked about a Cuba-Turkey missile trade, 27 October 1962

It was a moment when the United States and the Soviet Union stood, to use Andrei Gromyko's memorable mistranslation, "balls to balls." Most observers agree it was the instance in the Cold War when the world came closest to the nuclear abyss (although exactly how close remains a fruitful area for discussion). It was the Cuban missile crisis of October 1962, an episode that has understandably continued to inspire more Kennedology than anything except the assassination. For all this work, however, remarkably few authors have thoroughly exploited the many documents declassified in recent years. One of the results has been an incomplete understanding of the Jupiter story. Just as most existing accounts have underestimated the Jupiters' role in the origins of the crisis, so have they missed the key role the missiles played in its development and conclusion.[1]

The Jupiters entered into the top secret discussions of Kennedy and his famous NSC Executive Committee ("ExComm") on the first day it met, 16 October. At one point the president asked how many were stationed in Turkey, and at another occurred the following curious exchange, as Kennedy puzzled over Khrushchev's missile deployment in Cuba:

> JFK: Why does he put these in there though? . . . It's just as if we suddenly began to put a major number of MRBMs in Turkey. Now that'd be goddamn dangerous, I would think.
> BUNDY?: Well, we *did*, Mr. President.
> U. A. JOHNSON?: We *did* it. We . . .
> JFK: Yeah, but that was five years ago . . . that was during a different period then.

The president may have inexplicably forgotten between the first and second meetings that the Jupiters were in Turkey. Or, perhaps he had convinced himself that Eisenhower was solely responsible for the Turkish deployment. Whichever is the case, the exchange recalls nothing so much as the scene in *Dr. Strangelove*, in which President Muffley asks General Turgidson about the attack plan that has allowed General Ripper to launch SAC bombers against the Soviet Union.

MUFFLEY: Plan R????

TURGIDSON: That's right, sir. Plan R. . . . You approved it, sir. You must remember.

As with Muffley, so with JFK: in a real sense, the chickens were coming home to roost. Although the Jupiters made only fleeting appearances on the first day of the emerging crisis, the missiles Kennedy had helped deploy now quickly returned to haunt him. Over the tense, potentially disastrous days to follow, these *other* "missiles of October" would reappear repeatedly—as a key influence in private and public discussion, as the pivot when things turned for the worst, and yet then, in the ultimate irony, as an important means toward a peaceful resolution.[2]

THE CUBA–TURKEY ANALOGY REVISITED

During the crisis, the Kennedy administration both accepted and rejected the analogy between Soviet SS-4s under construction in Cuba and U.S. Jupiters in Turkey, sometimes in the same sentence. "Retorts from either our European allies or the Soviets that we can become as accustomed as they to accepting the nearby presence of MRBM's have some logic," Ted Sorensen wrote on 17 October, "but little weight in this situation."[3]

Publicly, the administration felt it had to deny the analogy during (and after) the crisis in order to help justify the dramatic U.S. response to the Cuban deployment. Acceptance of any parallel between U.S. missiles in Turkey and Soviet missiles in Cuba would expose the United States to charges of hypocrisy, of bringing the world to the brink of nuclear war over the same situation to which the Soviets had reacted with relative restraint. Moscow might thus win its case in the "court of world opinion." Anxious to avoid such a result, and clearly sensitive to the comparison, the United States Information Agency (USIA) prepared on the eve of Kennedy's 22 October speech a "policy guidance" memo directing that official statements were to deny the analogy *"only* if hostile comment compares Cuban bases to U.S. bases in other countries."[4]

Accepting the Analogy

It is difficult to agree with Allyn, Blight, and Welch that the "supposed symmetry between the two deployments was far from obvious" to Kennedy and his advisers.[5] In private, the administration acknowledged or tacitly accepted the Cuba-Turkey analogy in four distinct ways. As the audio transcript for 16 October reveals, three of these variations emerged at the beginning of the crisis deliberations. The fourth, in the form of a missiles-for-missiles trade, was not raised until the next day; it warrants separate treatment (see below).

First, ExComm acknowledged the analogy in its attempts to discern Khrushchev's motives and predict his response to various U.S. moves. Secretary of State Rusk guessed, "[Khrushchev] knows we don't really live under fear of nuclear weapons to the extent that . . . he has to live under ours. . . . Khrushchev may feel that it's important for us to learn about living under medium-range missiles, and he's doing that to sort of balance . . . that political, psychological [plank?]." Ambassador-at-Large and Soviet expert Llewellyn Thompson predicted on 17 October that Khrushchev would "justify [his] actions because of [NATO] missiles in Italy and Turkey." McCone, the DCI, believed that one of Khrushchev's "political objectives" was the "establishment of a 'trading position' " to force the United States out of its overseas bases and Berlin. Thompson and Charles ("Chip") Bohlen went further; they thought the Soviets were preparing "for a confrontation with President Kennedy at which time they would seek to settle the entire subject of overseas bases as well as the Berlin question."[6]

Second, the analogy cropped up when ExComm considered military scenarios, in which the Jupiters appeared as logical targets for Soviet retaliation after a U.S. attack on Cuba. On 16 October, Robert Kennedy asserted that if U.S. air strikes destroyed the missiles in Cuba, it would be "almost incumbent upon the Russians, then, to say, Well, we're going to send [the SS-4s] in again, and if you [attack Cuba] again . . . we're going to do the same thing to Turkey." At the evening meeting, another policymaker raised the issue of "points of vulnerability around the world," such as Turkey, and the following day Rusk recommended the United States "be alert for an attack on Turkey" and elsewhere after a U.S. attack on Cuba. On 19 October, in this vein, among "steps that would make [an] air strike more acceptable to the blockade group," Thompson listed "prior notice to our principal Allies, particularly Italy and Turkey."[7]

Finally and most fundamentally, officials drew the analogy in general, politico-military terms—under which Cuba and Turkey contained similar weapons and constituted similar political contexts. As we have seen, the general analogy predates October 1962, so its immediate appearance at the outset of the crisis should come as no surprise. On 16 October, the president inadvertently but flatly validated the analogy by commenting on Khrushchev's policy, "It's just as if we suddenly began to put a major number of MRBM's in Turkey." The CIA, similarly, at one point concluded that the Soviets might respond to the U.S. blockade with one of their own—"perhaps against a nation such as Turkey." In exploring the pros and cons of the blockade then emerging as the preferred policy, McCone included among the cons the notion that "sustaining [the U.S.] position in world opinion" would be difficult "because of its own complex" of missile and other bases abroad. Such concern led someone to commission an NSC staff member to draft a memo devoted to rebutting "Attempts to Equate Soviet Missile Bases in Cuba with NATO Jupiter Bases in Italy and Turkey." The obvious nature of the general analogy explains why Kennedy and other officials repeatedly chose Turkey rather than some other country to illustrate the points they made. At times they were also more direct: on 27 October, JFK simply referred to the Jupiters as being "the same" as the Soviet missiles in Cuba.[8]

Rejecting the Analogy

Despite their tacit acceptance of the Cuba-Turkey analogy, administration officials also rejected it, at certain points in private and uniformly in public. On 16 October, after being reminded that the Jupiter deployment was not hypothetical but factual, the president backed away and denied the analogy. "Yeah," he accepted the reminder, "but that was five years ago . . . that was during a different period then." The phrase "a different period" is ambiguous. It may have been a denial of responsibility for the Jupiters' presence, or an assertion that NATO's 1957 agreement in principle, concluded in a different international context, somehow was not "goddamn dangerous." In any case, JFK had quickly recovered and declared the analogy invalid.

Kennedy's 16 October response belongs in the first category of denial, that of simple contradiction. Sorensen, too, as mentioned, rejected the analogy out of hand as having "little weight in this situation." On 18 October, in a draft message intended to be from Kennedy to Khrushchev but never sent, he also asserted that NATO and Cuban missiles were "in no way comparable in the eyes of either history, international law or world opinion." On 26 October, DCI McCone objected to the linking of Cuba and Turkey. "[The] Soviet weapons in Cuba were pointed at our heart," he said, "and put us under great handicap in continuing to carry out our commitments to the free world." McCone, too, was offering an argument bereft of self-awareness; NATO weapons in Turkey were equally pointed at the Soviets' heart and equally hampered fulfillment of their responsibilities to the socialist world. Probably because they sensed the "logic" of the analogy, McCone, Sorensen, and perhaps Kennedy were forced to argue by assertion: the analogy does not hold because it does not hold.[9]

A second way to deny the analogy was to point out how the Jupiter deployment had been undertaken by a free alliance (NATO), whereas the Soviet infusion of missiles was not. The NSC staff memo held the Jupiter deployment up as resulting from a "unanimous and publicly affirmed decision of the NATO Heads of Government" into which they had "freely entered." And on 18 October, according to an official top-secret postmortem, ExComm members agreed that a "basic principle of the balance of power in the nuclear age . . . was that sensitive areas, such as Berlin, Iran, or Laos, should not be turned into missile bases, and that missile installations only be established pursuant to open military alliances, such as NATO." Needless to say, they did not deem Turkey a "sensitive area."[10]

Third, the administration drew the offensive-defensive distinction. Whereas the missiles in Cuba could "only be assumed to be aggressive," according to U.S. officials, the Jupiters had been installed "only after Moscow [had] threatened Western Europe with nuclear attack." The USIA's "policy guidance" argued that Soviet bases in Cuba were "clearly for offensive purposes and not to defend the USSR which ha[d] sufficient strength to protect itself—as Khrushchev ha[d] so often noted—without Cuban bases." With the lack of political discretion that repeatedly chagrined his boss, however, Secretary McNamara remarked in the meeting with congressional leaders on 22 October, "One might question whether the [Soviet] missiles are or are not offensive." McCone noted that this was the first time a policymaker had doubted the offensive character of the SS-4s. When it came to public relations, at times policymakers strayed from the policy guidance, but usually they said the right thing: ours are defensive, theirs are offensive.[11]

Fourth and finally, the administration emphatically contrasted openness on one hand and secrecy and deception on the other. Kennedy did this in his famous televised address of 22 October, in which he appeared, as the novelist Robert Kelley puts it, "perhaps as emcee of the end of the world," to reveal the Soviet missile buildup in Cuba and announce the U.S. blockade of the island. The president intoned, "Our own strategic missiles have never been transferred to the territory of any other nation under a cloak of secrecy and deception." As the NSC staff memo concluded, the NATO policy's "contrast with the secretly-emplaced Soviet missile bases in Cuba [was] self-evident." U.S. policymakers viewed the secrecy and deception of the Cuban deployment as the most important difference, and clearly it was a great propaganda advantage the Soviets yielded to the Americans heading into the crisis. ExComm veterans have acknowledged how difficult it would have been to justify the vigorous U.S. response and secure global support for it had the Soviets deployed their missiles openly.[12]

Such were the elements of an emerging official line on the Cuba-Turkey analogy. "It has to be made clear that there's a big difference between offensive Soviet nuclear weapons in Cuba and our own in Turkey and elsewhere," Kennedy told his press secretary, Pierre Salinger, ending a list of instructions for handling the press after the televised address. "Ours are an attempt to redress the balance of power in Europe," he continued, the "locations and capability" of which were known to the Soviets. The Cuban deployment, by contrast, represented "a provocative change in the delicate status quo in this hemisphere." Its "very secrecy," moreover, posed an "obvious danger" to the United States that it couldn't ignore. McNamara now toed the line more effectively when he briefed the press right after Kennedy's speech. "There is a very, very basic difference between these two situations," he answered to a question on the subject. It "was the Soviet threat to Western Europe . . . that led to . . . [the United States'] arming the Turks and Italians with certain nuclear weapons." He continued, "There is no similarity between arming nations under threat, on the one hand, versus the arming of Cuba on the other, which obviously was not under the threat of nuclear attack or attack from this country."[13]

Were these distinctions the administration drew valid? This is a somewhat theological question over which scholars have differed and will differ. Some have adopted the administration's denials of the analogy and even supplemented them with their own. Allyn, Blight, and Welch, for example, note the larger size of the Cuban deployment, the absence of a dual-control arrangement in Cuba, and the covert nature of Khrushchev's move. By referring to the Soviets' "cloak of deception" and "cloak of secrecy," they even appropriate Kennedy's language.[14]

The denials, however, do not stand up to scrutiny: as Richard Betts has written, it is difficult to imagine "a man from Mars" believing that the SS-4s were less legitimate than the Jupiters. For one thing, one must question how meaningful a difference exists regarding the "free alliance" issue. True, Cuba was not a member of the Warsaw Pact, but it welcomed the missiles and "freely entered" into an agreement to deploy them. Surely host-country consent is more important than the technical question of whether the deployment occurs within a formal alliance. And, in a related sense, the Soviet deployment was perfectly legal under international law, and U.S. officials knew it. In fact, *"our* legal problem," State Department legal adviser Abram Chayes recalls, "was that their action *wasn't* illegal."[15]

Furthermore, the offensive-defensive distinction is questionable because it is purely subjective. SS-4s and Jupiters had much in common, apart from their essential characteristics. The United States had deployed IRBMs near the hostile superpower, to protect its friends, to compensate for the adversary's enormous local conventional superiority, and to serve as stopgap ICBMs; the Soviets, although they reacted fiercely, did not attempt to force them out with a blockade, massive military preparations, or the like. In Cuba, the Soviet Union was in part following the American precedent. In addition, considering such U.S. policies as the Bay of Pigs invasion, the economic embargo, the anti-Castro covert action program (Operation Mongoose), and the repeated, large-scale military maneuvers staged nearby—one directed against a mythical leader "Ortsac," a letter string suggestive if reversed—it was not at all "obvious" that Cuba was not under threat of attack.[16]

Finally, the openness-versus-secrecy distinction is equally dubious. This is the case, first, because the NATO deployments were not as aboveboard as one might think. The Jupiter policy was decided on publicly, but its execution was far more clandestine. The *New York Times* reported in October 1962 that the number and location of NATO bases in Turkey had "never been officially stated." Ankara (as well as Rome) consistently strained to limit publicity surrounding the deployments to an absolute minimum. The *Times* stated that "the Turkish Government had never officially said for domestic publication that Turkey possessed missiles." Officials never even identified these strange, sixty-foot cylinders for local inhabitants and kept them from getting close enough to find out for themselves; they thus soon believed, understandably in view of the similarity in appearance, that the Jupiters were minarets. One USAF general caused a minor stir when he referred publicly to the Jupiter base when visiting Turkey; he had not been told to avoid such statements. To be sure, anyone interested enough could have learned about the Jupiters and their status at any given point with little effort, and their presence was an open secret among Turkish elites. The Kremlin certainly knew about the deployment before it began. Nevertheless, the claim that the deployment was public should be heavily qualified.[17]

The U.S. stance on secrecy is also suspect because it suggests that secrecy is somehow abnormal and unacceptable in international relations, or that the United States eschewed secret policies. The administration did have a right to be angry about the Soviets' *deception.* Not only did they publicly deny they were putting missiles in Cuba, but they also did so using—and thus corrupting—the highly secret and trusted diplomatic channel maintained through Robert Kennedy and Soviet secret agent Georgi Bolshakov. The *secrecy* of the deployment, on the other hand, is a different matter. Every nation has executed certain foreign policies in secret, including the United States. It had not warned the Soviets, for example, about the Bay of Pigs operation or its plots to assassinate foreign leaders; Eisenhower did not tell Khrushchev about the U-2 overflights he had ordered, and then he tried more than once to deceive the Soviets once they shot down one of the spy planes in 1960. In the end, to object to the secrecy of the adversary's policies is to betray a remarkable naïveté, one that recalls Secretary of State Henry Stimson's comment as he disbanded the U.S. code-breaking unit in 1929: "Gentlemen," he sniffed, "do not open each other's mail."[18] It is also suddenly to rewrite the rules of international behavior when it is convenient.

Perhaps most significant, however, the Kennedy administration's stance implies that it would have tolerated the Soviet deployment in Cuba had it been conducted in the open or under the rubric of a formal defense pact, which is obviously not the case. ExComm's public rejection of the analogy was perfectly understandable; it was trying to justify, before domestic and international audiences, its attempt to force withdrawal of the SS-4s. And if such an effort was necessary, it was at least adequate to the task. But the rejection was neither logical nor consistent, and U.S. officials sensed this—as their multifaceted, tacit acceptance of the analogy would suggest.

COMMAND AND CONTROL REVISITED

From early on in the crisis, ExComm worried about an unauthorized Jupiter launch. This was at least in part because the custody and control problems identified by the JCAE subcommittee in 1961 remained unremedied. First, although in June 1962 Kennedy had ordered installation of PALs on all U.S. nuclear warheads in Europe, with top priority going to the QRA aircraft and Jupiter warheads, the military received authorization to begin modifying the latter only on 18 September and did not issue an installation schedule for the Jupiters until November. Thus PALs had not been installed on any Jupiter warheads when the missile crisis erupted. And second, the Alert Procedures under which the U.S. warheads sat atop the missiles at all times, and which the JCAE subcommittee had noticed in 1960, remained in effect through October 1962. The Jupiters, in short, continued to represent one of the gravest command and control problems in the Western arsenal.[19]

That the Jupiters were now on alert—a temporary, urgent status, as opposed to the existing Alert Procedures described above—and thus by definition more readily launched, did not make the situation any less precarious. Early in the crisis, Norstad had placed all his forces in a state of "awareness," which would facilitate an alert should he order one, but he was given discretion in this matter and declined to do so. Despite this, on 22 October individual service commanders in Washington circumvented him and directly ordered some units of the U.S. Air Forces Europe (USAFE) to go to Defense Condition (DEFCON) 3. Whether the Turkish Jupiters were placed on DEFCON 3 as well is unclear, but as of 22 October, all fifteen of them were on some higher level of alert than normal. In addition, Jupiter commanders may even have had some "predelegated" authority to launch under attack. Thus did unauthorized-launch scenarios retain their frightening plausibility—especially now, in the midst of a crisis that might lead to a Soviet attack on the Jupiter bases. On 22 October, Kennedy worried about a particular form of the famous "use-it-or-lose-it" dilemma. Even though suffering only a "spot reprisal," Jupiter commanders, perhaps having lost contact with higher authority, might assume a full-scale nuclear war had erupted and launch their missiles without orders to do so. He did not accept JCS assurances that the commanders' standing orders were sufficient.[20]

Therefore, that same day Kennedy ordered the Joint Chiefs to take precautions. They directed Norstad "to destroy or make inoperable JUPITERs if any attempt [was] made to fire them without specific authorization of [the] President" and that he so inform "US custodians and their commanders" in USAFE. Presumably U.S. personnel would have an opportunity to disable the missiles during an unauthorized launch procedure or in case a launch attempt failed. We do not know what precautions Jupiter personnel took to comply with the Joint Chiefs' order; the Jupiters did remain at some heightened level of alert. ExComm's fears of such a launch from Italy or Turkey may have been more justified than it realized.[21]

There is another, more intriguing aspect to ExComm's efforts to assert tight control over the Jupiters during the missile crisis. A document that appears to be McNamara's order to the Joint Chiefs, which they then passed on to Norstad on 22 October, read, "The President has ordered me to make certain that the Jupiters [in Italy and Turkey] will not be fired without his further authorization, *even in the event of a selective nuclear or non-nuclear attack on these units by the Soviet Union in response to actions we may be taking elsewhere.*" This elaboration takes on new meaning when paired with another fragment of evidence, from 27 October. On that day Bundy remarked, "We were going to *let* [Khrushchev] have his strike in Turkey, as I understood it last week . . . at one point at least that was the way we talked about it." McNamara confirmed this, although he added that it had been "one alternative." Early in the crisis, in short, working from the assumption that a U.S. air strike on Cuba would provoke Soviet retaliation against the Turkish Jupiters, ExComm developed an option whereby it would tolerate such retaliation without proceeding any farther up the escalatory ladder. The idea was clever: liquidate one's least valuable military assets in order to eliminate one of the most glaring drawbacks of the air strike option—the possibility that it would trigger an escalatory spiral culminating in World War III. This option, of course, might not have prevented escalation. Nevertheless, the fact remains that ExComm seriously considered sacrificing the Turkish Jupiters to Soviet retaliation and leaving it at that—a sharply limited tit for tat, reminiscent of the New York–for–Moscow exchange in Eugene Burdick and Harvey Wheeler's best-selling novel *Fail-Safe*. ExComm's consideration of this avenue demonstrates how hard it struggled to make the air strike option viable—and how deeply it feared the possibility of escalation that helped lead it to opt for the naval blockade first.[22]

MISSILE MARKET RESEARCH

ExComm devoted much more attention to a nonviolent sacrifice of the Jupiters: a trade for the SS-4s in Cuba. Doing so represented the committee's most obvious tacit acknowledgment of the Cuba-Turkey analogy. For the first few years after the crisis, Kennedy's confidants categorically denied that such a missile swap had even been considered. The first major modification of this version appeared with Robert Kennedy's *Thirteen Days* (1969), in which he revealed his meeting with Soviet ambassador Anatoly Dobrynin on the evening of 27 October. According to RFK, he told Dobrynin that although there could be no "quid pro quo," the president "had been anxious to remove those missiles"; further, "It was our judgement that, within a short time after the crisis was over, those missiles would be gone." Thereafter, many observers concluded that the Kennedys had implicitly agreed to remove the Jupiters as part of the crisis settlement.[23]

Since then, evidence has emerged that clearly indicates, first, that beginning on 17 October, several members of ExComm repeatedly considered a Cuba-Turkey trade to be necessary or even desirable. Second, at the end of the crisis, President Kennedy not only argued for the trade option but was by far its most ardent proponent, repeatedly returning the discussion to that

Meeting of the Executive Committee, National Security Council, October 1962. Far from avoiding the subject, ExComm considered the benefits or necessity of a Cuba-for-Turkey missile trade on virtually every day of the crisis. (Cecil Stoughton; courtesy John F. Kennedy Library)

subject on 27 October. Third, Kennedy put in place a contingency plan, apparently for use in case the Soviets rejected the U.S. offer of 27 October, in which he would have the United Nations propose a public trade that the United States would then accept. And fourth, the 27 October offer that Moscow did accept included a secret but explicit trade under which the Jupiters would be withdrawn some five months after the crisis.

Only by tracing the administration's discussions of a trade can one fully appreciate their impressive scope. To be sure, on the first day, 16 October, Kennedy's initial impulse was to advocate a swift air strike against Cuba, and he does not appear to have considered a trade. Yet by the following day, administration officials began to suggest or expect a missile swap. *"I feel you should [make] it clear,"* UN ambassador Stevenson underlined in a memo to the president on 17 October, *"that the existence of nuclear missile bases anywhere is negotiable before we start anything."* On that and the following day, Theodore Sorensen included a trade in an early list of options for the president.[24]

On 18 October ExComm reconvened, and members wondered if Khrushchev's objective was to force a withdrawal of the Turkish Jupiters. "The only offer we would make . . . that would have any sense . . . [and give Khrushchev] an out," Kennedy said, "would be Turkey." According to the minutes, everyone "readily agreed" the Jupiters "were not much use but a political question was involved." Bundy said JFK's point was "equally valid" as well in conjunction with an air strike and doubted if they could "keep this Turkish base in this context." McNamara argued that the "price" of eliminating the Soviet missiles in Cuba "at the very least" would be the missiles in Italy and Turkey. In light of this discussion, Sorensen drafted a letter to Khrushchev for the president's signature—which was never sent—in which Kennedy offered to discuss removal of the Jupiters after the Soviets halted work on their SS-4s.[25]

At five o'clock that same afternoon, Kennedy welcomed to the White House Foreign Minister Gromyko, who denied that his country was supplying any "offensive" weapons to Cuba. Neither the Jupiters nor the Cuba-Turkey analogy came up during the conversation, but Gromyko did broach the issue that evening over dinner with Dean Rusk. Rusk could not deny the presence of U.S. bases and advisers "in such countries as Turkey, Pakistan, Japan," and others, said Gromyko. Thus the United States apparently had the right to maintain such bases, whereas the Soviet Union was not allowed to bolster Cuba's economy or "defense capability." "The Soviet Union," Rusk replied, "is exaggerating the significance of American foreign military bases."[26]

"More than once" during a meeting of all the principals except the president on 19 October, Secretary McNamara again said "that the U.S. would have to pay a price to get the Soviet missiles out of Cuba"—it would "have to give up [its] missile bases in Italy and Turkey and . . . probably . . . more besides."[27]

McNamara restated this opinion during an ExComm meeting on Saturday, 20 October. But this session is more famous for the contribution of Ambassador Stevenson, who had come down from New York. He recommended, after the Soviets removed their missiles, "a settlement involving the withdrawal of [U.S.] missiles from Turkey and [U.S.] evacuation from Guantánamo." The president opposed discussing an ultimate political settlement in Stevenson's opening UN presentation, but he "agreed that at an appropriate time [the United States] would have to acknowledge that [it was] willing to take strategic missiles out of Turkey and Italy if this issue was raised by the Russians." He was "firm," however, in saying the United States should only make such a proposal "in the future." Stevenson disagreed, insisting that the administration "must be more forthcoming" about a missile trade. Paul Nitze, generally an ExComm hard-liner, joined the president in opposing a trade initiated by the United States. However, far from being "outraged" by

Stevenson's "attempt at total appeasement," as he later claimed, Nitze according to the minutes "said he would not object to discussing this question in the event that negotiations developed" from U.S. establishment of the blockade. True, several members, especially McCone, Eisenhower holdover Douglas Dillon, and early–Cold War veteran Robert Lovett, in fact "jumped on Stevenson," as Schlesinger puts it. But they did so for several reasons— because the ambassador advocated beginning with a trade, because he was taking the discussion back to square one when ExComm had virtually settled on the blockade option, because he had thrown in Guantánamo, because he seemed too critical of U.S. policy, because most of those present disliked him anyway—not because they considered a missile trade per se to be out of bounds.[28]

Ironically, on Sunday, 21 October, while a perhaps chastened Stevenson removed Turkey and Italy from his proposal for an initial presentation, consideration of a trade among his colleagues reached a high point. Nitze's deputy William P. Bundy submitted an analysis of U.S. overseas bases that pointed out the Jupiters' drawbacks and limited value compared with other bases; from a military standpoint, the United States could abandon such bases without significantly weakening national security. In addition, a State Department group working on UN matters, chaired by Stevenson and attended by Rusk, discussed a missile trade. Then, Robert Kennedy called together various ExComm members that evening. According to legal adviser Chayes, who attended the meeting, those present "almost unanimously" accepted the necessity of a missile trade. McNamara again said the United States "would be lucky to get out of the crisis with only a trade of the Turkish missiles." Robert Kennedy polled the others for their responses, and "there was no disagreement with McNamara's evaluation." What JFK thought at this moment is unclear; one of his doodles indicates that he spoke on the phone that day about "being prepared to accept" withdrawal of the Jupiters. But among his advisers, anticipation of a trade had become widespread.[29]

Perhaps it comes as no surprise, then, that talk of a swap continued the next day, 22 October. The attorney general worried that Stevenson would offer a trade at the UN prematurely, but it was just that, a question of timing. "We will have to make a deal in the end," he explained to Arthur Schlesinger, "but we must stand firm now. Our concessions must come at the end of negotiation, not at the start." Averell Harriman, now serving as assistant secretary of state for Far Eastern Affairs, implied in a memo to the president that a missile trade might facilitate a settlement by helping Khrushchev to save face. And in a rough draft for a speech with which JFK would announce an air strike should it come to that, Sorensen also had the president declaring his readiness "promptly" to "withdraw all nuclear forces presently based in Turkey."[30]

At a formal NSC meeting on the afternoon of the 22d, however, officials did not discuss a trade (perhaps because Kennedy considered it a topic too sensitive for this much larger and less reliable group). Rusk did confront the analogy at one point, arguing that the administration should justify an attack on Cuba (should it come to that) using the UN Charter broadly, and not its Article 51, "which might give the Russians a basis for attacking Turkey." The president discussed the analogy too, stating that "it was most important that everyone be fully briefed as to why" the deployments did not "match" and emphasizing the Soviets' secrecy and deception. And yet while about this time he confided to British ambassador David Ormsby-Gore that the IRBMs "had become more or less worthless," whether a deal involving them was politically possible "was hard to tell" at this point. Active consideration of a trade largely subsided for the moment, as the preparation, announcement, and impact of the blockade took center stage.[31]

Rather, in the first few days following the announcement of the blockade, officials spent some time crafting scenarios intended to make a trade more palatable within the alliance. On 23 and 26 October, for example, Rusk, two of his assistant secretaries, and Walt Rostow all proposed plans in which Washington would have the Turks offer the Jupiters' withdrawal after they were replaced by a multilateral seaborne nuclear force.[32]

On 25 October, various strains of the administration's thinking found expression. Some officials, such as Rostow, continued to believe that the Soviets might seek a missile trade. Rusk, asked at a background news conference whether the Jupiter bases were negotiable, did not rule out "general disarmament arrangements" in the future but declared that for purposes of the current crisis the Cuban situation was "a special problem." Nitze, by this point, had come to oppose a trade; he said there was "nothing to negotiate" with Khrushchev until his missiles were gone from Cuba. Then the United States should be willing to discuss NATO's bases. One of McGeorge Bundy's assistants advised him against trading missiles because that would "play havoc with the Alliance." Proponents of an air strike, in continuing to draft their "scenario," listed as one of the air strike's advantages its implication that the United States would not "bargain bases in Cuba for positions in Berlin, NATO and elsewhere." But most intriguing was a report received by the British Foreign Office that Adlai Stevenson and other "top level persons" in the U.S. government had intimated to former UN official Andrew

Cordier that they might be willing to agree to UN surveillance of the Turkish (and perhaps other) bases in return for similar observation of the SS-4s in Cuba. Whether this suggested an actual trade of missiles is unclear.[33]

By 26 October, the crisis had entered a new phase. The U.S. naval blockade had succeeded in preventing further Soviet shipments from reaching Cuba, but work on the existing missile sites continued, and ExComm now had to anticipate—or try to decide—what would happen next. In its meeting that morning, according to the minutes, Stevenson predicted that the Russians would ask the United States "for a new guarantee of the territorial integrity of Cuba and the dismantlement of U.S. strategic missiles in Turkey." President Kennedy, for his part, painted the U.S. options in stark colors: "We will get the Soviet strategic missiles out of Cuba only by invading or trading." John McCloy, whom Kennedy had assigned to bolster Stevenson at the UN and who was sitting in, echoed the president's assessment.[34]

That ExComm on 26 October fully expected the Soviets to demand a missile trade was confirmed at its 10:00 P.M. meeting. Policymakers had just received a letter from Khrushchev in which the premier offered to withdraw the SS-4s from Cuba merely in return for a no-invasion pledge (and an end to the blockade). According to the administration's crisis history, the president and his advisers were struck by "the fact that the letter did *not* condition withdrawal of the missiles on a *quid pro quo* fulfillment of Soviet demands in other parts of the world such as Berlin, elimination of U.S. bases, or, most importantly, the Jupiters in Italy and Turkey." As the meeting adjourned, Kennedy entertained real hope that his fears were unjustified—that he might need neither a missile trade nor an invasion to get out of the crisis.[35]

NUISANCE OF DECISION: 27 OCTOBER 1962

Khrushchev erased such hope the next morning, 27 October, when he sent a second letter to Kennedy—and simultaneously had it broadcast publicly—proposing a missile trade. If Khrushchev had not come up with this new offer on his own—which he most assuredly did—he might have arrived at it by listening to public discussion of the crisis over the previous week. The halls of the United Nations, for example, had echoed with chatter about a trade, particularly among delegates from nonaligned nations. Similarly, speaking at a political rally in Vienna on 25 October, Austrian foreign minister Bruno Kreisky proposed a missile swap. Voices in the press chimed in. "What is sauce for Cuba, is also sauce for Turkey," the *Manchester Guardian* had editorialized. If Khrushchev had really brought nuclear missiles into Cuba, he had "done so primarily to demonstrate to the U.S. and the world the mean-ing of American bases close to the Soviet frontier." The most important opinion in the press, however, came from the dean of American journalists, Walter Lippmann, who first discussed the Turkish Jupiters in his column on 23 October. "These advance bases of ours," he argued, "are more hostage than ally," thus allowing Khrushchev to defend Cuba by attacking Turkey. Two days later, Lippmann sought to convert the liability into an asset. Argu-ing that the U.S. blockade would fail to dislodge those Soviet missiles already in Cuba, that the Turkish and Cuban missiles—sitting on the adversary's frontier and having little military value—were comparable, and that mutual dismantlement would not affect the balance of power, Lippmann proposed a missile trade as a way to resolve the crisis.[36]

More important, Soviet readers of the *New York Times* may have noticed the articles of Max Frankel. He reported on 24 October that Kennedy ad-ministration officials rejected the Cuba-Turkey analogy but acknowledged "the appeal of the argument" and said "it was conceivable that the United States might be willing to dismantle one of the obsolescent American bases near Soviet territory." The following day, he noted "unofficial" interest in a trade among top U.S. officials, to whom Frankel clearly enjoyed access in writing both articles.[37]

The Soviets, meanwhile, had called attention to the possibility that they might demand a Cuba-Turkey trade, mostly by repeatedly invoking the analogy. Defense Minister Malinovsky told a Western diplomat in Romania on 23 October, "[In] Turkey, the Americans are holding a dagger at our chest. Why can't we hold a dagger at the American chest in Cuba?" Back in Mos-cow the following day, Khrushchev had a conversation—reported to Rusk on the 26th—with William E. Knox, president of Westinghouse Electrical International. In defending his Cuban move, the Soviet premier discussed the offensive-defensive distinction. "The U.S. said that its Turkish bases were defensive," he said, "but what was the range of the missiles there?" He also "told his familiar story about a man who learned to get along with a smelly goat" despite his dislike for it. "The Soviet Union had its goats in Italy, Greece, etc. and was living with them. The U.S. now had its goat in Cuba." On 25 October, Marshal Malinovsky told the French military attaché that if the Soviets could "put up with Turkey and Iran," then the United States "should be able to put up with Cuba." On 26 October, the official Red Army organ *Red Star* went further, declaring that if the Soviets withdrew their missiles from Cuba, the U.S. should reciprocate in Turkey.[38]

U.S. officials thus had reason—before Lippmann's 25 October proposal—

to suspect that the Soviets might demand a trade. The importance of the Lippmann article, and of the Frankel articles as well, lies in the possibility that the Kremlin interpreted them as enjoying official sanction. After all, Lippmann had visited Khrushchev in April 1961 bearing a Berlin proposal that the premier assumed was from Kennedy. A hint of the Soviet perception emerged when KGB Washington station chief Aleksandr Feklisov (aka Fomin) had one of his now famous meetings with ABC correspondent John Scali on the 27th—in which Feklisov probed for a settlement, it is now clear, on his own authority. When Scali angrily declared Khrushchev's second letter "a stinking double-cross," Feklisov replied that the Soviet trade demand was "not new. After all, Walter Lippmann . . . and many other prominent Americans" had mentioned it. Scali "didn't give a damn if Walter Lippmann or Cleopatra mentioned it—it was completely, totally, utterly and perpetually unacceptable." Ironically, if the Soviets viewed Lippmann's piece as an official trial balloon, they were not completely off base: Lippmann had visited George Ball at the State Department and told him about the article the day before it ran, and Ball had not tried to stop him. Moreover, trial balloon or not, the administration could have easily ended any such speculation among the Soviets by attacking the article publicly, but it did not.[39]

The question then becomes whether Lippmann's, Frankel's, or similar statements influenced Khrushchev's decision between late 26 October and early 27 October (Washington time) to up the ante. On the 27th, Llewellyn Thompson speculated that the Soviets viewed Lippmann's piece and the Kreisky speech as officially inspired trial balloons and that this explained the shift in Soviet demands. As Lebow and Stein observe, however, if Soviet diplomats in Washington considered the Lippmann column important, a cable describing it would probably have landed on Khrushchev's desk on Friday morning at the latest, well before he sent his first message, silent on the Jupiter issue. The same is true of the Frankel articles. On the other hand, Khrushchev may have been motivated by the articles but only after a delay, for whatever reason. One of his assistants, Oleg Troyanovski, recalls that the Lippmann and other statements were decisive. Other Soviet officials attribute the second message to changing assessments of how much bargaining time remained before a U.S. attack on Cuba. A definitive answer, unfortunately, awaits the release of secret Kremlin documents.[40]

In any case, Stevenson had thus predicted correctly, and Khrushchev's first message had indeed proven too good to be true. Moreover, the Soviet premier precipitously presented his second offer in public, placing the White House in an awkward position. ExComm met at 10:00 A.M. to discuss the new development, and President Kennedy immediately began to lean toward a trade, or at least to reconcile himself to the apparent lack of any alternative. "To any man at the United Nations or any other rational man," he said, "it will look like a very fair trade." Nitze, Ball, Rusk, Bundy, and Dillon raised objections to a trade: this concession would only lead to additional demands; the Jupiters were a European and thus separate issue; and the Turks were not threatening the peace. Robert Kennedy argued both points of view. First he advocated consideration of a trade if "some assurances" could be given to the Turks and other NATO allies "for their own security." But then, according to the minutes covering the period that was not tape-recorded, he stressed how the Turkish and Cuban missiles were "entirely separate" problems.[41]

The president remained steadfast in his support of a trade despite such dissent. Although wishing to avoid getting bogged down in elaborate negotiations while construction of the SS-4s proceeded, JFK said the Soviets had "a very good proposal," which was why they made it publicly. "Most think . . . that if you're allowed an even trade you ought to take *advantage* of it." The minutes have him arguing, toward the end of the morning session, "We have to face up to the possibility of some kind of a trade over missiles."[42]

At this point, accordingly, Kennedy ordered Roswell Gilpatric to spend the afternoon with State and JCS representatives in Bundy's basement office drafting a "scenario" for early removal of the Jupiters. It included separate plans for Italy and Turkey, owing to those countries' contrasting attitudes on the subject, as well as the manner in which to approach the allies and present the withdrawal in public. Gilpatric undertook this mission, however, with the understanding that the removal was for negotiation after the Soviets stopped work on and rendered inoperable their missiles in Cuba.[43]

Kennedy resumed his pro-trade stance at the 4:00 P.M. ExComm meeting. He repeatedly expressed his conviction that a trade would be necessary and acceptable (again, if work ceased on the Cuban missiles), particularly in contrast to the military action he saw as unavoidable otherwise. At one point, he was quite forceful. "I'm just thinking about what . . . we're going to have to do in a day or so . . . possibly an invasion, all because we wouldn't take missiles out of Turkey, and we all know how quickly everybody's courage goes when the blood starts to flow, and that's what's going to happen in NATO . . . and [the Soviets] grab Berlin, and everybody's going to say, 'Well, that was a pretty good proposition.' . . . By negotiation," Kennedy concluded a few moments later, "—we're going to have to take our weapons out of Turkey." He recognized that the Turks would resist, but he added, "We may just decide we have to do it in our own interest."[44]

A few advisers continued to point out the drawbacks of a trade. Bundy, Ball, and the new JCS chair, Maxwell Taylor (no doubt accurately reflecting the views of the other Chiefs), worried about NATO rejecting a trade or being seriously damaged by it. But Ball seems to have shifted in the latter part of the meeting toward accepting a trade. "If we're going to get the damned missiles out of Turkey anyway," he argued, "say we'll trade you the missiles . . . we're going to put Polaris in there, [so you Soviets are] not going to benefit by this." In response to a question by Bundy, Ball said he did not think NATO would be "wrecked," and further, "[If the alliance] isn't any better than that, [then] it isn't that good to us." Rusk wondered whether the Soviets were really seeking a trade or merely trying to undermine U.S. standing in global public opinion.[45]

Secretary McNamara suggested that if the United States announced it was "defusing the Jupiters . . . and replacing them with Polaris submarines," then it would be "in a much better position to present this whole thing to NATO." This would remove them as a target for Soviet military retaliation in case the United States attacked Cuba (it did not occur to McNamara that the Soviets, in responding to an attack on Cuba, might disregard or disbelieve such an announcement). Then, rather than presenting it as a trade, Washington could say it was "relieving the Alliance of a threat that is presently upon [it]." McNamara stated clearly that he did not oppose a trade, but he also said, "[I want to avoid being in a] position where we haven't traded . . . and we *are* forced to attack Cuba, and the missiles remain in Turkey." Vice President Lyndon Johnson—who earlier in the crisis had favored an air strike— argued that if the United States was willing to defuse the Jupiters and thus effectively remove them as weapons, then why not go ahead and trade?[46]

Neither Robert Kennedy nor Llewellyn Thompson opposed a trade outright at the afternoon meeting, but they both counseled against it in favor of the famed "Trollope ploy." In this scheme, first suggested by Bundy (not RFK, who took the credit in *Thirteen Days*), President Kennedy would respond to Khrushchev's first offer and essentially ignore his second. At that same 4:00 P.M. meeting, JFK approved the Trollope ploy in the form of a letter to Khrushchev, sent and released publicly just after 8:00 P.M. It offered an end to the U.S. blockade and a U.S. pledge not to invade Cuba in return for the removal of the Soviet missiles, but it did not, as is often assumed, ignore Khrushchev's second letter. In fact, it stated that the offered settlement would relieve "world tensions" and thus facilitate "a more general arrangement regarding 'other armaments,' as proposed in [Khrushchev's] second letter." A "continuation" of the Cuban "threat," on the other hand, "or a prolonging of this discussion concerning Cuba by linking these problems to the broader questions of European and world security, would surely lead to an intensification of the Cuban crisis and a grave risk to the peace of the world." Of course, the main point was that Kennedy's message accepted Khrushchev's 26 October letter, which had asked for only a U.S. no-invasion pledge, and rejected the 27 October letter, which had sought a missile trade. Such was the U.S. response—in public. There was more to it than that.[47]

THE TURKS, THE ITALIANS, THE ALLIANCE

In the meantime, ExComm could scarcely go about its business without considering the NATO allies, most of all Turkey. Not that it felt compelled to consult with even the major allies on its big decisions during the crisis; it merely kept them informed. "We did not want," Dean Rusk later admitted, "multilateral management of the Cuba crisis." But administration officials did have to reckon with the Europeans' potential reaction to a missile trade.[48]

As early as 23 October, the Turkish Foreign Office had expressed to the Americans its concern that the Soviets would attempt to amend a resolution then before the UN Security Council to include dismantlement of the Jupiter bases as well. Such suspicions were in the ballpark but overestimated the Soviets' subtlety. At a reception in Ankara on 23 October, the Soviet ambassador to Turkey, Nikita Ryzhov, apparently acting on his own initiative, told the Turks that their country "was in this just as much" as the United States because the Soviet Union "considered Turkey its 'Cuba'"; the bases on its soil "were just as menacing as anything in Cuba." Then, on 25 October, Ryzhov called on Turkish foreign minister Feridun Erkin and demanded removal of the Jupiters and other NATO bases from Turkey. Premier Ismet Inönü personally drafted a note of rejection. Ryzhov fired back an ultimatum: Dismantle the Jupiters or Turkey's cities become the priority targets for Soviet nuclear weapons in case of war. "If you don't think we are ready to make war over Cuba," Ryzhov added, "you are mistaken." With characteristic disdain, Inönü retorted, "Don't make me laugh."[49]

On 23–24 October, citing Cuba-Turkey comparisons in the Western press, Erkin urged the United States to increase and expedite military aid to his country, particularly aircraft and aircraft parts; the aid was "desperately needed" before the Soviets pressured Turkey to give up its Jupiter bases. The U.S. embassy in Ankara was instructed to reply that top U.S. officials were discussing ways of accelerating MAP deliveries. Despite such opportunities the crisis created, however, it also generated fears among the Turks that Washington might bargain away the Jupiters behind their backs.[50]

ExComm's early consideration of a trade led it to solicit the views of Ambassadors Raymond Hare in Ankara, Reinhardt in Rome, and Thomas Finletter, the U.S. representative at NATO, in Paris. It was "possible that [a] negotiated solution for removal [of the] Cuban offensive threat," Rusk cabled on 24 October, might "involve dismantling and removal [of the] Jupiters." Rusk recognized that "this would create serious politico-military problems for U.S.-Turkish relations and with regard to Turkey's place in NATO alliance," and so he asked Hare in particular for his assessment of the "political consequences" of "outright removal, removal accompanied by stationing of Polaris submarine in area, or removal with some other significant military offset, such as [a] seaborne multilateral nuclear force within NATO."[51]

Ambassador Reinhardt's response to Rusk's inquiry, which arrived from Rome late in the afternoon of 26 October, was notably optimistic about the feasibility of a trade, in line with the precrisis indifference of Italian officials toward their Jupiter squadrons. Reinhardt began by asserting that removal of the Italian Jupiters would probably be manageable but the United States should consult Rome early on should a trade involving them appear likely. The Italian people and government greatly valued the U.S. military presence on their soil, he added, but not any particular weapon system and certainly not the Jupiters, the continued stationing of which the public was only minimally aware. Under some "combination of offsetting circumstances"—such as a clear demonstration that its security would be safeguarded without the Jupiters, assurances as to the presence of Polaris submarines in the Mediterranean, and public emphasis of Italy's importance in NATO—Rome "would agree to withdrawal [of the] Jupiters," Reinhardt concluded.[52]

As for Finletter, when his Belgian counterpart argued at a Paris dinner party on 25 October that the alliance should offer a missile trade, he responded that making or agreeing to such an offer was impossible at this point, "for reasons of prestige and American public opinion." His reply to Rusk, however, was more nuanced. On the one hand, he stressed the great symbolic importance the Turks attached to the missiles, the severe damage that would result from a trade without their prior consent, and their likely resentment at being openly equated with Cuba. A trade might establish a dangerous precedent for the alliance or seriously disrupt it by demonstrating that Washington was willing to sacrifice the allies' security for its own security in the Western Hemisphere. On the other hand, he argued that establishment of a "small southern command multilateral seaborne force on a 'pilot basis,'" if it was packaged properly, supported fully by the United States, and included Turks in its crews, would adequately compensate the Turks for loss of the Jupiters in a trade. Moreover, some NATO countries, especially Norway and Denmark but perhaps Britain as well, might tolerate a trade if it seemed the only alternative to nuclear war.[53]

Hare submitted a lengthy response from Turkey, arriving in Washington between late morning and early afternoon on the 27th, that was gloomier but still did not rule out a trade of some kind. In his view, a trade would create a "major problem" in U.S.-Turkish and U.S.-NATO relations. The United States would risk losing the Turks' value as a staunch ally were they to "get the impression that their interests . . . were being traded off in order to appease an enemy." Should Washington insist on a trade, their "demand for arms to fill the vacuum would be specific and sizeable." He then outlined four alternatives "in order of increasing difficulty": (1) (obviously) avoiding a trade altogether; (2) a trade in which Turkey and Cuba were not at all visibly coupled—the Jupiters gradually phased out and replaced with something such as a multilateral seaborne nuclear force, a deal the Turks might buy but the Soviets, because it would be sequential and secret, might not; (3) a trade in which Turkey and Cuba were more explicitly linked but which still was a U.S.-Soviet secret—the Jupiters would be quickly phased out, but Turkish suspicions and demands for compensatory military aid would grow; and (4) most difficult of all, an open trade—a devastating blow to U.S. credibility and Turkish morale. Presenting the solution chosen through NATO, making use of the IRBM-doubting British and Italians, and emphasizing the military aspect would all ease the process, Hare added, but he concluded that only his second option, gradual decoupled withdrawal, would fit the bill without profoundly damaging bilateral and alliance ties while stimulating further Soviet demands.[54]

ExComm discussed the cables from Hare, Reinhardt, and Finletter. One snag the committee hit was its ignorance of the allies' opinions: the U.S. ambassadors, following instructions, had not actually canvassed the Europeans, a move that obviously would have tipped Kennedy's hand and perhaps blown up in his face. Yet while officials thus had only the ambassadors' assessments to go on, these still exerted influence in ExComm. Echoing the divide-and-rule tactic Norstad had tried during the search for hosts in 1958, McNamara advocated using Italian and British attitudes toward IRBM removal to pressure the Turks to accept a trade. Similarly, Kennedy at one point suggested approaching the Turks first, but if that failed, then convening a NATO meeting, which might "put enough pressure" on the Turks. More frequently, those who opposed or raised questions about a trade invoked potential Turkish or alliance reactions to bolster their case.[55]

Again, however, the president was unswayed by such objections, as is evident from one exchange early in the morning meeting.

BALL: [We have only asked the ambassadors to give their judgments because] if we talked to the Turks, I mean this would be an extremely unsettling business.

JFK: Well *this* is extremely unsettling *now* George, because [Khrushchev has] got us in a pretty good spot here, because most people will regard this as not an unreasonable proposal, I'll just tell you that.

Or, consider this segment of the afternoon session:

BUNDY: [Hare's and Finletter's cables] make the same proposition, that if we appear to be trading our—the defense of Turkey for the threat to Cuba we . . . just have to face a radical decline in the . . .

JFK: Yes, but I should say that also, as the situation is moving, Mac . . . this trade has appeal. Now if we reject it out of hand and then have to take military action against Cuba, then we also face a decline.[56]

At no point, certainly, did the president eagerly embrace a public missile trade; nor did he dismiss concern for the alliance or U.S.-Turkish relations, which he rightly viewed as legitimate. He even felt that the transfer of the first launch position to TAF control was an additional difficulty. The Turks put to rest any doubts about Hare's assessment on the 27th, when they flatly rejected Khrushchev's public call for a trade. It was "out of the question," Foreign Minister Erkin announced. "We did not even discuss the matter at the Cabinet meeting." In NATO as a whole, as Barton Bernstein persuasively argues, several governments would have welcomed a public trade; Prime Minister Macmillan had even suggested to Kennedy that he could immobilize the sixty Thor missiles as part of a settlement, or as a means of facilitating the Turks' giving up their Jupiters. Others in the alliance, to be sure, would have proven difficult. Certainly no one in ExComm savored the prospect of forcing a trade on Turkey or NATO. Yet Kennedy even more strongly sensed the legitimacy of Khrushchev's trade offer and the perils of a military solution to the crisis. Even a complete disruption of the alliance was small potatoes compared with a nuclear exchange, which would have

been, as the president had aptly termed it, "the final failure." From this difficult dilemma would emerge Kennedy's attempt to square the circle.[57]

THE SECRET TRADE

After the 4:00 P.M. meeting in which he had okayed the letter to Khrushchev,
Kennedy met in the Oval Office with a smaller group of advisers to discuss how best to complement the letter using the secret RFK-Dobrynin back
channel opened earlier in the week. Dean Rusk suggested telling Dobrynin
that while there could be no missile deal, the United States would remove
the Jupiters after the crisis was settled. The president and everyone else
quickly approved and agreed to keep knowledge of this aspect in the room,
being especially sensitive to repercussions in Turkey should it be revealed.[58]

Robert Kennedy phoned Dobrynin and asked him to come to see him
at the Justice Department, where they met at 7:45 P.M. Kennedy told the
ambassador, as he reported to Rusk shortly after the crisis, that the United
States "had to have a commitment" by at least the next day that the Cuban
bases would be removed. "He should understand that if [the Soviets] did not
remove those bases then we would remove them." He then reiterated the
U.S. offer of a no-invasion pledge. Dobrynin—on his own initiative—raised
the Jupiter issue. As RFK recounted to Rusk on 30 October, "I replied that
there could be no quid pro quo—no deal of this kind could be made. . . . It
was up to NATO to make the decision. I said it was completely impossible
for NATO to take such a step under the present threatening position of the
Soviet Union. If some time elapsed—and per your instructions, I mentioned
four to five months—I said I was sure that these matters could be resolved
satisfactorily." He then wrote that he had added an unequivocal rejection,
"that there could be no deal of any kind." Such was what he reported on
30 October. Nonetheless, many observers have long interpreted RFK's account in *Thirteen Days* as describing an implicit missile trade. Now it is clear
that even these do not go far enough, for as Ted Sorensen revealed in 1989,
the secret trade was *explicit*. Sorensen had edited Robert Kennedy's notes
for publication as *Thirteen Days* in 1969, and now he admitted that they
were "very explicit that [the Jupiter concession] was part of the deal." Dobrynin's reports of the conversation, recently released, confirm this admission. So one should take Robert Kennedy's first choice of words literally—
"no deal *of this kind* could be made." A different sort of deal, one explicit
but secret, was another matter. This is what the Kennedys offered that evening (along with the no-invasion pledge JFK had tabled publicly), keeping its

Attorney General Robert F. Kennedy and President Kennedy, October 1962. On Saturday the 27th, Robert met with Soviet ambassador Anatoly Dobrynin and concluded an explicit trade, SS-4s in Cuba for Jupiters in Italy and Turkey, known to only two other U.S. policymakers besides the Kennedys. The deal helped defuse the most dangerous crisis of the Cold War. (Cecil Stoughton; courtesy John F. Kennedy Library)

true character concealed from all of ExComm except for Rusk and Llewellyn Thompson. Incidentally, the Kennedys included the thirty Italian Jupiters in the exchange as well, which may reflect their adoption of the intra-alliance pressure tactic suggested by Hare and McNamara.[59]

After Dobrynin left the Justice Department, ExComm reconvened at 9:00 P.M. Here, the smaller group of top officials kept the RFK-Dobrynin meeting and its content secret from the rest of ExComm, while the Kennedys kept the explicit nature of their Jupiter concession secret from the smaller group (again, save Rusk and Thompson). Thus the meeting, as Bernstein notes, was "a kind of charade"—indeed, a charade within a charade. The president did go so far as to admit that he was still holding a Jupiter swap in reserve. "We're trying to get it back on the original proposition of last night," he summarized. "We don't want to get into this trade, [but if the Trollope ploy were to fail,] then . . . it's *possible* that we may have to get back on the Jupiter thing." At one point he read aloud a cable he had just received from General Norstad. Norstad, who according to C. L. Sulzberger was "a bit worried about the judgment and sangfroid of the team in control in Washington," predictably argued against a trade. But it is striking that his views had no discernible effect on the discussion.[60]

At the same time, Dobrynin returned to the Soviet embassy and reported his meeting with Robert Kennedy to Moscow. Khrushchev and other members of the Presidium nervously concluded that they had no choice but to withdraw the Soviet missiles from Cuba immediately. They were receiving reports that an attack on Cuba was imminent, and they feared that events were spinning out of control. They also saw the Jupiter offer as Kennedy's "last concession." Thus at 3:00 A.M. Washington time, 28 October, Khrushchev ordered his subordinates to draft a positive reply to Kennedy's letter. They broadcast it over Radio Moscow, delivered it to the U.S. embassy in Moscow, and rebroadcast it over American radio at 9:00 A.M. McGeorge Bundy relayed the good news to JFK shortly thereafter.[61]

Of course, in this form, the trade failed to meet an important objective of Khrushchev's second letter: to end the crisis before the eyes of the world with an equitable quid pro quo, not a Soviet retreat. The exchange, first of all, was secret, not open, denying Khrushchev the chance to save face beyond the no-invasion pledge. And second, the missiles in Cuba and Turkey were not removed simultaneously. The United States would only withdraw the Jupiters months later, providing a "decent interval" with which Washington could additionally avoid the appearance of a trade. Moreover, from the Kremlin's standpoint, there was theoretically nothing preventing Washington from reneging on the agreement. Khrushchev had to pull his missiles out and then hope without recourse that Kennedy would uphold his side of the bargain. Still, it was another significant carrot to accompany the sticks. Arthur Schlesinger would downplay the concession as merely helping to "sweeten" the Soviet "retreat." Khrushchev himself would stress its "symbolic nature," although he seemed to appreciate that "Kennedy was creating the impression of mutual concessions." It is true, moreover, that his fear of war was Khrushchev's main reason for settling. But Soviet officials nevertheless recall that the "question was not trivial"; the Jupiter concession was "extremely welcome" for Khrushchev and "made it possible to justify" the Soviet retreat. After all, the Turkish missiles had profoundly irritated him for years, and it would thus come as a surprise had their imminent departure not provided him now with some genuine satisfaction.[62]

THE CORDIER OPTION

In 1987, Dean Rusk revealed another striking new detail about the president and the Jupiters at the end of the crisis:

> It was clear to me that President Kennedy would not let the Jupiters in Turkey become an obstacle to the removal of the missile sites in Cuba because the Jupiters were coming out in any event [sic]. He instructed me to telephone the late Andrew Cordier, then at Columbia University, and dictate to him a statement which would be made by U Thant, the Secretary General of the United Nations, proposing the removal of both the Jupiters and the missiles in Cuba. Mr. Cordier was to put that statement in the hands of U Thant only after further signal from us. That step was never taken and the statement I furnished to Mr. Cordier has never seen the light of day. So far as I know, President Kennedy, Andrew Cordier and I were the only ones who knew of this particular step.

Rusk's account was revealed at a March 1987 conference at Hawk's Cay, Florida, and according to George Ball, Kennedy's advisers present "were astonished. None of them knew of it." Indeed, the strict secrecy of the "Cordier option" appears undeniable.[63]

In view of the evidence, the Cordier option is not so astonishing. It is compatible with Kennedy's role, unmistakable in the 27 October ExComm transcripts, as leading advocate of a trade. Its form, moreover, in which the United Nations and not the United States would propose a trade, reflects Kennedy's preference. At one point during the afternoon meeting, Kennedy asked, "[If a trade is offered,] wouldn't we rather have NATO saying it[?]" And a bit later, when Bundy commented that defusing the Jupiters and replacing them with a Polaris submarine would be widely viewed as a trade, Kennedy responded, "Well what we'd like to do is have the Turks come and offer this." Mindful of the hazards involved in trading, or appearing to trade, Kennedy wanted a third party to propose the deal, hoping to turn concession into compromise. The Cordier plan, in which the UN would propose the exchange, thus has Kennedy's mark on it.[64]

The Cordier option is also consistent with Kennedy's doubts about the Trollope ploy. These are clear from the ExComm transcript and from RFK's account, in which he and the president had "a hope, not an expectation," that the Soviets would back down without achieving a public trade. With such misgivings, Kennedy logically wanted a channel ready through which he could make a public trade in the less painful way described by Rusk.[65]

Just because Kennedy installed an apparatus with which he could have traded publicly does not necessarily mean he would have traded publicly, at least not immediately. He had alternatives to an air strike or invasion of Cuba if the Soviets stuck to their demand for a public missile trade. On 27 October, during the afternoon and evening meetings, ExComm discussed measures short of attack or invasion to apply more pressure to the Soviets. These included tightening the blockade to include "POL" (petroleum, oil, and lubricants), mobilizing NATO forces, deploying more warships, and calling up additional air reserve squadrons, the last of which Kennedy did approve that night. "I'd rather go the total blockade route," Kennedy said at one point, "which is a lesser step than military action."[66]

The audio transcript shows clearly that Kennedy was deeply concerned about the risk of war. This suggests that Kennedy would have reached for alternatives before resorting to military action. Now the question becomes, Which would he have considered worse—the additional risk of war, if any, residing in the options above, or the political costs of a public Jupiter trade through the UN? The answer may never be known. What is known is that on 27 October, Kennedy was sufficiently willing to trade missiles openly that he readied the Cordier contingency plan, but not so willing that he would not give the Trollope ploy, and perhaps other actions, a chance first. Had these additional measures failed to dislodge the missiles from Cuba, Kennedy may well have opted for a public trade. Even accounting for the spin control his administration would have employed, the political costs at home and abroad would have been substantial. If Kennedy was willing to incur those, then his desire to avoid military action was far stronger than we have ever suspected. Fortunately for Kennedy, the success of the Trollope ploy on 28 October allowed him to avoid a decision on a public deal, leaving historians with fascinating but unanswerable counterfactual questions.[67]

CONCLUSIONS

When the Cuban missile crisis began, President Kennedy and his advisers quickly, if tacitly, acknowledged the analogy between the Jupiters and Premier Khrushchev's SS-4s in Cuba, while at times denying it in private and consistently straining to dismiss it in public. The tacit acceptance probably explains why the administration, with equal speed, began discussing a missile trade as a possible or necessary solution to the crisis and continued to do so through 27 October. The administration also worried about command and control of the Jupiters, particularly because it expected Soviet retaliation against them in response to the air strike on Cuba it was considering. It even went so far as to consider tolerating such retaliation without further extending the hostilities.

Khrushchev publicly demanded the Jupiters' removal as part of a trade on 27 October. In the ExComm sessions that Saturday, Kennedy repeatedly argued, more strongly than any of his advisers, in favor of accepting a trade. Moreover, had Khrushchev not backed down, the president might have traded publicly, via the Cordier ploy, rather than invade Cuba, although he might have chosen other actions first. It is a moot point, because despite his advocacy of a public trade, on the 27th he agreed to try the Trollope ploy, coupled with an explicit but secret missile trade, first. This combination successfully secured Khrushchev's agreement to withdraw his MRBMs from Cuba. The U.S. concession—viewed by both sides as an explicit part of the settlement—was not decisive, to be sure. Khrushchev was far more impressed by the threat of an attack on Cuba, which he viewed as both imminent and profoundly dangerous. Nevertheless, both he and Kennedy viewed the Jupiter concession as important, and the role it played in the final deliberations of both parties to the crisis should not be underestimated.

The importance of the Turkish Jupiters in ExComm's deliberations only grows with every release of new evidence. The traffic in proposals for a Cuba-Turkey trade in and around ExComm is especially remarkable and deserves elaboration. These trade proposals were:

Consistently discussed. Top U.S. officials consistently kicked around trade proposals throughout the crisis. It is plainly incorrect to argue, for example, that in "early sessions the notion of a swap had been dismissed as unthinkable."[68] Despite the flux of events—consideration of an air strike, decision on a blockade, public exposure of the Soviet move, maneuvers at the United Nations—on virtually every day of the confrontation, during its beginning, middle, and end, several top officials repeatedly returned to the possibility or eventual necessity of a trade.

Widely discussed. A trade was considered throughout the Kennedy administration. The number of ExComm and other high-ranking officials who participated in discussions of this option is impressive. Clearly the administration was not unified; there were several shades of opinion. Depending on the instance and the conditions, some favored a trade, and some opposed it; some rejected it while anticipating it, or were certain of its approach and sought more palatable forms of it. What is indisputable is that the notion of a trade, broadly speaking, was neither restricted to a few "doves" like Adlai Stevenson nor a taboo subject in memoranda or ExComm sessions. Far from it: various bureaus of State and Defense repeatedly commissioned specific explorations of a trade. The president himself received memos on the subject and demonstrated his own willingness to discuss it, so clearly it was acceptable for his subordinates to do likewise. In fact at one point, an apparent majority of ExComm members accepted the necessity of a trade.

Independently conceived. Several ExComm members expected or were reconciled to a trade before Khrushchev's first letter. Kennedy and his advisers undoubtedly hoped the Soviets would not raise the Jupiter issue publicly, and mostly avoided doing so themselves. But before the first Soviet proposal arrived, they considered a Soviet demand on the Jupiters a real possibility; were relieved by its absence from that first proposal; and were not in the least surprised when Khrushchev included it in his second message.

Variably and unpredictably supported. Some policymakers are difficult to pigeonhole on the Jupiter issue because they shifted positions during the crisis. President Kennedy changed his opinion of a trade between 20 and 26 October, Paul Nitze his between 20 and 25 October, McGeorge Bundy his between the 18th and the 27th, and George Ball his within one day, 27 October. In this regard, the ironies are rich. John McCloy, hard-bitten cold warrior sent to stiffen Stevenson at the UN (as well as to render the U.S. team bipartisan), supported a missile trade, whereas Stevenson, the notorious dove, flip-flopped on the 27th and opposed a Jupiter trade. McCone, director of the CIA, easily one of the administration's staunchest hawks, not only supported a trade at one point but recommended forcing Khrushchev to accept a trade.[69]

On the 27th, the crucial day, moreover, some officials remained silent on the Jupiter issue. But it is safe to say that some, such as Nitze and Bundy, opposed a trade. Others, such as Ball, McNamara, and Johnson, either supported or reluctantly accepted a swap. The claim of Nitze and others that a majority opposed it is almost certainly untrue and definitely unsubstantiated by the evidence.[70] And there is no doubt that on 27 October no one was more open to a trade than the president.

The Jupiter subplot in its latest form necessitates other modifications of missile crisis history, with regard to several issues.

Superpower symmetry. In ending the crisis, the United States and Soviet Union behaved more alike than we have thought. Both superpowers cut a secret deal behind the backs of their clients, Cuba and Turkey, in effect agreeing with each other at the expense of existing agreements with Ankara and Havana. Both risked serious difficulties with those clients in so doing; both decided they would confront such difficulties afterward. In the emergency cooperation that only a desperate crisis could produce, both clearly were willing to sacrifice the interests of their friends—and some nuclear weapons to boot—in order to help avoid war.

The role of ExComm. The above account can only diminish the importance of ExComm as a deliberative, decision-making body. The point should not be overstated; the discussion on 27 October clearly helped Kennedy decide on the Trollope ploy, for example, and the amount of thinking aloud and idea bouncing that took place undoubtedly had some beneficial effect. Still, the audio tapes reveal that meetings of JFK's "high-priced help" were often muddled and circular, and on the 27th, opponents of a missile trade had no discernible effect on Kennedy's commitment to it. Rather than relying on the free marketplace of ideas to generate the best decision, it seems that the president was seeking to build a consensus for and render workable an option he had already chosen. And, when he failed to obtain that consensus, he ceased treating ExComm as a single group and in effect broke it up into concentric circles in order to facilitate his own dual, public-private solution. The outer ring, occupied by Nitze, McCone, Dillon, and others, Kennedy completely excluded from the crucial Oval Office meeting in which he approved RFK's approach to Dobrynin. The middle circle, containing advisers such as McNamara and Bundy, was on hand in the Oval Office and thus in on the decision to inform the Soviets that the Jupiters would ultimately be removed—but then denied knowledge of the explicit missile deal and the Cordier option. Only Dean Rusk and Llewellyn Thompson, not generally considered insiders, made it into the inner circle. The Kennedy brothers made Rusk and Thompson privy to the explicit missile trade, and only Rusk to the preparation of the Cordier back channel. Leaks, especially by those who raised objections to a missile trade, an issue replete with potential pitfalls, were something Kennedy naturally wanted to avoid, so he limited knowledge of important decisions to certain advisers. It is pure speculation, but perhaps the Kennedys viewed Rusk and Thompson as the most reliably tight lipped. Regardless, with these moves, JFK accepted a more complicated and more deceitful relationship with his advisers in exchange for less complicated and less risky execution of policy. Far from being Schlesinger's "brilliant instrument of consideration and coordination," therefore, ExComm increasingly deserves the diminished stature recent scholarship assigns to it. It follows, moreover, that Kennedy's stature as an independent decision maker is significantly enhanced.[71]

The advent of arms reduction. Most observers view the missile crisis as a major watershed in postwar international relations. Few entertain romantic notions of a "Gettysburg" of the Cold War, but many see it as an important, short-term impetus for the two relieved superpowers to reduce bilateral tensions and thus as a catalyst for the first major step in controlling the global nuclear arms race, the Limited Test Ban Treaty of 1963. In light of what we now know, however, the missile crisis itself deserves recognition as the first arms control agreement—indeed, first arms *reduction* agreement—between the Soviet Union and the United States.[72]

Of course, the IRBM deal differs from subsequent pacts such as the Limited Test Ban, SALT I, and Intermediate Nuclear Forces treaties in several important respects. The Jupiter–SS-4 swap was verbal, informal, secret, spontaneous, sequential, unevenly verified, and subsumed under a larger tacit agreement. Like most arms control agreements, it did not appreciably affect the superpowers' arsenals, which in fact grew at an accelerated pace during the 1960s. Nevertheless, it is the first agreement in the history of the arms race under which both sides dismantled a portion of their operational nuclear delivery systems. The missile crisis was many things; it was a landmark of informal arms control as well. In the oddest possible way, Kennedy had finally put the Jupiters to some good use. He had sacrificed them to help end a crisis that they—and he—had helped cause in the first place.

Five years earlier, as we have seen, the December 1957 IRBM offer to NATO had been only the prelude to a long and involved effort to locate host countries and deploy the Jupiters. In the Cuban missile crisis, the reverse process began, but in a similar way. Even though the RFK-Dobrynin missile trade of 27 October 1962 helped resolve the most dangerous international crisis of the postwar period, it too was merely a beginning: President Kennedy now had to make good on the deal, to remove the Jupiters within a specific time span without letting anyone—neither the Turks, the NATO allies, the Congress, the public, nor most of the U.S. government itself—know why he was doing so.

6

A VERY TIDY JOB

I feel as though we [have] won. This is the
payoff for our policy of strength and reliance
on the United States.
A Turkish newspaper editor, reacting to the
publicly announced settlement of the missile
crisis, 28 October 1962

Those [Jupiters] are going to be out of there
by April 1 if we have to shoot them out.
John McNaughton, 29 October 1962

The Cuban missile crisis did not abruptly end on 28 October 1962. American and Soviet negotiators in New York wrangled over issues such as verification and the removal of Soviet IL-28 bomber aircraft from Cuba, and not until 20 November could Kennedy announce that the IL-28s would also leave Cuba and that he was lifting the naval blockade of the island. The Jupiter missiles remained an important issue during this last phase of the crisis and for months beyond. Kennedy had to clarify the nature of the missile deal with the Soviets, keep the agreement secret from just about everybody, and, of course, see that the Jupiters were actually dismantled.[1]

FINALIZING THE DEAL, LAUNCHING THE REMOVAL

On 29 October, Dobrynin presented the attorney general with a letter from Premier Khrushchev to President Kennedy. In it, Khrushchev acknowledged that removal of the Jupiters was a delicate issue for the United States, but he also expressed the hope that an accord on it would "mean taking a step—a far from unimportant one, too—toward easing international tensions." This in turn might "serve as a welcome incentive to the solution" of other problems of international security. The Kennedys read the letter, and then RFK met again with Dobrynin the next day. Robert Kennedy's notes recall what he told the Soviet ambassador:

Read letter—Studied it over night.
No quid pro quo as I told you.
The letter makes it appear that there was.
You asked me about missile bases in Turkey. I told you we would be out of them—4–5 months. That still holds. . . . You have my word on this & that is sufficient.

Take back your letter—Reconsider it & if you feel it is necessary to write letters then we will also write one which you cannot enjoy.

Also if you should publish any document indicating a deal then it is off & also if done afterward will further affect the relationship.

In Dobrynin's report to Moscow on the meeting, rather than declaring "no quid pro quo," RFK twice stated that the president "affirm[ed] the agreement" on removal of the Jupiters. Nor did RFK appear as threatening as he portrayed himself, and he added, interestingly, that any written agreement "could cause irreparable harm to [his] political career in the future" should it surface. However, the two accounts agree that the Kennedys returned Khrushchev's letter and flatly refused to create any paper trail.[2]

Dobrynin informed RFK on 1 November that Khrushchev agreed not to press for a formal agreement and "had no doubt that the President would keep his word." Indeed, because of the damage he expected to Soviet relations with Cuba—Castro, like the Turks, made it clear he would have deeply resented his relegation to pawn status—Khrushchev soon came to appreciate the absence of a public trade. In their busy correspondence over the following weeks, neither leader raised the Jupiter issue again, although while drafting Kennedy's letters, ExComm had to remind itself about the Cuba-Turkey analogy. This was undoubtedly the reason why the committee excised from JFK's 6 November letter a paragraph in which the president asks Khrushchev how he "would have felt if the situation had been reversed and if a similar effort had been made by [the United States] in a country like Finland."[3]

The day after Khrushchev came to terms, Defense Secretary McNamara summoned DOD general counsel John McNaughton, already becoming the trusted assistant who would later immerse himself in policy making on Vietnam. "John," McNamara remembers saying, "get those missiles out of Turkey. . . . Cut them up. Saw them up. Take photographs of them. Deliver the photographs to me. . . . Do it!" "I don't want you to ask any questions about it," he also told McNaughton. "I don't want you to say to anybody else why it's being done, 'cause I'm not going to tell you." Thus began the effort to remove the Jupiters.[4]

McNamara claims that he ordered the Jupiters photographed so that he "could personally see that those missiles had been destroyed." Still, this request is curious in light of several facts: the secretary of defense was obviously not in the habit of demanding photographic proof that his directives had been carried out; the Jupiter–SS-4 trade was explicit, and the United

States verified removal of the Soviet missiles using low-level aerial reconnaissance; and yet clearly Washington was not about to let the Soviets reciprocate by overflying Turkey and Italy. Is it possible, then, that McNamara
passed the photos of the dismantled Jupiters on to the Soviets, to prove to
them that Kennedy had upheld his side of the deal? McNamara writes that
he does "not believe copies of the photos were ever given to the Soviets," but
the intriguing possibility that they were remains.[5]

In any case, McNaughton formed and chaired an interdepartmental task
force in accordance with his chief's instructions. Virtually no information is
available about this task force, but clearly haste was its hallmark; it first met
immediately after the crisis, on 29 October. Even more striking, McNaughton opened the session by proclaiming, "Those missiles are going to be out
of there by April 1 if we have to shoot them out." The date 1 April is not co-
incidental; it lay five months ahead, the outside length of time RFK had told
Dobrynin the administration would need to take the Jupiters down. Moreover, at least superficially the U.S. removal effort was conforming to superpower symmetry: with urgent talk of photographic verification and "shoot-
ing them out," ironically, administration officials were referring to NATO
Jupiters in Turkey as they had to Soviet SS-4s in Cuba.[6]

TWO INTERNAL COVER-UPS

In reality, the U.S.-Soviet missile agreement of 27 October existed not between the two governments but between only the highest levels of each
government, to the exclusion and deception of all levels below. This fact led
to two-tiered behavior among both Soviets and Americans. At the highest
level, the Americans sought to fulfill their part of the missile bargain and
dismantle the Jupiters by 1 April, and the Soviets sat and watched, hoping
that Kennedy would keep his word. At the lower levels, in the dark as to
what had transpired at the top, U.S. and Soviet officials understandably continued to act as they had before—the Soviets raised the issue of immediate
Jupiter removal, and the Americans refused to discuss it.

Most of the Americans, that is. An exception was George Kennan, whose
1957 warning about the IRBM deployments had proven so astoundingly
accurate. Now, five years later, from his ambassadorial post in Yugoslavia, he
suggested to Rusk that the resolution of the missile crisis had created an ex-
cellent opportunity for improving U.S.-Soviet relations through "a series of
reciprocal unilateral concessions." An example of such a move Washington

could make to start the ball rolling, he cited in his ignorance of the missile trade, was a statement that it proposed to raise with the Turks and NATO the question of the future of the Turkish Jupiters.[7]

The dominant attitude, however, was that which drove Lauris Norstad, soon to step down as SACEUR, to launch a preemptive strike against any postcrisis Jupiter withdrawal. "To permit the question of missiles in Turkey to be raised again," he wrote to the president personally on 1 November, "would seem to deny the soundness of your position on the Soviet missiles in Cuba." Even to discuss the issue would divide, demoralize, and provoke opposition in the alliance. In his reply to Norstad, however, Kennedy avoided the IRBM issue altogether.[8]

Norstad's warning was ahead of its time by only a few days. Although the explicit missile trade remained a tightly held secret, during the first week of November word of the impending Jupiter removal could not help but spread swiftly throughout the administration. Opposition to the new policy arose just as quickly, as is clear from a memo Assistant Secretary of State for European Affairs William Tyler sent to Dean Rusk on 9 November. Tyler argued that although the Jupiters were "obsolescing," they remained "a significant military asset of NATO." More important, "from a political point of view, it would be highly inadvisable for the U.S. to associate itself" with a withdrawal effort *at any time in the near future*," although it could do so ultimately—*after* a substitute force in which the Italians and Turks could take part was up and running. Tyler stressed that his admonition had gained newfound urgency because he and his colleagues at State had just gotten wind of McNamara's instructions for removal before May 1963. He added that Paul Nitze too was "vigorously opposed" but felt he was "under direct orders" from McNamara. Tyler appended a seven-page supporting memorandum that he suggested Rusk send to the president.[9]

Rusk followed the recommendation the same day. "Though I share your concern about maintaining the Turkish and Italian Jupiter missiles," he wrote to JFK in his cover memo, "I have concluded that, [on] balance, it would be undesirable to undertake action leading to their being phased out in the near future." Rusk's action is strange considering his knowledge of the explicit missile deal and the "four- to five-month" time frame RFK had agreed on with Dobrynin on 27 October. Perhaps Rusk did not consider four to five months to be "in the near future," or had changed his mind about the advisability or feasibility of withdrawing the missiles so quickly, or accepted the policy but was creating a false paper trail in case it went awry, or sent the memo to appease his subordinates, knowing that it would have no effect.[10]

Whichever the case, Tyler and Rusk were quickly joined by other officials. Jeffrey Kitchen, a midlevel State Department official, wrote to Robert Komer, one of Bundy's most influential NSC assistants, that even though he had long considered the IRBM deployments "military and deterrence nonsense," he nevertheless felt "more strongly than on any single problem since [he] returned to government . . . that precipitate attempts to obtain removal of these weapons would do the U.S. great damage." Komer, in turn, seconded the objections from State; early withdrawal, he warned Bundy, would harm the credibility of the United States with Pakistan and Iran as well as NATO, while encouraging Khrushchev. It could, in short "create one hell of a mess" and "undermine [the United States'] whole success in Cuba."[11]

Although the evidence is spotty, Kennedy clearly ignored or deflected these worries bubbling up to his office. He went ahead with "precipitate" removal of the Jupiters and did nothing to lessen the ignorance of the foreign policy bureaucracy. In speaking to subordinates, some top officials denied the existence of a trade while indicating that removing the Jupiters "on grounds of obsolescence [would] soon require attention," as McNamara had to the Joint Chiefs on 29 October. Midlevel officials in the State Department objected to the firm 1 April deadline, and they must have wondered when top policymakers continued to insist on that date. But U.S. officials would continue to coinhabit this split-level house even beyond the removal of the missiles. Just before leaving for Moscow to negotiate a nuclear test ban treaty in July 1963, Averell Harriman "was sure the Russians would not agree to an inspection quota acceptable to [the United States] unless he had, as he liked to put it, 'some goodies in his luggage,'" Arthur Schlesinger later wrote. Harriman "thus regretted the fact" that the United States had unilaterally withdrawn the Jupiters from Turkey and Italy three months earlier: "If he only had them to trade now!"[12]

Soviet diplomats and propagandists, having been similarly denied knowledge of the trade, acted as if removal of the Jupiters was still a goal they should pursue. On 29 October, for instance, the Soviet chargé d'affaires in Budapest asked a U.S. diplomat when Washington was going to reply to Khrushchev's trade offer of the 27th. The Soviet ambassador in Bonn raised the issue with West German diplomats as well. On the 29th and 30th, Soviet radio demanded liquidation of the Turkish bases. And Deputy Foreign Minister Vasily Kuznetzov, head of the Soviet delegation sent to New York to hammer out a final settlement of the crisis with Stevenson and McCloy, said he wanted to discuss broader issues including the Turkish bases. The president, understandably concerned, instructed his delegation to keep the focus narrow, which it did. McCloy, as ignorant of Kennedy's missile concession as Kuznetzov was, warned him over lunch on 4 November against dragging the Jupiter issue into their talks. "It bears no relation," he said, "to the Caribbean or the Western Hemisphere." It was a lunch of the mutually uninformed.[13]

Even Anastas Mikoyan, whom Khrushchev would have let in on the secret if anyone, was either clueless or careless enough to resurrect the Jupiter issue in a meeting with JFK on 29 November. Kennedy had stumbled upon the broader issue in an equally careless way, according to Mikoyan's memorandum of conversation, by asking his visitor "half in jest" whether the Soviets "would be able to sleep soundly if in, say, Finland there unexpectedly turned out to be 100 missiles targeted on the Soviet Union." Mikoyan replied that Soviets "slept soundly" because the only missiles stationed "next door" were those in Turkey, which he incorrectly thought were "in the hands of the Americans." Kennedy then merely remarked that the "missile bases in Turkey and Italy did not mean much," and that his administration "was studying the expediency of keeping those bases." It is as if the president was unsure whether Mikoyan was in on the secret and thus thought it best to assume he was not. Understandably, Kennedy and Khrushchev had not coordinated the remarkable cover-ups they were directing against their own subordinates.[14]

ONE EXTERNAL COVER-UP

On the missile-deal aspect of the Cuban crisis resolution, at least, Khrushchev had it easy. Having neither made any concessions nor acted from any motives that were not already public, and leading a closed government responsible to no independent institutions, all he had to do was keep quiet about the U.S. Jupiter concession. Kennedy, by contrast, had to work to drape a "cloak of secrecy" over it, although because he held the secret so closely, he could rely on most of his subordinates to help cover it up unwittingly—and convincingly, because they sincerely thought there had been no trade. Enduring in its intensive version for several months—and then lingering more subtly for several years—this subterfuge assumed several forms.

First and foremost, the administration directed the cover-up toward the U.S. Congress. Soon after Kennedy's public announcement of the impending Jupiter removal, some lawmakers on Capitol Hill began suspecting that it bore some relationship to the Cuban missile crisis. They asked about this in committee, and the administration denied it unequivocally.

SENATOR STENNIS: [Withdrawal of the Jupiters] has nothing to do with
    the Cuban situation or anything like that.
MCNAMARA: Absolutely not . . . the Soviet Government did raise the
    issue . . . [but the] President absolutely refused even to discuss it.
    He wouldn't even reply other than that he would not discuss the
    issue at all.

Dean Rusk was not to be outdone.

SENATOR HICKENLOOPER: The removal of the missiles from Turkey . . .
    was in no way, shape or form, directly or indirectly, connected
    with the settlement, the discussions or the manipulations of the
    Cuban situation?
RUSK: That is correct, sir.

"We denied in every forum that there was any deal," Bundy later wrote,
adding a monument to qualification, "and in the narrowest sense what we
said was usually true, as far as it went."[15]

Besides flat denials, the administration used other tactics on Congress.
One was to cite the Jupiters' maintenance costs, which McNamara put at $1
million per missile per year. When faced with a particularly good question—
why was the administration taking the Jupiters out so quickly?—officials
either ducked or explained that they did not want to be caught in another
crisis, which might erupt any moment at a flashpoint like Berlin, with these
vulnerable missiles still in place. Nor did they shy away from torturous
logic, which they used in written answers to the questions of Senator Mil-
ward Simpson (R-Wyo.). "The replacement of the obsolescent Jupiters could
scarcely be part of any agreement . . . with Khrushchev," they argued, "since
the net effect of this replacement will be to strengthen [NATO's] military
capabilities." But the approach they took most often was also their best: invoke modernization. The crisis had driven home the Jupiters' obsolescence,
they argued, and this was only one system among many that should be replaced with newer, less vulnerable weapons, in this case the Polaris SLBM.[16]

In approaching Congress, the administration also dusted off the February
1961 JCAE subcommittee report. In his testimony, McNamara quoted the
portions of it that had recommended cancellation of the Turkish deployment
and substitution of Polaris submarines. Indeed, he mentioned the spring
1961 contacts with the Turks and then said, "It has taken from then until
now to work this out"—implying that negotiations had been continuous,

which of course was not the case. The secretary suggested that the report "was the foundation" for the administration's attempts at removal. By citing the JCAE's earlier work as extensively as they did, administration officials deftly, if disingenuously, shifted some of the responsibility for removal back onto the same lawmakers who were asking awkward questions about the new policy.[17]

A second approach to the cover-up involved emphasizing or exaggerating all elements in the resolution of the crisis apart from the Jupiter deal. In April 1963, for example, Robert Kennedy gave a speech in which he claimed that on 27 October, the president had notified Khrushchev that "strong and overwhelming retaliatory action would be taken unless he received immediate notice that the [Cuban] missiles would be withdrawn." This, the first public reference by any administration official to a U.S. ultimatum, is particularly interesting in light of preponderant evidence indicating RFK and Dobrynin's agreement that the U.S. demand for a swift withdrawal of the missiles from Cuba was *not* to be understood as an ultimatum. In a similar vein, after again completely denying the existence of any missile deal, McNamara testified that on 27 October ExComm "faced . . . the possibility of launching nuclear weapons and Khrushchev knew it, and that [was] the reason, and the only reason, why he withdrew [his] weapons."[18]

Third, the Kennedy administration selected Adlai Stevenson as postcrisis scapegoat in such a way as to suggest that it had dismissed the idea of a missile trade. Stevenson was the obvious choice for fall guy; well known as dovish on international questions, outspoken in his support of a trade in early crisis deliberations, thoroughly disliked and distrusted by Kennedy and many of his top advisers, he fit the bill nicely. All it took was approval of a single leak to JFK's friend Charles Bartlett, who with Stewart Alsop was writing a major behind-the-scenes account of the crisis for the *Saturday Evening Post*. In their article, which hit newsstands on 1 December, a "nonadmiring official" leveled the worst possible charge: "Adlai wanted a Munich," that is, to "trade the Turkish, Italian, and British missile bases for the Cuban bases." The piece also had Stevenson as the lone peacenik bucking the ExComm consensus and Kennedy listening "politely" to his proposal and then rejecting it.[19]

"Adlai on Skids over Pacifist Stand in Cuba" read the subsequent *New York Daily News* headline, part of the international controversy the Alsop and Bartlett account had stirred. Angry and humiliated, Stevenson, like many others, assumed the accusation had been White House–inspired and probably intended to elicit his resignation. The latter supposition was wrong; for purely practical reasons, Kennedy did not want him to step down. But JFK's claim in a private consolation letter to Stevenson—"I did not discuss the Cuban crisis or any of the events surrounding it with *any* newspapermen"—was a lie. Indeed, Kennedy probably was the "nonadmiring official" supplying the Munich quip, and he did discuss the article with Bartlett before publication, prevailed upon him to make several changes, and yet let the depiction of Stevenson stand. Publicly and privately, the president expressed his regret over the rumpus and continuing support for his UN ambassador but never disputed the charge against him. Kennedy probably treated Stevenson so shabbily in order to contain the ambassador's popularity—which his famous "hell-freezes-over" performance during the crisis had enhanced immensely—and thereby his independence. But the leak also served the purpose of staking out a first history of the missile crisis that marginalized the trade proposal as a kooky attempt at appeasement and thus something that ExComm, naturally, had not seriously considered—much less adopted.[20]

Fourth, policymakers acted as if they had been surprised by Khrushchev's 27 October trade proposal and puzzled over where he could have gotten the idea. Before the Senate Foreign Relations Committee, Dean Rusk claimed that the administration "didn't know exactly why" Khrushchev demanded a trade, and again speculated about the Kreisky speech and Lippmann article. In early November, Kennedy feigned wonderment that Khrushchev had thought he could exact the abandonment of the Turkish bases. He also said he was annoyed and baffled by Lippmann's column advocating a trade.[21]

Fifth, when it came to suspicions that a trade had taken place, Kennedy's men were not above dismissing the messengers along with the message. In a letter to French political analyst Raymond Aron, Bundy wrote that those "who would spread rumors" about a Jupiter trade, "of course, must be pretty far gone in their mistrust of the United States to start with." This was an exception, however. Generally the administration did not resort to this approach, probably because it did not have to, with so many others available.[22]

Finally, the cover-up became institutionalized in the years after the removal, through a variety of means. One was the published government document, such as DOD's FY 1963 annual report, which made the incredible claim that Britain, Italy, and Turkey had "announced *their* decisions to phase out the IRBMs" stationed in their countries. Another technique was the interview. In one of these for a 1964 NBC White Paper on the missile crisis, for example, Bundy said that a missile trade "was the gravest kind of political danger" for the United States because if it had done that "at the point of a gun . . . the Atlantic Alliance might well have come unstuck." In

1967 Schlesinger went so far as to assert, according to an interviewer's notes, that "Turkey was Stevenson's idea." Interviews had a huge impact particularly through accounts that relied heavily on them, such as Elie Abel's *The Missile Crisis* (1966). But by far most useful and durable in preserving the cover-up, however inadvertent, was the insider history. In *A Thousand Days* (1965), Arthur Schlesinger allowed that "others" on ExComm had discussed the Jupiters besides Stevenson and that Stevenson had "changed his mind on this" by 21 October. But most important was his portrayal of the reaction to Khrushchev's "perplexing" trade offer: Kennedy "regarded the idea as unacceptable, and the swap was promptly rejected." Ted Sorensen, in *Kennedy* (1965), similarly wrote that the "President had no intention of destroying the alliance by backing down" and that it was the "vulnerable, provocative and marginal nature" of the Jupiters that "led to their quiet withdrawal" in 1963. *Kennedy* and *A Thousand Days*, both Book-of-the-Month Club selections, both dramatic, intimate, and authoritative, formed perhaps the sturdiest pillars of the cover-up. But they were only two among many.[23]

Fidel Castro, oddly enough, chiseled the first tiny crack in the cover-up. "One day, perhaps, it will be known," he said in an interview published in 1967, "that the United States made some concessions in relation to the October Crisis besides those which were made public." He was more direct in another interview, published in 1969: "Kennedy was willing to give up the Turkish and Greek [sic] bases." The first major, widely noticed break in the story appeared in RFK's *Thirteen Days*, and additional revelations have continued to seep out since. Only in 1989, however, did Ted Sorensen reveal the occurrence of an explicit missile trade. The cover-up had succeeded for more than a quarter century.[24]

THE DIPLOMACY OF WITHDRAWAL

On 10 December 1962, the president met with McNamara, Rusk, and Bundy to discuss strategy for the upcoming regular ministerial session of the North Atlantic Council in Paris. They agreed that Rusk and McNamara, who would attend the meeting, should use the opportunity to begin steering the alliance toward modernization of its missile force. But they also decided, according to the minutes, "that in light of the uncertainties surrounding the problem of multilateral and seaborne deterrents, it might be well to begin" side talks with the Turkish and Italian defense ministers "simply with an effort to clear up the problem of the Jupiters itself." This made sense, especially if the administration was to achieve removal of the Jupiters by 1 April; establishment of a multilateral force would surely take longer than that. McNamara added that he would attempt to persuade the Italians and Turks by pointing out that the missile crisis had underscored how "dangerous" the Jupiters were; that the IRBMs were expensive and thus diverted funds from other projects; that the United States would consider strengthening the Mediterranean deterrent, perhaps by redeploying U.S.-owned and -crewed Polaris submarines there; and that it was willing to discuss Italian participation in the manufacture of armored personnel carriers and Turkish acquisition of additional fighter aircraft. Armed with this array of arguments and enticements, Rusk and McNamara flew to Paris.[25]

Italy
The Italians immediately proved themselves the easier sell, which is understandable considering their positive response on the subject of IRBM removal even before the missile crisis. At the NATO ministerial conference, held 13–15 December, McNamara spoke with Defense Minister Andreotti and proposed dismantlement of the Jupiters by 1 April and their replacement with Polaris. He sweetened the pot by offering to replace Corporal tactical missiles in Italy with Sergeants (a promotion, of sorts, which would also serve to bury the Jupiter removal in a broader context of "modernization"). Andreotti responded that the move must be a U.S. initiative and should precede the spring elections in Italy, but otherwise he "appeared not overly disturbed" by it. Not until 5 January 1963, however, did McNamara follow up with a more formal proposal, which reiterated the Polaris substitution and 1 April target date.[26]

The U.S. initiative annoyed Italian political leaders, including Prime Minister Fanfani and Antonio Segni, now president. Although accepting the logic behind it, they worried that Italy would lose the elevated status it enjoyed over nonnuclear members of the alliance. They assumed that Kennedy had made his decision during the missile crisis and thus were irritated to learn of it only three months later. In a related sense, they suspected that it resulted from a secret superpower bargain. And finally, they felt Washington did not consider the domestic political problem withdrawal might create for them. With the Americans now making the same anti-IRBM arguments the opposition parties had made all along, and a 1 April pullout coming on the eve of parliamentary elections, the embarrassment and political costs might prove considerable. Fanfani's frustration showed in his quip to a colleague: when it came to the proposed multilateral force, "the United States would probably propose placing Italian cooks on the submarines and call it joint control."[27]

President Kennedy with Italian prime minister Amintore Fanfani, January 1963. Fanfani's smile concealed his resentment, shared by the Turks, of being treated as a pawn. Nevertheless, he agreed to give up his Jupiters. They would be replaced by Polaris missile-firing submarines under sole U.S. control. (National Archives)

Despite all this, however, no Italian leader seriously considered opposing the withdrawal. Thus on 16–17 January, when Kennedy proposed the withdrawal and Polaris substitution to the visiting Fanfani, the prime minister was amenable. Although according to their joint communiqué the two leaders had only "agreed on the need to modernize both the nuclear and conventional weapons and forces which their countries contribute[d] to the Alliance," newspapers correctly noted that this would entail dismantlement of the IRBMs.[28]

The rest was anticlimax. Fanfani's cabinet signed off on the decision on 24 January, and the Chamber of Deputies voted in favor of it the following day. On 12 February, Gilpatric and Andreotti agreed on various cooperative defense measures, including joint conventional weapons production, which were part of the Kennedy administration's attempt to appease the Italians. That same day, U.S. officials in Rome announced the 1 April Polaris deployment in the Mediterranean. Andreotti's public complaint a week later, that the missile substitution weakened his country's voice in NATO defense matters, was in vain.[29]

Turkey

The Turks provided a stark contrast. Unlike the Italians, they had been unwilling to give up their IRBMs before the missile crisis, and they were unwilling afterward. On 28 October, the same day Khrushchev gave in apparently without winning removal of the Jupiters, Turkish anxiety still led Foreign Minister Erkin to tell Hare that he "assumed [the] U.S. would do nothing which concerned Turkey without consultation." Rusk quickly authorized Ambassadors Hare and Finletter to tell the Turks that "no 'deal' of any kind was made with USSR involving Turkey," and U.S. diplomats such as Adlai Stevenson assured their Turkish counterparts that they would consult Turkey and NATO before Washington engaged in any talks on the Jupiters. Ankara tried to protect itself by reiterating publicly its desire to keep the missiles in place.[30]

At the December NATO conference, McNamara approached Turkey's defense minister, Ilhami Sancar, as he had Andreotti. Sancar expressed concern over how removal would affect Turkish morale and confidence in NATO; in general he did not respond favorably. Foreign Minister Erkin, on the other hand, told Rusk "that he saw no difficulty" as long as the United States provided alternative means of demonstrating its commitment to Turkish security. Whether Sancar and Erkin were performing a good cop–bad cop routine or genuinely disagreed on the U.S. proposal, the Turks clearly posed more of an obstacle than the Italians did.[31]

The Americans certainly recognized this, and in his 5 January letter to Sancar, McNamara bolstered the now standard arguments about modernization and vulnerability with an offer to accelerate deliveries of nuclear-capable F-104G aircraft to Turkey; Rusk authorized Hare to take a similar tack. Erkin presented the U.S. proposal to Prime Minister Inönü and his cabinet on 18 January, and although the government agreed in principle to the withdrawal, Erkin muddied the waters by suggesting to his colleagues that Turkish personnel would serve on board the Polaris submarines. This the U.S. government would not even consider; it had decoupled the Mediterranean Polaris force and the planned MLF, and blurring the line between the two might delay the former and jeopardize the latter. Despite this new potential stumbling block, Erkin made it clear to Hare after the cabinet meeting that Turkey did not want to be shown up on the issue by Italy, and Hare considered this the U.S. "ace in the hole." As it had during the search for IRBM hosts, the United States might again enjoy an opportunity to play one NATO ally off another.[32]

Frustration continued for U.S. officials, however, as an agreement continued to elude them despite tantalizing progress. The Turks did effectively tie their own hands by announcing publicly on 23 January that their Jupiters would be dismantled and replaced, but complications persisted. One was conflicting responses coming from the Turkish Foreign and Defense Ministries; another, more grave, was the need for some tangible evidence of the United States' continued strategic commitment with the Jupiters gone and joint Polaris crews out of the question. "[The] problem is essentially psychological," Hare reported, "and something more obviously demonstrable [is] required than visits to Turkish ports or visits [by] Turkish officers to Polaris subs." On 9 February, Erkin informed Hare that the Turkish government had accepted the missile substitution without conditions, but the types of compensatory military aid Turkey would receive—that is, the conditions—remained unresolved. It took a visit to Ankara by Major General Robert Wood, acting as McNamara's representative, to achieve closure. Wood succeeded in hashing out the final details of the U.S. compensation, which included additional F-104Gs (which would mean a six-month delay in F-104G deliveries to Taiwan) and other, wholly conventional armaments, by 15 March.[33]

The broader alliance posed the only other potential diplomatic obstacle. Technically, the North Atlantic Council had to approve the IRBM removals, but the White House had no intention of allowing it to get in the way. Any illusions about this on the NAC were no doubt shattered when its members first learned of the Italian Jupiter removal from press reports. As briefing papers for JFK's early February press conference stated, the administration wished to meet its "obligation to the North Atlantic Council in this matter without providing the Council an opportunity for divisive discussion or action." It thus recommended reference to NAC "endorsement" rather than "approval." Apparently no real effort was necessary, however, to realize this preference; the NAC met sometime around 22 February and concluded that because the Jupiter removal decision was an accomplished fact, there was no need for the council to approve it. Many of its members doubtless considered all this business as usual, that is, nonconsultation.[34]

POT PIE: WITHDRAWAL

The USAF removal operation, dubbed with minimal wit POT PIE, went fairly quickly; after all, taking missiles down is much easier than putting them up. The air force did receive what one general later called "the goddamnest instructions from Mr. McNamara's office": do not merely dismantle the IRBMs, but salvage them in the "most economical" way. Unfortunately,

Operation POT PIE: dismantled Italian Jupiter missile being readied for transport, April 1963. The period for which the missiles were actually deployed turned out to be far shorter than the time required to deploy them. (National Archives)

dismantled Thors alone were more than the air force or NASA could usefully convert into space boosters, and no one else in the government was interested in the leftover Jupiters. So, the air force destroyed the missile bodies and returned the warheads, guidance systems, and mobile equipment to the United States. This attempt to reap more buck for the bang recovered multipurpose items worth only $14 million, which was, as one DOD official admitted, a disappointingly small sum.[35]

The IRBM dismantlement began on 1 April 1963 and thus was complete a few weeks after the 1 April target date. The thirty Italian Jupiters lay in pieces by 23 April. McNamara, well aware of the president's special interest in the subject, scrawled a note to him on 25 April: "The last Jupiter missile in Turkey came down yesterday. The last Jupiter warhead will be flown out of Turkey on Saturday." The sixty British Thors, incidentally, were carted off by September, and the short-lived Western arsenal of IRBMs was no more.[36]

The first of the substitutes, a sixteen-missile Polaris submarine, was on station in the Mediterranean by 30 March, and the second by 12 April. One of them, the USS *Sam Houston*, paid a visit to the Turkish port city of Izmir on 14–15 April. This played a major role in a well-orchestrated effort, which included the visits by General Wood before and others of high rank after, like the new SACEUR Lyman Lemnitzer, to reassure the Turkish government and public of Washington's continuing strategic commitment to them. And, as Ambassador Hare argued persuasively, the goal was largely achieved. "Submarine Which Scares Soviets Is In Izmir" read an Ankara headline that typified the Turks' enthusiasm. They did not have their Jupiters any more, and like the Italians they resented being on the receiving end of an unequal partnership with Washington and, as they saw it, being informed rather than consulted about important decisions affecting their security. But with the official attention and increased aid, they did have a renewed sense of their importance in the alliance, at least for the moment, and the Jupiter removal had certainly not caused any serious rift in the Turkish-American relationship.[37]

REACTIONS

Overall, public reaction was rather mild in the United States. Many stories in major newspapers framed the issue as one of missile replacement or even Polaris deployment rather than Jupiter retirement, no doubt to the relief of administration officials. A solid majority of editorials welcomed the move as strengthening—or accepted it as not weakening—Western defense or expected it to reduce tension in U.S.-Soviet relations. *Time* gave the administration's version of events and in its accompanying photo caption described the Polaris substitution as "sending lethal fish to replace sitting ducks." Only a handful of observers charged Kennedy with having concluded a secret trade or viewed the dismantlement as a surrender to Soviet demands. Some on the Far Right were certainly outraged, including New Orleans private investigator Guy Banister, one of the shadowy figures many authors tie to Kennedy's assassination. His files on what he considered JFK's most nefarious policies included one labeled "Missile Bases Dismantled—Turkey and Italy." But more broadly, the new policy neither generated significant public controversy nor stayed in the news for very long.[38]

The worst reaction was that of U.S. Air Force leaders, who were upset by what they saw as a premature withdrawal of the IRBMs. The "concrete for some of the launching pads had just been poured," air force chief of staff Curtis LeMay later complained. He was exaggerating, but he and his colleagues did feel that the deployment, on which they had worked so hard and for so long, was just beginning to bear fruit. Indeed, although the Turkish Jupiters had become operational by March 1962, construction of the facilities was deemed 100 percent complete only in December of that year. U.S. Air Force officials still valued the missiles and did not share civilian concerns over command and control. Thus they were understandably irked by the removal, as well as by the additional aid to Rome and Ankara used to achieve it. "We objected to it at the time," LeMay remembered, "but in vain"—this the unhappiness, oddly, of one who in early 1962 had remarked that the British Thor program was "entirely political; there was no military requirement for it and the RAF had never wanted the program." Regardless, the timing of the Jupiter removal, coming so soon after the missiles had gone on line, convinced them the president had cut a secret deal with Khrushchev. LeMay's key congressional testimony is heavily censored, but in the portions released he hinted darkly that "other factors" besides modernization had affected the IRBM withdrawal, about which the inquiring congressman should "ask the Secretary of Defense." Years later, top air force officers were more blunt. "We gave away everything," recalled General Disosway, negotiator of the Italian deployment in 1958–59. "We lost our fannies on that Cuban deal."[39]

Congress, for the most part, accepted the administration's policy and its explanations for it. Several legislators asked questions, sometimes insightful, about the removal decision. But only a few Republicans wondered aloud whether Kennedy had made a secret trade, like Barry Goldwater (R-Ariz.). "Mr. President," he asked on the Senate floor, "what goes on?" Were the IRBM removals and other Kennedy defense policies "part of some kind of deal involving Cuba and disarmament plans?" And only a few senators objected to the removal, like Armed Service Committee chair Richard Russell (D-Ga.), who belonged to the more-is-simply-better school of nuclear deterrence (and even suggested secretly retrieving the nuclear warheads but leaving the missiles in place armed with dummies). At no point was congressional opposition to removal anything more than a nuisance easily contained via artful testimony.[40]

The effect on NATO and other individual European countries is difficult to assess, although the French reacted sharply. They chose to interpret the Jupiter withdrawal as proof that the United States was disengaging from Europe. "To pretend that any new arrangement, such as moving the deterrent to sea, is a way of modernizing [it]," said General Pierre Gallois, one of de Gaulle's military advisers, "is a swindle." The semiofficial *Revue Militaire d'Information* accused the United States of having made a missile deal with the Soviets and thus having demonstrated its willingness to sacrifice the security of its allies. The Gaullist press, predictably, cited this as justification for France's independent nuclear force. Yet overall, the impact of the removal on the alliance appears to have been negligible, certainly in the long run and certainly compared with the fears of many U.S. officials. Some other Europeans joined the French in suspecting American disengagement, but their reactions to the Jupiter removals scarcely affected transatlantic relations.[41]

Kennedy's recent experience with Turkey and its Jupiters continued to influence his thinking. In February 1963 he confided in Ben Bradlee that "the presence of 17,000 Soviet troops in Cuba . . . was one thing viewed by itself, but it was something else again when you knew there were 27,000 U.S. troops stationed in Turkey." He warned Bradlee not to repeat the observation. "It isn't wise politically," JFK said quietly, "to understand Khrushchev's problems quite this way." He returned to the subject the following evening over dinner, almost accepting the case for tolerating Soviet troops in Cuba because of the U.S. forces in Turkey. One of the dinner guests, ambassador to Greece Henry Labouisse, raised the issue of Hawk surface-to-air missiles that were slated for Crete and might create a political problem. The president quickly became irritated. "What the hell do we need those missiles for, anyway?" he asked. Formally he was more polite, asking for a DOD report on the deployment, because he did "not understand the justification for it at this time." The fact that the missiles in question were short range, indisputably defensive, and for training purposes merely underscores the eagerness with which Kennedy sought to avoid other bad missile experiences in the Mediterranean.[42]

CONCLUSIONS

The Jupiter withdrawal was in a real sense, as McGeorge Bundy noted in May 1963, "a very tidy job."[43] The Kennedy administration came rather close to fulfilling its promise to remove the Jupiters four to five months after the missile crisis. Several lawmakers were asking hard questions about the removal, but even the most suspicious soon dropped the subject. For the White House, public exposure of the missile trade would have been a political nightmare, if not an outright disaster, and yet it remained a secret even for years after Kennedy's death. Italy, Turkey, and NATO agreed to the withdrawal, raising little fuss and demanding little compensatory military aid relative to what one might have expected. For all these reasons, the administration must have been pleased with how quickly and smoothly it had completed the operation.

The diplomacy of withdrawal did not prove nearly as nettlesome as had the diplomacy of deployment. The understandable opposition within the Turkish government presented the main difficulty. Negotiating deployment with the Turks in 1959 had been easy, because they shared the U.S. desire for a Turkish deployment. Negotiating withdrawal in 1963 was tougher, because now the Americans wanted them out and many Turks, particularly in the military, did not. The resulting split in the Turkish government, whether feigned or real, hampered the process. Nevertheless, reaching a removal agreement with the reluctant Turks of 1963 required no more than four months—still significantly less time than that needed to achieve a deployment accord with the enthusiastic Turks of 1959.

The removal in addition brought tangible, even mutual, benefits. The Italians and Turks, although they were excluded from the real underlying decision and may have lost some short-term political capital in the alliance, gained conventional and dual-purpose weaponry they might not otherwise have gained. They were relieved of their IRBMs, military lightning rods that had periodically ignited domestic political brushfires. In addition, the withdrawal freed up for each country more than two thousand skilled technicians, badly needed for other military and industrial projects. Western security and deterrence enjoyed marked improvement with the substitution of Polaris; according to calculations used by the JCS, the Polaris A-2 SLBM entailed 27 percent better reliability, 25 percent greater accuracy, a 65 percent less destructive warhead, 100 percent better survivability without warning, and 1,900 percent better with. In addition, of course, all allies on both sides of the Atlantic benefited from scrapping their most vulnerable and provocative nuclear systems, and doing so significantly earlier than they would have otherwise.[44]

For the Kennedy administration, however, withdrawing the Jupiters did have its costs. It had to come up with additional military aid to Italy and Turkey; it had to deceive those countries, the rest of NATO, the public, the U.S. Congress, and itself. It had to obtain the acquiescence or cooperation of these groups, and this required making excuses, allaying suspicions, warding off counterarguments, exaggerating other motives, and maintaining the cover-up over the long haul. These represented at least a major bureaucratic nuisance, entailing care, effort, and orchestration. More important, the United States went behind the backs of its minor allies, who depended on it for their security, and bartered away part of that security—however flawed the particular weapons—for the sake of its own. Those who sat on ExComm would have argued, and some indeed have argued, that these were small prices to pay to help extinguish the most perilous crisis of the postwar era and avoid World War III. Perhaps they are right. Nor can anyone deny that the administration pulled off what was politically an extraordinarily dangerous maneuver with some skill and great deal of luck. In a curious way, Kennedy had converted the militarily useless into the politically useful. But while the job of removing the Jupiters may have been tidy, it was not exactly clean.[45]

Kennedy and the Jupiters

This mixed portrait of skill and luck, of deceit and resourcefulness, of satisfactory ends and questionable means, is perfectly consistent with the larger, divided mural of Kennedy's entire Jupiter policy dating from January 1961. And this policy, in turn, neatly conforms to the profound ambivalence that acts as a consensus in recent scholarship on Kennedy's foreign policy.[46]

Kennedy's handling of the Jupiters is in large part a story of redemption. Like the missile crisis, the Jupiter policy encompassed a negative, probably avoidable beginning and a positive ending. Just as Kennedy deserves higher marks for his handling of the missile crisis once he found himself in it than he does for his contribution to touching it off in the first place, so does his liquidation of the provocative, obsolete Jupiters to help end the crisis far outshine his 1961 decision to proceed with their deployment. Continuing the deployment reflected a careless, timid drift with the existing flow of policy, whereas the secret trade with Khrushchev, if a bit obvious, was nevertheless relatively bold and efficient.

More broadly, JFK's management of the Jupiter issue exhibits numerous characteristics seen elsewhere in his foreign policy. First, it was alternately or simultaneously pragmatic, cynical, clever, improvised, risky, and conservative. Second, it was in keeping with Kennedy's use of nuclear weapons for political purposes. He saw nuclear weapons as tools useful for solidifying the Atlantic alliance, and in this regard his 1961 Jupiter deployment decision joins his flirtation with the Multilateral Force and his provision of Polaris missiles to Great Britain to settle the flap over Skybolt in late 1962. Third, Kennedy's use of the Jupiters during and after the missile crisis belongs in the context of his heavy reliance, throughout his presidency, on secret back channels, especially via Robert Kennedy, Dobrynin, and Georgi Bolshakov regarding such hot spots as Berlin and Laos. And fourth, it fits in with a similar pattern of tacit agreements and secret cooperation with the Kremlin, such as the administration's part in forming a reconnaissance satellite regime, its alleged proposal of a joint U.S.-Soviet military strike against the Chinese nuclear complex, and its deliberate leak of information on PALs to the Soviets. In light of these various foreign policy methods, Kennedy's Jupiter policy suddenly appears less extraordinary.[47]

Yet equally in step with many of Kennedy's initiatives, his Jupiter policy could not escape the powerful pull of credibility. This was definitely the case in late spring of 1961, when the administration decided, amid conflicting recommendations, to proceed with the Turkish deployment. Here its concern over U.S. credibility in the shadows of the Vienna summit and the Berlin crisis, in conjunction with its related worry over relations with Turkey, played a decisive role. During the Cuban missile crisis, credibility of course had everything to do with Kennedy's determination to remove the Soviet missiles from Cuba, although it coexisted with more pressing matters, namely settling the crisis and avoiding a military clash that might escalate uncontrollably. Still, even before the crisis ended, credibility dictated the manner in which the Jupiters figured in the settlement. After all, fear for U.S. credibility lay at the root of Kennedy's insistence that his Jupiter concession remain a secret. To be sure, credibility with Turkey and the other allies had supplanted credibility toward the Soviet Union, but it is credibility that most influenced what decision was taken, in the first instance, and how the decision was carried out, in the second. It left its telltale marks on JFK's Jupiter policy at every stage.

CONCLUSION

But that Jupiter missile! . . . That sure was a
provocative weapon. It gives me the willies to
think we ever deployed it over in Turkey and Italy.
A young weapons designer, 1965

Richard Nixon had a fine sense of history. In September 1970,
his administration discovered that the Soviets were constructing a submarine base at Cienfuegos, a port on Cuba's southern coast. His first impulse
was to fire off a handwritten note to his national security adviser, Henry
Kissinger, in which he asked for "a report on a crash basis" on possible U.S.
responses to the Soviet initiative. These included: "(3) Most important, what
actions can we take, covert or overt, to put missiles in Turkey—or a sub base
in the Black Sea—anything which will give us some trading stock." Nothing
came of the request—Nixon neither relived the missile crisis nor concluded
another secret missile trade. But the incident suggests that the Jupiter missiles had maintained some presence in official memory years after Kennedy
had scrapped them.[1]

Since then, the closest thing to an encore has been the inclusion of Jupiter
test-flight footage in a television commercial for Coast soap (1994). Apart
from advertising executives, only scholars have remained interested in the
Jupiters, and they have mostly limited their inquiries to the question of the
missiles' role in the Cuban crisis. And small wonder—the question is important. This study, however, has sought to broaden the focus by telling the
entire Jupiter story—its beginning and end as well as its high point.

At one level, the latest evidence only confirms what many observers and
former policymakers have long suggested: the Jupiter deployment was a
highly dubious policy. These "Model-T's of the missile age" were vulnerable
and provocative like few strategic systems in U.S. nuclear history and were

virtually obsolete before they became operational. When they finally did go on-line, the more advanced delivery systems for which the IRBMs were supposed to have served as stopgaps were already entering the U.S. arsenal. In view of the Jupiters' negligible military utility and the multiple political problems they caused, McGeorge Bundy does not exaggerate when he declares them to have been "worse than useless."[2]

It is important to add, moreover, that this is not mere Monday-morning quarterbacking. Eisenhower, Kennedy, and almost all of their civilian subordinates assigned little military value to the IRBMs from the very start, and their doubts only grew with time. The broader focus of this study has thus spawned a broader question: Why did successive administrations—different from each other in many ways—pursue the Jupiter deployments when they themselves increasingly questioned that policy? The answer revolves around a key issue in U.S. foreign relations during the Cold War: credibility.

"Throughout the post–World War II period," Robert McMahon has written, "American leaders have explained, defended, and justified a wide range of diplomatic and military decisions by invoking the hallowed principle of credibility." Concern for U.S. international credibility influenced or dominated foreign policy making from the formation of NATO to interventions in Korea, Vietnam, and the Persian Gulf. To this list now belongs the IRBM policy of Eisenhower and Kennedy. Credibility is the issue, more than any other, that runs like a thread through U.S. policy making on the Jupiters between 1957 and 1963.[3]

"Credibility" is a loose, intangible concept. It exists in the realm of psychology; it is difficult to track or measure with any precision. Yet clearly it manifests itself in two basic forms: the credibility of threats and the credibility of commitments. Even though the Jupiters were strategic nuclear weapons, at issue here is the credibility of commitments. But this latter category should be further subdivided into credibility toward the adversary, the Soviet Union, and credibility toward the NATO allies. Indeed, the particular shape credibility assumed in this case is one in which U.S. leaders were constantly attempting to preserve credibility with either NATO or the Soviet Union or both.

Credibility made its presence felt from the outset. Eisenhower and Dulles offered IRBMs to NATO in late 1957 for a complex jumble of reasons, large and small, but primarily to address an existing lack of U.S. strategic credibility among the NATO allies that *Sputnik* had only exacerbated. That lack of credibility is beyond question; the particular solution the Americans chose, however, was unnecessary and thus questionable.

Credibility remained on center stage during the search for host countries, 1957–59. Eisenhower's doubts about the NATO deployment deepened significantly during this period, leading him and some of his subordinates to flirt briefly with cancellation or even use of the undeployed Jupiters as bargaining chips with Khrushchev. But afraid in 1959 that appearing to cave in to the Soviets' threats and complaints might only embolden them, and equally worried that withdrawing even a questionable offer might damage the allies' confidence, Eisenhower went ahead and placed missiles in Turkey in addition to those already committed to Italy. As it came to a close in January 1961, Ike's administration only reconfirmed the credibility bind in which it had placed itself, a situation that the proliferating doubts about the deployments had rendered additionally absurd.

Early in his term, John F. Kennedy received well-reasoned recommendations to cancel the Turkish deployment just getting under way and, I have argued, had a good opportunity to do so. Like Ike, he passed up the opportunity, and like Ike, credibility made him do it. Facing Turkish resistance, and then alarmed by the Vienna summit and Khrushchev's reopening of the Berlin crisis, Kennedy and his advisers decided that cancellation would be a sign of weakness that would distress Ankara and encourage Moscow.

In October 1962, credibility with allies, adversaries, and the domestic public led Kennedy to decide that he must force the Soviet SS-4s out of Cuba. At the end of the ensuing crisis, the secret missile deal that meant the Jupiters' eventual removal—the first superpower arms reduction agreement of the Cold War—had little to do with credibility and a great deal to do with avoiding war. But the nature of the trade on which JFK insisted and the nature of the removal reflected the power of credibility, at least in one of its guises. Credibility toward the Soviets was now moot, but credibility with the allies, Turkey in particular, demanded that the administration conceal the trade with a shroud of secrecy and lies—at the time and for years thereafter.

As other cases have demonstrated, the tricky thing about credibility is that policymakers have based their understanding of it, and unavoidably so, on their assumptions. Dulles and Eisenhower assumed that the European allies immediately needed concrete reassurance in the realm of nuclear weapons, that IRBMs would do the trick, that to withdraw their IRBM offer would shake the alliance and encourage the Soviets, and that the political costs of terminating the policy would far exceed those of preserving it. Similarly, Kennedy assumed that canceling the Turkish deployment would dangerously undermine credibility with the Turks and the Soviets at a critical moment. Then he assumed that a secret missile trade was preferable to a public one—although it is striking testimony to his fear of all-out war that he may have been willing to go the latter route.

To point out these assumptions, however, is not to assess their quality. Some clearly rested on firmer ground than others. In a related sense, it is easy to exaggerate how bad the Jupiter policy was, and it is easy to condemn Eisenhower and Kennedy for having seen it through, for not having acted on the signals and criticisms that pointed toward cancellation of the deployments. Credibility, however fuzzy a construct, was not something any policymaker could dismiss out of hand. It was, and is, vitally important to any great power trying to manage an alliance. Moreover, to reverse any policy, much less one booby-trapped with sticks of credibility, is always a difficult thing. "To recognize error, to cut losses, to alter course," as Barbara Tuchman has written, "is the most repugnant option in government."[4]

That is why such action requires leadership, but in the case of the IRBMs, leadership was in short supply. Indeed, it is fair to conclude that this was no shining moment for either Eisenhower or Kennedy. Ike failed to consider allied demand or Soviet reactions before offering the missiles. Both men had feasible options before them that they considered, or could have considered, at the time; both failed to question their assumptions about credibility; and both deployed nuclear missiles that they knew to be provocative, vulnerable, and obsolete. These missiles then came back to haunt Kennedy when they helped touch off, and then complicated, the Cuban missile crisis. In the clutch, JFK did make good (if politically risky) use of them and withdrew them without too much trouble. But they need not have constituted such a liability in the first place.

Thus Kennedy and Eisenhower, for all their many differences, also had some things in common. One of those was the Jupiter policy, which they handled similarly and for similar reasons. That policy was, of course, only one of many, but it was more significant, and played a larger role in some key events of the Cold War, than existing histories of that era have supposed. Today, more broadly, with Americans often repainting the history of the Cold War in triumphalist hues, the Jupiters also serve as a useful reminder that the United States survived its adversary not only because of its policies, but sometimes in spite of them.

NOTES

Abbreviations Used in Notes

AESP	Adlai E. Stevenson Papers, Seeley G. Mudd Library, Princeton University, Princeton, New Jersey
AFHRC	United States Air Force Historical Research Center, Maxwell Air Force Base, Montgomery, Alabama
AlphSS	Alphabetical Subject Series
AMSP	Arthur M. Schlesinger Jr. Papers, John F. Kennedy Library, Boston, Massachusetts
AS	Administrative Series
AWF	Dwight D. Eisenhower, Papers as President of the United States, 1953–61 (Ann Whitman File), Dwight D. Eisenhower Library, Abilene, Kansas
CDF	Central Decimal File
CDSP	*Current Digest of the Soviet Press*
CF	Central File
CIADCMC	McAuliffe, *CIA Documents on the Cuban Missile Crisis*
CN	Office of the Administrative Assistant, Secretary of the Air Force, *Current News*, White House Central Files, Presidential Papers, 1961–63, John F. Kennedy Papers, John F. Kennedy Library, Boston, Massachusetts
CMC	National Security Archive, *The Cuban Missile Crisis, 1962*
CPSU	Communist Party of the Soviet Union
CS	Chronological Series
CSF	Classified Subject Files
CSM	*Christian Science Monitor*
CWIHP	Cold War International History Project
DDEDS	Dwight D. Eisenhower Diary Series
DDEL	Dwight D. Eisenhower Library, Abilene, Kansas
DDRS	*Declassified Documents Reference System*
DF	Decimal File
DHS	Dulles-Herter Series
DODSubS	Department of Defense Subseries
DOS	Department of State
DSB	*Department of State Bulletin*
ESSFRC	*Executive Sessions of the Senate Foreign Relations Committee*
EUR	Bureau of European Affairs, U.S. Department of State
FAOHP	Foreign Affairs Oral History Program, Lauinger Library, Georgetown University, Washington, D.C.
FBIS	*Foreign Broadcast Information Service*, Daily Reports
FR	*Foreign Relations of the United States*
GC	General Correspondence

GHI	General and Historical Information
HCA	House Committee on Appropriations
HCAS	House Committee on Armed Services
HCFA	House Committee on Foreign Affairs
HCT	Welch, "Proceedings of the Hawk's Cay Conference on the Cuban Missile Crisis," Hawk's Cay, Florida, March 1987
IS	International Series
ISA	International Security Affairs, Office of the Secretary of Defense
JBMFAES	John B. Martin Files on Adlai E. Stevenson, Seeley G. Mudd Library, Princeton University, Princeton, New Jersey
JFDOHP	John Foster Dulles Oral History Program, Seeley G. Mudd Library, Princeton University, Princeton, New Jersey
JFDP	John Foster Dulles Papers, Dwight D. Eisenhower Library, Abilene, Kansas
JFKL	John F. Kennedy Library, Boston, Massachusetts
JIC	Joint Intelligence Committee
JJMP	John J. McCloy Papers, Amherst College Archives, Amherst, Massachusetts
LBJ	Lyndon B. Johnson
LBJL	Lyndon B. Johnson Library, Austin, Texas
LF	Lot Files
LMP	Lawrence McQuade Papers, Lyndon B. Johnson Library, Austin, Texas
LNP	Lauris Norstad Papers, Dwight D. Eisenhower Library, Abilene, Kansas
MCP	Memorandum of Conference with the President
MemCon	Memorandum of Conversation
MFA	Ministry of Foreign Affairs, USSR
MM	Meetings and Memoranda
MTC-JFD/CH	*Minutes of the Telephone Conversations of John Foster Dulles and Christian Herter*
NASD	Notes as Assistant Secretary of Defense, 1961–63
NFTP	Nathan F. Twining Papers, Manuscript Division, Library of Congress, Washington, D.C.
NIC	National Indications Center
NIE	National Intelligence Estimate
NNP	National Security Archive, *Nuclear Non-Proliferation, 1945–1990*
NSA	National Security Archive, Gelman Library, George Washington University, Washington, D.C.
NSCS	National Security Council Series
NSF	National Security File, Presidential Papers, 1961–63, John F. Kennedy Papers, John F. Kennedy Library, Boston, Massachusetts
NYT	*New York Times*
OAPMA	Office of Atlantic Political and Military Affairs, U.S. Department of State
OCBS	Operations Coordinating Board Series
OHC	Oral History Collection
OSANSA	Office of the Special Assistant for National Security Affairs
OSD	Office of the Secretary of Defense
OSS	Office of the Staff Secretary
PFS	Policy File Series
PIS	Preparedness Investigating Subcommittee
POF	President's Office File, Presidential Papers, 1961–63, John F. Kennedy Papers, John F. Kennedy Library, Boston, Massachusetts
PPP	*Public Papers of the Presidents*

PREM	Records of the Prime Minister's Office, Public Record Office, Kew, London, England
RA	Office of European Regional Affairs, Bureau of European Affairs, U.S. Department of State
RD	Records of the Director
RG 59	Record Group 59, Records of the Department of State, National Archives, College Park, Maryland
RG 128	Record Group 128, Records of the Congressional Committees, National Archives, Washington, D.C.
RG 218	Record Group 218, Records of the Joint Chiefs of Staff, National Archives, College Park, Maryland
RG 273	Record Group 273, Records of the National Security Council, National Archives, College Park, Maryland
RPPS	Records of the Policy Planning Staff
RRA	Records of the Office of European Regional Affairs
RRN	Records Relating to NATO
RSF	Regional Security File
S/AE	Special Assistant for Atomic Energy
SAS	Special Assistant Series
SCAS	Senate Committee on Armed Services
SCFR	Senate Committee on Foreign Relations
SGML	Seeley G. Mudd Library, Princeton University, Princeton, New Jersey
SNF	Subject-Numeric File, February–December 1963
SS	Subject Series
SSubS	Subject Subseries
SubS	Subseries
TCSP	Theodore C. Sorensen Papers, John F. Kennedy Library, Boston, Massachusetts
TDWP	Thomas D. White Papers, Manuscript Division, Library of Congress, Washington, D.C.
TUSLOG	Turkish-U.S. Logistics Group
USAFOHP	United States Air Force Oral History Program, Air Force Historical Research Center, Maxwell AFB, Montgomery, Alabama
USIA	United States Information Agency
USIB	United States Intelligence Board
WHCF	White House Central File
WHF	White House Files
WHO	White House Office
WP	*Washington Post*

Introduction

1. Chet Holifield, interview by Enid H. Douglass, 25 April and 7 May 1975, OHC, JFKL, pt. 1, 106. Holifield refers to the Hercules missile but clearly means the Jupiter.

2. Newhouse, *De Gaulle and the Anglo-Saxons*, 23; MemCon, 26 November 1957 (drafted 2 December), midafternoon, Missiles and Satellites, vol. 1 (3) (September–December 1957), DODSubS, SS, OSS, WHO, DDEL, 3; MCP, 13 January 1961 (drafted 17 January), Staff Notes January 1961, DDEDS, AWF.

3. McNamara in WGBH, *Cuban Missile Crisis*; Bundy, *Danger and Survival*, 435; Rusk in Blight and Welch, *On the Brink*, 172; Ormsby-Gore to Macmillan, 23 October 1962, PREM 11/3689, courtesy Philip Zelikow; Allison, *Essence of Decision*, 142.

Chapter One

1. Trade adviser Clarence Randall, 22 October 1957, quoted in Divine, *Sputnik Challenge*, xv.

2. Ambrose, *Eisenhower*, 2:436–40; Divine, *Sputnik Challenge*, 58–60; Eisenhower quoted in Larson, *Eisenhower*, 176, emphasis in original; *NYT*, 11 December 1957, 1, 8; Hoopes, *Devil and John Foster Dulles*, 429.

3. "Statement by Secretary Dulles, December 16," *DSB* 38 (6 January 1958): 9.

4. Zuckerman, *Scientists and War*, vii–viii.

5. "Meeting the Threat of Surprise Attack," Report to the President by the Technological Capabilities Panel of the Science Advisory Committee, 14 February 1955, in Trachtenberg, *American Strategic Thought*, 370, 405–6. On the development of the IRBMs, the only full-length study remains Armacost, *Politics of Weapons Innovation*; for a sense of the classified sources, see relevant portions of Neufeld, *Ballistic Missiles*; on the IRBMs' origins, see the latter, 121–22, 143–47, and the former, 22–81.

6. Eisenhower, *Mandate for Change*, 456–57; Killian, *Sputnik, Scientists, and Eisenhower*, 76–77; MemCon, 257th NSC meeting, 4 August 1955, and MemCon, 258th NSC meeting, 8 September 1955, both in *FR* 1955–57, respectively 19:100–102, 19:119–21.

7. Department of State, "U.S. and Soviet Missiles," n.d. [30 November 1955], and MemCon, 268th NSC meeting, 1 December 1955, both in *FR* 1955–57, respectively 19:154–61, 19:167–69; Bundy, *Danger and Survival*, 327.

8. Neufeld, *Ballistic Missiles*, 160–61; Botti, *Long Wait*, 169–71, and Melissen, *Struggle for Nuclear Partnership*, 64–67.

9. MemCon, 16 July 1956, *FR* 1955–57, 27:663–65; editorial note, ibid., 665 n. 2; Neufeld, *Ballistic Missiles*, 160–65; Botti, *Long Wait*, 172–73; Clark, *Nuclear Diplomacy*, 47–51.

10. Botti, *Long Wait*, 171–74; Melissen, *Struggle for Nuclear Partnership*, 68. On the aftermath of Suez in Anglo-American relations, see Lucas, *Divided We Stand*, 298–330.

11. Department of State, Bureau of European Affairs, "Bermuda Meetings—March 21–24, 1957," 13 February 1957, *FR* 1955–57, 27:693; Macmillan, *Riding the Storm*, 240–41; Melissen, *Struggle for Nuclear Partnership*, 38.

12. Melissen, *Struggle for Nuclear Partnership*, 36–38, 70. The McMahon Act, or Atomic Energy Act of 1946, revised in 1954 and 1958, governed all atomic energy matters in the United States.

13. MCP, Bermuda, 22 March 1957, 1:00 P.M., MCP, Bermuda, 3:20 P.M., both in *FR* 1955–57, respectively 27:733, 27:737; Eisenhower, *Waging Peace*, 124; MemCon, 317th NSC meeting, 28 March 1957, *FR* 1955–57, 19:454–55. For the communiqué, see *NYT*, 25 March 1957, 5; for the discussion of other nuclear matters in Bermuda, see Melissen, *Struggle for Nuclear Partnership*, 39.

14. Melissen, *Struggle for Nuclear Partnership*, 22–23, 70; Baylis, *Anglo-American Defense Relations*, 89–90; Clark, *Nuclear Diplomacy*, 53–55. On differences within the British government over the IRBM proposal through 1958, see Navias, *Nuclear Weapons and British Strategic Planning*, 214–25.

15. Herter and Wilson to Eisenhower, "Intermediate Range Ballistic Missiles for the U.K.," 14 March 1957, IRBM for UK (March 1957), AlphSS, SS, OSS, WHO, DDEL, enclosure (tab A), 1; Melissen, *Struggle for Nuclear Partnership*, 68; MemCon, "Bipartisan Congressional Meeting," 25 March 1957, Mar 1957 Staff Memos (1), DDEDS, AWF, 3; text of Dulles background conferences held 24 March 1957 in Bermuda, 28 March 1957, box 113, JFDP, 4; Clark and Angell, "Britain, the United States," 157–58; MCP, Bermuda, 22 March 1957, 3:20 P.M., 737.

16. MCP, Bermuda, 22 March 1957, 1:00 P.M., 735.

17. MemCon, "Bipartisan Congressional Meeting," 25 March 1957, 4; Murphy to Gordon Gray, 15 January 1957, quoted in Clark, *Nuclear Diplomacy*, 53; see also edito-

rial note, *FR 1955–57*, 19:410. When asked publicly, Eisenhower denied the existence of and Dulles denied knowing of plans to base IRBMs on the Continent as well, but Dulles left open the possibility should IRBM production increase. The Department of Defense was at the same time "studying what additional deployments . . . should be undertaken in the U.K. and/or in other areas." "President's News Conference of April 17, 1957," *PPP 1957*, 286; text of Dulles background conferences, 3, 4; Herter and Wilson to Eisenhower, 14 March 1957, 1.

18. Eisenhower, *Waging Peace*, 124–25; MemCon, "Bipartisan Congressional Meeting," 25 March 1957, 1; Macmillan, *Riding the Storm*, 317.

19. Clark, *Nuclear Diplomacy*, 57–74; Melissen, *Struggle for Nuclear Partnership*, 72–73; Botti, *Long Wait*, 182–83, 192–97. For the draft agreement, see Wilson to Eisenhower, 17 April 1957, 711.56341/4-1157, DF, RG 59, tab A, and for a glimpse of where matters stood in September, see MemCon, "IRBM Project," 17 September 1957, 711.56341/9-1757, DF, RG 59.

20. See Trachtenberg, *History and Strategy*, 153–68; Wampler, "Eisenhower, NATO, and Nuclear Weapons," 162–90; Ireland, "Building NATO's Nuclear Posture," 12–13.

21. The best description of the immediate impact on U.S. government policies is Divine, *Sputnik Challenge*, but see also Killian, *Sputnik, Scientists, and Eisenhower*.

22. On the "loss of confidence," see Schwartz, *NATO's Nuclear Dilemmas*, 35–61.

23. MemCon, 339th NSC meeting, 10 October 1957, *FR 1955–57*, 19:602–3; see also MCP, 11 October 1957, 8:30 A.M., Department of Defense, vol. 2 (2) (September–October 1957), DODSubS, SS, OSS, WHO, DDEL, 2; Melissen, *Struggle for Nuclear Partnership*, 76.

24. Macmillan to Eisenhower, 10 October 1957, *FR 1955–57*, 27:785–86; Macmillan, *Riding the Storm*, 315–16; Divine, *Sputnik Challenge*, 34–35.

25. Steinbruner, *Cybernetic Theory*, 176–79; Norstad, interview by Richard D. Challener, 1 February 1967, JFDOHP, 7–9; Thurston to Fessenden, 9 September 1959, IRBM-General, December 1957–December 1958, 1959, box 1, RRN 57–64, OAPMA, EUR, LF, RG 59, 2; Facon, "U.S. Forces in France," 246–47; MemCon, 11 July 1957, *FR 1955–57*, 27:134–35; Elbrick to Murphy, 30 September 1957, 711.56351/9-3057, DF, RG 59; Twining to McElroy, 14 November 1957, CCS 334, Guided Missiles Committee (1-16-45) sec. 21, CDF 57, RG 218; Quarles to Dulles, 7 December 1957, 711.56351/12-757, DF, RG 59.

26. MCP, 22 October 1957 (drafted 31 October), October 1957 Staff Notes (1), DDEDS, AWF, 1. *FR 1955–57*, 27:800–801, drawing from the same source, inexplicably declares the two key quotations "not declassified." See also MemCon, 348th NSC meeting, 12 December 1957, and Dulles to Eisenhower, 21 October 1957, both in *FR 1955–57*, respectively 19:708 and 27:796–99.

27. "Secretary Dulles' News Conference of July 16," *DSB* 37 (5 August 1957): 234. "You can't operate on the theory of big allies and little allies," he would remark rather disingenuously in December. "You would lose each ally one by one." Quoted in Sulzberger, *Last of the Giants*, 438.

28. MemCon, 24 October 1957, 10:30 A.M., *FR 1955–57*, 27:816–21; Macmillan, *Riding the Storm*, 319–24; "Declaration of Common Purpose by the President and the Prime Minister of the United Kingdom," 25 October 1957, *PPP 1957*, 768–72; White House statement, ibid., 773; Divine, *Sputnik Challenge*, 34; Melissen, *Struggle for Nuclear Partnership*, 75–77.

29. "Declaration of Common Purpose," 771; MemCon, 17 October 1957, 5:00 P.M., MemCon, 24 October, 7:00 P.M., MemCon, 25 October, 2:05–2:32 P.M., all in *FR 1955–57*, respectively 27:791, 27:823, 27:835–36; ibid., 4:183–84 n 9; MCP, 22 October, 2; Macmillan, *Riding the Storm*, 324–25; *NYT*, 26 October 1957, 1, 4, and 31 October 1957, 1, 11; Spaak, *Continuing Battle*, 265–66; Divine, *Sputnik Challenge*, 73.

30. MemCon, 28 October 1957, ca. 11:00 A.M., folder 9, October 1957 (1), JFD-DDEL CS; see also MCP, 28 October 1957 (drafted 30 October), October 1957 Staff Notes (1),

DDEDS, AWF, 2–3; MemCon, 7 November 1957, 5:30 P.M. (drafted 8 November), #353, *NNP*, 2–3; see also Dearborn to Cutler, 13 November 1957, #3458, 1986, *DDRS*.

31. Frank C. Nash, Report to the President, "United States Overseas Military Bases," [24] December 1957, Nash Report—U.S. Overseas Mlty Bases (1), AS, AWF, 9–10, 17, 52; Security Resources Panel of the ODM Science Advisory Committee, Report to the President, "Deterrence and Survival in the Nuclear Age," 7 November 1957, *FR* 1955–57, 19:642–43, 657–58; Gilpin, *American Scientists*, 173; Memorandum, "Discussion with Paul Nitze," 29 May 1958, HO Chron—May–August 1958, box 182, RPPS 57–61, RG 59; see also McElroy to Dulles, "IRBM for NATO," 12 November 1957, 396.1/11-1257, DF, RG 59, and Armacost, *Politics of Weapons Innovation*, 186. Opposition Democrats of the Democratic Advisory Council urged nuclear sharing with NATO but did not refer to IRBMs. Statement by the Democratic Advisory Council, 17 November 1957, in *New York Herald Tribune*, 18 November 1957, 9.

32. "Secretary Dulles' News Conference of November 5," *DSB* 37 (25 November 1957): 830; *NYT*, 16 November 1957, 1–2.

33. *NYT*, 18 November 1957, 1, 8; 7 December 1957, 10; 11 December 1957, 1, 3; 12 December 1957, 1, 5; 14 December 1957, 3; 15 December 1957, 30, 33; Herblock cartoon, *WP*, 21 November 1957; *Time*, 2 December 1957, 22. The president referred to IRBM deployment in his first post-*Sputnik* "chins-up" address on 7 November, but only in terms of placing the missiles at "forward positions, some of them in the lands of [U.S.] allies." Eisenhower, "Science in National Security," 7 November 1957, *DSB* 37 (25 November 1957): 820.

34. *NYT*, 22 December 1957, E5; *Time*, 23 December 1957, 17–18; see also MemCon, 27 December 1957, 396.1-PA/12-2757, DF, RG 59, 2; MemCon, 16 December 1957, 3:30–8:00 P.M. (sent U.S. Delegation to DOS, 17 December), and MemCon, 18 December 1957, A.M. & P.M. (sent U.S. Delegation to DOS, 19 December), both in *FR* 1955–57, 4:232–42 and 4:253–55.

35. MemCon, 26 November 1957, 3; see also MemCon, "IRBMs for NATO," 22 November 1957, 2:00–2:30 P.M., 740.5/11-2257, DF, RG 59, 3.

36. "Secretary Dulles' News Conference of November 19," *DSB* 37 (9 December 1957): 916; see also "Transcript of Dulles' News Conference . . . ," 10 December 1957, *NYT*, 11 December, 4. For claims that NATO partners would not have a veto, see "Secretary Dulles' News Conference of November 19," 921; MemCon, "Bipartisan Congressional Meeting," 3 December 1957, Legislative Leaders Meetings 1957 (5), Legislative Meetings Series, AWF, 4; for admissions that they would, see *NYT*, 11 December 1957, 1, 3; 12 December 1957, 5.

37. Armacost, *Politics of Weapons Innovation*, 172–79; Divine, *Sputnik Challenge*, 61–70; MemCon, 26 November 1957, 1–3; see also MemCon, 27 November 1957, 9:45 A.M., *FR* 1955–57, 19:697–98.

38. MemCon, 346th NSC meeting, 22 November 1957, *FR* 1955–57, 19:693; McElroy testimony, 20 November 1957, HCA, *Ballistic Missile Program*, 6; "December 15, Defense Cooperation" (conducted 28 November–4 December), *Gallup Poll*, 1528–29; see also McElroy testimony, 27 November 1957, PIS, SCAS, *Inquiry into Satellite and Missile Programs*, 194.

39. MCP, 22 November 1957, ca. 9:00 A.M., *FR* 1955–57, 19:688; MemCon, 346th NSC meeting, 691; MemCon, "IRBMs for NATO," 22 November 1957, 2–3; Divine, *Sputnik Challenge*, 69; see also Armacost, *Politics of Weapons Innovation*, 187–88.

40. MCP, 2 December 1957, ca. 5:00 P.M., folder 18, December 1957 (3), JFD-DDEL CS; MemCon, 348th NSC meeting, 12 December 1957, *FR* 1955–57, 4:217; Dulles to Eisenhower, 23 October 1957, October 1957 (1), Dulles, John Foster, DHS, AWF; Ambassador and Mrs. W. Randolph Burgess, interview by Philip A. Crowl, 24 August 1965, JFDOHP, 26–27.

41. Macmillan, *Riding the Storm*, 334. Dulles's mood could not have been helped by reading the report produced by the NATO members' chiefs of staff on the eve of the summit; even among them there was little enthusiasm for the IRBMs. *U.S. News and World Report*, 20 December 1957, 31.

42. "Statement by Secretary Dulles, December 16," 8–12; "Bipartisan Congressional Meeting," 3 December 1957, 3.

43. Dearborn to Cutler, 10 December 1957, NATO, SSubS, Operations Coordinating Board Series, OSANSA, WHO, DDEL; MemCon, 29 November 1957 (drafted 2 December), 3:30 P.M., 1, 5, and Dulles to Cutler, 18 November 1957, enclosure, both in NATO, SS, Special Assistant Series, OSANSA, WHO, DDEL; Elbrick to Murphy, 30 January 1958, FW 711.56351/12-757, DF, RG 59, 1; MemCon, "IRBMs for NATO," 22 November 1957, 3; "Draft of President's Speech in Closed Session," 10 December 1957, North Atlantic Treaty Organization (5), SS, CF, WHCF, DDEL, pt. 2, 3; Norstad, interview by Thomas Soapes, 11 November 1976, OHC, DDEL, 47–48; "Statement by Secretary Dulles, December 16," 9.

44. Excerpts of speeches from first closed session, 3:30–8:00 P.M., 16 December 1957, *NYT*, 17 December, 13, and *Keesing's Contemporary Archives*, 18–25 January 1958, 15965–68.

45. Excerpts of Bulganin Notes, 10–11 December 1957, *Keesing's Contemporary Archives*, 18–25 January 1958, 15976–78; Bulganin to Eisenhower, 10 December 1957, *DSB* 38 (27 January 1958): 127–30. The Rapacki Plan was named after the Polish foreign minister Adam Rapacki, who first introduced the proposal at the United Nations on 2 October 1957.

46. Appleby, "Eisenhower and Arms Control," 222–25; Divine, *Blowing on the Wind*, 174–76; *NYT*, 12 December 1957, 1, 4. Ike did not respond to the Bulganin letter until a month later.

47. Macmillan, *Riding the Storm*, 336–37; *NYT*, 19 December 1957, 12; MemCon, 18 December, 254.

48. "Text of Declaration and Communiqué, December 19," *DSB* 38 (6 January 1958): 13.

49. Ibid., 13–14.

50. "Transcript of Dulles' News Conference," 10 December; *NYT*, 19 December, 12. Attempting to clean up after Dulles, State hastily instructed U.S. NATO representatives to assert, however lamely, that he had been referring only to agreements on the *location* of IRBM bases. Department of State to Embassy Paris, 10 December 1957, 396.1-PA/12-1057, DF, RG 59.

51. This only reinforces the existing consensus on the centrality of *Sputnik* to the NATO IRBM offer, e.g., Melissen, *Struggle for Nuclear Partnership*, 74–77; Armacost, *Politics of Weapons Innovation*, 172–87, 217–18; Schwartz, *NATO's Nuclear Dilemmas*, 61–65; Divine, *Sputnik Challenge*, esp. 69–70, 73–74; Kaplan, *NATO and the United States*, 79; and Loeb, "Jupiter Missiles in Europe," 27–28.

52. Armacost, *Politics of Weapons Innovation*, 189; Divine, *Sputnik Challenge*, 69–70; NIE 11-4-57, "Main Trends in Soviet Capabilities and Policies, 1957–1962," 12 November 1957, *FR 1955–57*, 19:671.

53. MCP, 28 October 1957, 2–3.

54. See the first epigraph, above, as well as Wentworth to Joint Intelligence Committee, 6 December 1957, CCS 471.6 (5-31-44) sec. 12, CDF 1958, RG 218; Twining to McElroy, 15 December 1957, 333.1 (2) European Trip 9–23 Dec 57, General Twining 1957–60, Chairman's File, RG 218; Trachtenberg in HCT, 108.

55. A major high-level study in 1957 compared IRBMs with other weapons systems and discussed production issues but again, like its 1955 counterpart, ignored the question of deployment. See MemCon, 317th NSC meeting, 454–56; MemCon, 327th NSC meeting, 20 June 1957, *FR 1955–57*, 19:528–30.

56. Eisenhower letter quoted in Ambrose, *Eisenhower*, 435.

57. Eisenhower, *Mandate for Change*, 457; Eisenhower, *Waging Peace*, 124, 254; Mem-Con, 346th NSC meeting, 692.

Chapter Two

1. Eisenhower, *Waging Peace*, 232; Divine, *Sputnik Challenge*, 73–74; "The NATO Conference at Paris: Report by President Eisenhower and Secretary Dulles," 23 December 1957, *DSB* 38 (13 January 1958): 47–52; Truman quoted in *Time*, 6 January 1958, 10–11; Allen, *Eisenhower and the Mass Media*, 157–58. Other works that discuss the search for hosts are Melissen, *Struggle for Nuclear Partnership*, 100–106; Tocchet, "Sending Nuclear Weapons to Europe," 18–27; Armacost, *Politics of Weapons Innovation*, 180–218; and Schwartz, *NATO's Nuclear Dilemmas*, 66–74.

2. Twining to McElroy, 3 January 1958, CCS 471.6 (5-31-44) sec. 12, CDF 1958, RG 218, emphasis added; Thurston to Dulles, 11 February 1958, IRBM-General (3), PFS, LNP; Neufeld, *Ballistic Missiles*, 175; Divine, *Sputnik Challenge*, 116.

3. Dulles, "Telephone Call to Senator Johnson," 23 December 1957, 3:45 P.M., frame 16, reel 7, *MTC-JFD/CH*; MemCon, 348th NSC meeting, 215; see also the Dulles quotation prefacing this chapter; Armacost, *Politics of Weapons Innovation*, 176; JCS 2101/301, *Report by the Joint Strategic Plans Committee* to the Joint Chiefs of Staff on *Report to the President by the Security Resources Panel of the ODM Science Advisory Committee (IRBM Operational Status)*, 26 March 1958, #832, 1983, *DDRS*, enclosure B, 2659. On the completion of the Thor deal, see Melissen, *Struggle for Nuclear Partnership*, 74–86.

4. Reprinted in *NYT*, 31 May 1959, pt. 4, 3.

5. MemCon, 319th NSC meeting, 11 April 1957, *FR 1955–57*, 19:473–74; for the Soviet threats, see *NYT*, 27 March 1957, 4; 28 March 1957, 8; 31 March 1957, 35; 5 April 1957, 2; 10 April 1957, 11; 28 April 1957, 27.

6. MemCon, 358th NSC meeting, 13 March 1958 (drafted 14 March), NSCS, AWF, 16; James S. Lay Jr. to NSC, "U.S. Overseas Military Bases," 14 February 1958, Mill-191, 3 of 3, Mill Papers 191, RG 273, attachment, 3–4. The BNSP paper of that year stated only that "the determination as to whether to position IRBM's around the Sino-Soviet periphery outside the NATO area [would] be made by the President." NSC 5810/1, 5 May 1958, in Trachtenberg, *American Strategic Thought*, 198.

7. ONE, SNIE 100-4-58, "Probable Sino-Soviet Reactions to US Deployment of IRBMs on the Soviet Bloc Periphery," 15 April 1958, in Koch, *CIA Cold War Records*, 271–79; see also JCS 1924/102, *Report by the Joint Intelligence Committee* to the Joint Chiefs of Staff on *Soviet Reaction to U.S. Deployment of Intermediate Range Ballistic Missiles (IRBMs)*, 24 March 1958, CCS 471.6 (5-31-44) sec. 17, CDF 1958, RG 218, 1400–1407, which had the same basic thrust (the JIC had some input into the drafting of SNIEs). Military leaders had already arrived at this same assessment earlier; see Thomas D. White and Maxwell D. Taylor testimony, 4 and 7 February 1958, HCA Subcommittee, *Department of Defense Appropriations for 1959*, 232, 392–93.

8. Armacost, *Politics of Weapons Innovation*, 203.

9. Excerpts of Bulganin notes, 15976–78; Bulganin to Eisenhower, 127–30; Bulganin to Adenauer, 11 December 1957, Gromyko, Khrushchev speeches, 21 December 1957, Khrushchev, replies to questions of V. Sindbaek, 15 January 1958, Khrushchev speeches, 22 January 1958 and 24 May 1958, Khrushchev, answers to questions of Christos Lambrakis, 4 May 1958, TASS statement, 1 May 1958, *Izvestia* article, 26 February 1958, Khrushchev, interview by Giuseppi Palozzi, 24 March 1958, all in *CDSP*, respectively 9 (29 January 1958): 20–21; 10 (12 February 1958): 4, 7; 10 (19 February 1958): 19; 10 (5 March 1958): 16, 20; 10 (2 July 1958): 13; 10 (11 June 1958): 20, 22; 10 (2 April 1958): 15; 10 (7 May 1958): 30; Soviet Foreign Ministry statement, 21 January 1958, *NYT*, 22 January 1958, 4; see also, for example, Supreme Soviet appeal to FRG Bundestag, 31 March

1958, *CDSP* 10 (4 June 1958): 8; *NYT*, 13 December 1957, 9, 15 January 1958, 8, 4 May 1958, 3.

10. Soviet note to the United States, 21 April 1959 (see also U.S. note to the Soviet Union, 8 May), both in *DSB* 40 (25 May 1959): 740–42; Trachtenberg, *History and Strategy*, 172–73; DOS, *Foreign Ministers Meeting*, 31, 40–41, 44, 64, 82, 107, 128, 133, 147, 168–70, 185, 202, 206, 307, 337–39, 357, 400, 516–17. Whether the campaign's resurgence bore any relationship to Khrushchev's initiation of the Berlin crisis in November 1958 is unclear. The State Department confidentially dismissed the 21 April note as "routine," a "crude and obvious propaganda effort." Herter circular, 22 April 1959, 396.1-GE/4-2259, DF, RG 59.

11. *Keesing's Contemporary Archives*, 11–18 July 1959, 16907–9; *NYT*, 30 April 1959, 5; Khrushchev speeches, 26 May, 30 May, and 6 June 1959, *CDSP* 11 (24 June 1959): 13–14, and 11 (1 July 1959): 5, 7; Bloomfield, Clemens, and Griffiths, *Khrushchev and the Arms Race*, 158–59; see also DOS, *Notes: Soviet Affairs*, no. 241 (1960), "The Quotable Khrushchev (April 1959–March 1960)," USSR-General, 1959–1960, Countries, POF, 49; joint Soviet-Polish declaration, 22 July 1959, *NYT*, 23 July 1959, 2. Khrushchev also supported creation of a "missile-free and atom-free zone on the Scandinavian Peninsula and the Baltic" at the same time. Khrushchev speech, 11 June 1959, *CDSP* 11 [15 July 1959]: 4. Yugoslavia joined the call for banishing nuclear weapons from the region. On Khrushchev's visit to Albania in which he waged part of this campaign, see also *FR 1958–60*, 10, pt. 2:86–96.

12. MemCons, 5 January 1959, 12:03–1:45 P.M., and 16 January 1959, 4:00–5:30 P.M., both in *FR 1958–60*, respectively 8:239 and 10, pt. 1:232–33; Eisenhower, *Waging Peace*, 340. Mikoyan also asked whether the United States intended to arm the FRG with nuclear weapons, and although Dulles answered that U.S. law forbade nuclear proliferation, the Soviets were unconvinced. In Geneva, Gromyko attacked FRG nuclearization in private as well. MemCon, 16 January 1959, 234; MemCons, 17 January 1959, 9:00 A.M., 21 May 1959, 8:00 P.M., and 22 May 1959, 11:30 A.M., all in *FR 1958–60*, 8:279, 743, 748.

13. MemCon, 23 June 1959 (sent Embassy Moscow to DOS, 25 June), *FR 1958–60*, 8:942 (see also ibid. and Thompson to DOS, 29 June 1959, both in *FR 1958–60*, 10, pt. 1:271, 283); Harriman, "Memorandum on Kremlin Reactions," 22 October 1962, NATO-Weapons, RSF, NSF, 1. On Harriman's trip, see also Abramson, *Spanning the Century*, 571–74.

14. MemCon, 26 July 1959, 3:30 P.M., *FR 1958–60*, 10, pt. 1:363, 365–66 (see also 360, 364, and Khrushchev speech, 28 July 1959, *CDSP* 11 [26 August 1959]: 14–15); *Newsweek*, 3 August 1959, 17. The toastmasters' squabble that ensued was only resolved by a toast "to the ladies." In his address broadcast on Soviet television on 1 August, Nixon countered that U.S. bases were purely defensive, born of past Soviet provocations, massive Soviet defense spending, and NATO fears of Soviet intentions. *Newsweek*, 3 August 1959, 17; *NYT*, 2 August 1959, 24.

15. *NYT*, 24 December 1957, 4; Norstad, television interview, 25 February 1958, *NATO Letter* 6 (March 1958): 13; Wolf to Timmons, 17 January 1959, IRBM General (2), PFS, LNP, 1. The lead phrase is Dulles's view of the administration's response to *Sputnik*, 3 March 1958, quoted in Divine, *Sputnik Challenge*, 120.

16. MemCon, 363d NSC meeting, 24 April 1958 (drafted 25 April), NSCS, AWF, 2, 3–4, 6. Twice in early 1958, PSAC recommended cancellation of one of the "almost identical" IRBM programs, but although Ike said he had "no problem with dropping" one of them, he never resolved to do so. Divine, *Sputnik Challenge*, 113, 121–23; MCP, 10 March 1958, 10:20 A.M. (drafted 11 March), Staff Notes March 1958 (2), DDEDS, AWF, 2.

17. Divine, *Sputnik Challenge*, 126–27; Trachtenberg, *History and Strategy*, 42, 202 n. 127, 42 n. 92. Department of Defense officials agreed on plans for distribution of the twelve squadrons: four would be placed in Britain, three in France, two in Italy, and one each in Turkey, Alaska, and Okinawa or the Near East. Historical Division, Joint Secre-

tariat, Joint Chiefs of Staff, "Chronology of Significant Events and Decisions Relating to the U.S. Missile and Earth Satellite Development Programs, Supplement I, October 1957 through October 1958," 15 December 1958, courtesy NSA, 58.

18. Spaak quoted in his *Continuing Battle*, 263.

19. MemCon, 18 January 1958, 12:22 P.M., #761, 1986, *DDRS*, 1; Elbrick to Murphy, 30 January 1958; Sulzberger, *Last of the Giants*, 442.

20. Elbrick to Murphy, 30 January 1958; MemCon, 18 December 1957 (sent Embassy France to DOS, 20 December), *FR* 1955–57, 27:209–10.

21. MemCon, 18 January 1958, 12:22 P.M., 1; Elbrick to Murphy, 30 January 1958.

22. MemCon, 18 January 1958, 10:40 A.M., IRBM-General December 1957–December 1958, 1959, box 1, RRN 57–64, OAPMA, EUR, LF, RG 59, 5–6; MemCon, 6 February 1959, Turkey, box 142, RPPS 57–61, LF, RG 59, 2 (the paragraph containing discussion of the "Turkish temperament" and unauthorized launch, perhaps unsurprisingly, is excised in the *Foreign Relations* version; see *FR* 10, pt. 2:794); Macmillan quoted in Ball, *Past Has Another Pattern*, 267.

23. Department of State MemCon, 25 March 1958, 4:15 P.M., IRBM-General (3), PFS, LNP; ISA MemCon, 25 March 1958 (drafted 26 March), #440A, 1981, *DDRS*, 2. Officials mentioned several alternative deployment possibilities at one time or another: smaller NATO countries (especially the Netherlands); non-NATO countries (Spain, Libya, Iran, Pakistan, the Philippines, and Taiwan); and U.S. or U.S.-controlled territory (Guam, Okinawa, and especially Alaska). U.S. Air Force leaders became increasingly keen on this last (far simpler) option as the search for NATO hosts dragged on. However, at no time did the projected number of IRBMs become so great, or the shortage of higher-priority potential hosts so desperate, that these alternatives received serious high-level consideration. See Armacost, *Politics of Weapons Innovation*, 212–13, 217; on the Netherlands, see van der Harst, "Storage of US Nuclear Warheads," esp. 5, 7–8, 9–12.

24. MemCon, 18 December 1957 (sent 20 December), 209–11; MemCon, 16 December 1957, 3:30–8:00 P.M., 237–38; Harrison, *Reluctant Ally*, 82; Houghton to Dulles, 22 November 1957, 751.5611/11-2257, and MemCon, 27 December 1957, 2:00 P.M., 711.56351/12-2757, both in DF, RG 59; *NYT*, 8 February 1958, 2; MemCon, 18 January 1958, 12:22 P.M., 1.

25. Norstad to Quarles, 12 February 1958, CCS 471.6 (5-31-44) sec. 14, CDF 58, RG 218, 1–2; MemCon, 5 March 1958 (drafted 6 March), 751.5611/3-658, and Houghton to Dulles, 11 February 1958, 765.5611/2-1158, both in DF, RG 59; ISA MemCon, 25 March 1958, 2.

26. Houghton to Dulles, 11 March 1958, 711.56351/3-1158; 2 April 1958, 711.56351/4-258, 1; 28 March 1958, 711.56351/3-2858, 1–2; and 27 March 1958, 711.56351/3-2758, 2, all in DF, RG 59.

27. Houghton to Dulles, 16 May 1958, 711.56351/5-1658, DF, RG 59; Historical Division, Office of Information, HQ SAC, Historical Study No. 72, "Strategic Air Command Participation in the Missile Program, 1 January 1958–30 June 1958," n.d., K416.01-72, AFHRC, 1:27–28.

28. Scheinman, *Atomic Energy Policy in France*, 186–93.

29. Dulles to Thurston, 7 June 1958, 711.56351/6-658; Lyon to Dulles, 12 June 1958, 711.56351/6-1258; Houghton to Dulles, 17 July 1958, 751.5611/7-1758, all in DF, RG 59.

30. MemCon, 5 July 1958, 10:30 A.M., and MemCon, 5 July 1958, 6:00 P.M., both in *FR* 1958–60, respectively 7, pt. 2:59–61, and 7, pt. 1:354–55. De Gaulle did not, as he later claimed, demand French custody of any nuclear weapons (including IRBM warheads) on French soil "entirely and unreservedly." De Gaulle, *Memoirs of Hope*, 208–9.

31. *NYT*, 21 July 1958, 1; Houghton to Dulles, 17 July 1958; Herter to Thurston, 22 August 1958, 711.56351/8-2258, DF, RG 59; MemCon, 25 August 1958, IRBM-General (3), PFS, LNP; Houghton to Dulles, 25 August 1958, 711.56351/8-2558, DF, RG 59.

32. Lyon to Dulles, 10 October 1958, 751.5611/10-1058, Lyon to Dulles, 17 Novem-

ber 1958, 711.56351/11-1758, and C. Billingslea to Robert Magill, 20 November 1958, 740.5/11-2058, all in DF, RG 59; Dulles to DOS, 15 December 1958, *FR 1958–60*, 7, pt. 2:154; see also MemCon, 15 December 1958, *FR 1958–60*, 7, pt. 2:151, and de Gaulle to Eisenhower, 25 May 1959, de Gaulle (June 1958–October 1959) (Corresp with President) (3), IS, OSS, WHO, DDEL, 4.

33. General Gabriel P. Disosway, interview by Lt. Col. John N. Dick Jr., 4–6 October 1977, K239.0512-974, USAFOHP, AFHRC, 150.

34. Nuti, "L'Italie et les missiles *Jupiter*," 130; Nuti, "Italy and the Nuclear Choices," 231–32; for an early Italo-U.S. discussion of IRBMs, see MemCon, 19 December 1957 (drafted 26 December), IRBM-Italy 1958–1959, box 1, RRN 57–64, OAPMA, EUR, LF, RG 59. Nuti, "L'Italie et les missiles *Jupiter*," 124–30, is the only other detailed discussion of the Italo-American IRBM negotiations and the only one that makes use of Italian sources; my account differs from his mainly in emphasis.

35. Nuti, "Italy and the Nuclear Choices," 231; *NYT*, 25 January 1958, 3, 6 February 1958, 6, 13 April 1958, 33; Kogan, *Political History of Postwar Italy*, 131; Zellerbach to USIA, 26 March 1958, m. Weapons, 1957–59, 21.51 Country Files: Italy, Records Relating to Atomic Energy Matters 1944–63, S/AE, LF, RG 59; Jernegan to Dulles, 28 March 1958, 711.56365/3-2858, and 19 March 1958, 711.56365/3-1958; MemCon, 19 March 1958, 711.56365/3-1958; MemCon, 20 March 1958, 711.56365/3-2058; Dulles to Embassy Paris, 25 March 1958, 711.56365/3-1258, and 31 March 1958, 711.56365/3-1958, all in DF, RG 59.

36. Thurston to Jernegan, 15 July 1958, IRBM-General (3), PFS, LNP, 1; Dulles, "Telephone Call to Allen Dulles," 29 July 1958, 10:54 A.M., frame 719, reel 7, *MTC-JFD/CH*; MemCon, 30 July 1958, *FR 1958–60*, 7, pt. 2:473.

37. Embassy Rome to DOS, 23 June 1958, and Zellerbach to Dulles, 23 June 1958, both 711.56365/6-2358; Zellerbach to Dulles, 21 July 1958, 711.56365/7-2158, and 28 July 1958, 711.56365/7-2858; and R. A. Fearey to Jandrey, 8 August 1958, 611.657/8-858, all in DF, RG 59.

38. Houghton to Dulles, 8 August 1958, IRBM-General (3), PFS, LNP; Zellerbach to Dulles, 5 September 1958, 711.56365/9-558; 26 September 1958, 711.56365/9-2658; and 3 September 1958, 711.56365/9-358, 1, all in DF, RG 59; O'Hara to Norstad, 12 September 1958, #436B, 1981, *DDRS*, 1.

39. Zellerbach to Dulles, 3 October 1958, 711.56365/10-358; "Memorandum to Ambassador Zellerbach," 12 November 1958, 765.5612/11-1258; MemCon, 13 November 1958 (1 of 2), 711.56365/11-1358; Merchant to Murphy, 30 December 1958, 611.657/12-3058; Dillon to Quarles, 20 February 1959, 711.56382/2-1259, table 2, all in DF, RG 59; Bell to Dillon, 26 January 1959, #520, *NNP*, 1.

40. MemCon, 11 January 1959 (drafted 16 January), #144, 1987, *DDRS*, 1; Zellerbach to Murphy, 11 February 1959, 711.56365/2-1159; Zellerbach to Dulles, 27 February 1959, 711.56365/2-2759, and 4 March 1959, 711.56365/3-459, 1, all in DF, RG 59. Because some felt the agreement could have been concluded before the Fanfani government fell, accusations and denials of foot dragging also flew within the State Department. Timmons to Merchant, 18 March 1959, 611.657, DF, RG 59.

41. Zellerbach to Dulles, 4 March 1959, 1–2, and 5 March 1959, 711.56365/3-559, 1; MemCon, 10 March 1959, 740.5/3-1059, all in DF, RG 59; Wollemborg, *Stars, Stripes, and Italian Tricolor*, 46–47.

42. Berding, *Dulles on Diplomacy*, 79; Dulles, "Telephone call from Secretary to Mr. Greene," 27 March 1959, 4:49 P.M., frame 460, reel 8, *MTC-JFD/CH*, 1.

43. Horace G. Torbert, interview by Charles S. Kennedy, 31 August 1988, FAOHP, 23.

44. Smith to Dulles, 31 March 1958, HO Chron—January–April 1958, box 181; Owen to Smith, 1 May 1958, HO Chron—May–August 1958, box 182; Smith to Dulles, n.d. [ca. late June 1958], HO-Chron—May–August 1958, box 182; all in RPPS 57–61, RG 59; see also Smith to Dulles, 16 June 1958, Owen, H., Chron, box 204, and Smith to Dulles, 24 July 1958, HO Chron—May–August 1958, box 182, both in RPPS 57–61, RG 59.

Policy Planning Staff officials were neither the first nor the last to view IRBMs as potential bargaining chips. The FRG Foreign Office and Harold Macmillan had both done so in December 1957, and Dulles's successor Christian Herter would in Geneva in May 1959, in light of Gromyko's complaints. Schwartz to DOS, 16 December 1957, 740.5/12-1657, attachment, DF, RG 59, 1; Macmillan, *Riding the Storm*, 335; MemCon, 24 May 1959, 10:30 A.M. (drafted 29 May), *FR 1958–60*, 7, pt. 2:228–29.

45. WSEG, "First Annual Review of WSEG Report No. 23—The Relative Military Advantages of Missiles and Manned Aircraft," 8 August 1958, #1505, 1988, *DDRS*, 14–15, 17; "Presentation by the Director, Weapons Systems Evaluation Group to the National Security Council on the Subject of Offensive and Defensive Weapons Systems," 13 October 1958, #2027, 1991, *DDRS*, 23, 27. As early as January, WSEG had concluded that there was no remedy for the vulnerability of fixed IRBM sites. Trachtenberg, *History and Strategy*, 202–3 n. 127.

46. Burke to McElroy, 31 October 1958, Memos—Oc 1958, box 106, NFTP; Norstad to JCS, 2 November 1958, CCS 333.1 (7) (Baghdad Pact Trip), Chairman's File, Gen. Twining 1957–60, RG 218; MemCon, 384th NSC meeting, 30 October 1958 (drafted 31 October), NSCS, AWF, 4–5 (this portion remains almost completely classified, but see Smith and Merchant to Acting Secretary, 8 November 1958, HO Chron—September–December 1958, box 182, RPPS 57–61, RG 59, 1–2, and Rountree to Murphy, 2 February 1959, #522, NNP, 4); McElroy press conference, 13 November 1958, 4:00 P.M., Public Statements of Secretary of Defense Neil H. McElroy, 1957–58, DDEL, 4:1751; *NYT*, 15 November 1958, 1, 10; Divine, *Sputnik Challenge*, 193–94. Department of State officials responsible cleared their statement with neither Dulles nor, much to McElroy's annoyance, DOD. Dulles, "Telephone call from Sec McElroy," 17 November 1958, 8:55 A.M., frame 327, reel 8, *MTC-JFD/CH*.

47. Merchant and Smith to Dulles, n.d. (ca. 18 November 1958), #352, *NNP*; MemCon, 5 December 1958, 740.5/1-659, DF, RG 59, 6.

48. Timmons to Thurston, 13 January 1959, RA Correspondence, 1959 (1), RRA, RD 55–60, LF, McElroy to Dulles, 17 January 1959, 711.56382/1-1759, DF, and Smith to Murphy, 2 February 1959, Turkey, box 142, RPPS 57–61, LF, all in RG 59.

49. MemCon, 28 November 1958 (drafted 9 December), Staff Notes Nov. 1958, DDEDS, AWF, 5; Divine, *Sputnik Challenge*, 200–202. With no State Department officials present, Deputy Secretary Quarles took the opportunity to pin the IRBM glut on them.

50. Divine, *Sputnik Challenge*, 200–202; Wolf to Timmons, 17 January 1959, 1–2; Neufeld, *Ballistic Missiles*, 223–24; Melissen, *Struggle for Nuclear Partnership*, 105. The administration allowed for an enlargement of up to two additional squadrons in the unlikely event that allied demand increased and if sufficient MSP funds became available, but it would have to make such a decision by 1 April 1959. The Bureau of the Budget also pushed for the program reduction; see Maurice Stans testimony, 20 May 1959, PIS, SCAS, *Major Defense Matters*, pt. 2, 245.

51. McElroy and Twining Testimony, 23 January 1959, HCA, *Department of Defense Appropriations for 1960*, pt. 1, 44–45; "United States Foreign Policy," 16 January 1959, ESSFRC 11:42–44. The overzealous Twining suggested that IRBMs were already operational, which would not be true of even the first British Thors for months.

52. Billingslea to Magill, 20 November 1958; Rountree to Murphy, 2 February 1959, 1, and Herter to Thurston, 3 January 1959, respectively #522 and #504, both in *NNP*.

53. Rountree to Murphy, 2 February 1959; Timmons to Merchant, 3 February 1959, 711.56382, DF, RG 59; see also Dulles to McElroy, 3 February 1959, #523, *NNP*, and Rountree to Murphy, 20 March 1959, Turkey, box 142, RPPS 57–61, LF, RG 59.

54. McElroy to Dulles, 17 January 1959; Bell to Dillon, 26 January 1959; Quarles to Murphy, 12 February 1959, 711.56382/2-1259, DF; Merchant to Murphy, 18 February 1959, 711.56382/2-1859, DF; Timmons to Thurston, 18 February 1959, RA Correspon-

dence, 1959 (1), RRA, RD 55–60, LF; Dillon to Quarles, 20 February 1959, 711.56382/2-1259, DF; and Timmons to Merchant, 23 April 1959, 711.56382, DF, all in RG 59 (these documents clearly represent only the tip of the funding-dispute iceberg); HQ USAF to CINCAL, 18 May 1959, Document 30, in HQ SAC, Historical Study No. 76, "History of Strategic Air Command, June 1958–July 1959," K4160.01-76, AFHRC.

55. Schwarz, *Adenauer*, 388–94; Richardson, *Germany and the Atlantic Alliance*, 57 n. 38.

56. Schwarz, *Adenauer*, 388–94. For claims that Adenauer opposed IRBMs for Germany, see Kelleher, *Germany and the Politics of Nuclear Weapons*, 130, and Boutwell, *German Nuclear Dilemma*, 22. In his memoirs, Adenauer wrote only that the IRBM decision was "one of the most important results" of the NATO conference. *Erinnerungen, 1955–1959*, 344, my translation.

57. MemCon, 26 November 1957, 740.5/11-2657, DF, RG 59, 3; MemCon, 21 November 1957, FR 1955–57, 4:205–6; NYT, 19 December 1957, 1, 12; Kelleher, *Germany and Nuclear Weapons*, 130–31; Boutwell, *German Nuclear Dilemma*, 22 n. 18; see also Schwartz to DOS, 3 January 1958, 396.1-PA/1-258, DF, RG 59, attachment. German leaders suggested that mobile IRBMs might be preferable instead, Adenauer particularly because of the protests he would expect in the areas around fixed bases. MemCon, 21 November 1957, 205; Schwarz, *Adenauer*, 389–90.

58. Schwarz, *Adenauer*, 393–94 (my translation); MemCon, 14 December 1957, 5:00 P.M., A–D (1), Memos of Conversation, General, General Correspondence and Memoranda Series, JFDP, 1; Felken, *Dulles und Deutschland*, 401–2; Dulles, "Telephone Call to Senator Knowland in Oakland," 23 December 1957, 12:40 P.M., frame 13, reel 7, *MTC-JFD/CH*; Macmillan, *Riding the Storm*, 335; *Time*, 30 December 1957, 19; NYT, 19 December 1957, 12. One can see why Macmillan was unsure exactly where Adenauer stood on the issue. See Macmillan to Eisenhower, 2 January 1958, FR 1958–60, 7, pt. 2:795.

59. Boutwell, *German Nuclear Dilemma*, 23–29; NYT, 7 November 1958, 5; Houghton to Dulles, 22 November 1958, #849, 1991, DDRS; on the nuclear debate, see also Cioc, *Pax Atomica*, 46–50, 62–65. Trachtenberg argues persuasively that FRG nuclearization was central to Khrushchev's decision to initiate the Berlin crisis. *History and Strategy*, 169–234. One wonders how much Adenauer supported Strauss's move; the FRG envoy at NATO said that Strauss had only "mentioned it" to the chancellor, "who had not specifically commented but had given [a] general gesture of approval." Houghton to Dulles, 22 November 1958.

60. George S. Vest, interview by Charles S. Kennedy, 6 July 1989, FAOHP, 38; Norstad, interview by Hugh N. Ahmann, 13–16 February and 22–25 October 1979, K239.0512-1116, USAFOHP, AFHRC, 339; MemCon, 17 December 1958 (drafted 31 December), #501, NNP, 1–2; MemCon, 18 December 1958 (drafted 30 December), #572, National Security Archive, *Berlin Crisis*, 1.

61. Houghton to Dulles, 3 January 1959, #1923, 1989, DDRS; Dulles to Thurston, 8 January 1959, 700.5612/1-859, DF, RG 59; Houghton to Dulles, 17 January 1959 (tel. 2612), #1927, 1989, DDRS; Houghton to Dulles, 22 November 1958; MemCon, 4 February 1959 (drafted 5 February), 740.5/2-559, DF, RG 59, 4.

62. Penfield to Dulles, 11 December 1957, 396.1-PA/12-1157, DF, and Prime Minister's Office, Information Department, "Daily News Bulletin," 17 December 1957, Greece/Paris NATO Summit Meeting, 1957, Subject Files Related to Greece and Cyprus, 55–58, LF, both in RG 59; MemCon, 18 December 1957 (sent 19 December), 255.

63. Couloumbis, *Greek Political Reaction*, 110–25; Lagani, "U.S. Forces in Greece," 327; Herter to Embassy Athens, 14 March 1958, also Riddleberger to Dulles, 8 March 1958, both 711.56381/3-858, DF, RG 59. Only the Greek military argued for acceptance.

64. Couloumbis, *Greek Political Reaction*, 125–32; Houghton to Dulles, 17 January 1959 (tel. 2614), #1928, 1989, DDRS; MemCon, 4 February 1959, 4; FBIS, no. 17 (1959),

p. J1, no. 49 (1959), p. J1, no. 64 (1959), p. J2, and no. 104 (1959), p. J2; McElroy to Eisenhower, 12 June 1959, McElroy, Neil H., Secy. of Defense, 1959 (2), AS, AWF, 1; Rountree to Murphy, 24 June 1959, and Berger to Jones, 4 June 1959, both IRBM-Greece, box 1, RRN 57–64, OAPMA, EUR, LF, RG 59; see also Berger to DOS, 26 June 1959, *FR* 10, pt. 2:666–67.

65. Ellis O. Briggs, "Proud Servant: The Autobiography of Ellis Ormsbee Briggs, Ambassador to Seven Countries and Career Ambassador of the United States of America," typescript, 1975, Hoover Institution Archives, Stanford, Calif., 358–59. After the meeting, Robert Murphy angrily accused Briggs of "rocking the boat." Ibid., 359. Brief accounts of this whole episode are found in Ambrose, *Eisenhower*, 532–34; Trachtenberg, *History and Strategy*, 202–4; Beschloss, *Crisis Years*, 439; and Melissen, *Struggle for Nuclear Partnership*, 105.

66. Eisenhower to McElroy, 3 June 1959, *FR* 10, pt. 2:661. Ike's obvious interest, speedy memo writing, and reference to issues not raised by Briggs suggest he was already troubled, and thus Briggs may have simply provided the decisive nudge in a direction in which Eisenhower was already leaning.

67. McElroy to Eisenhower, 12 June 1959. He made no reference to target coverage from Italy.

68. MCP, 9 June 1959, *FR 1958–60*, 7, pt. 1:464; MCP, 15 June 1959 (drafted 17 June), Staff Notes June 1–15 1959 (1), DDEDS, AWF, 1.

69. MCP, 16 June 1959, 1; MCP, 17 June 1959, Staff Notes June 16–30 1959 (2), DDEDS, AWF, 1–2.

70. MCP, 17 June 1959, 1–3; Trachtenberg, *History and Strategy*, 204.

71. NSC 5906/1, 5 August 1959, in Trachtenberg, *American Strategic Thought*, 234; Dillon to Herter, 16 June 1959, Dillon to Herter, 17 June 1959, and Herter to Dillon, 31 July 1959, all in *FR 1958–60*, respectively 10, pt. 2:663 n. 2, 663–64, and 671 n. 3; and Dillon to Consul Geneva, 1 August 1959, 781.5612/8-159, DF, RG 59.

72. "History, Air Force Chief of Staff for Guided Missiles, Headquarters, USAF, 1 Jul 1959 through 31 Dec 1959," n.d., K168.0321, AFHRC, 5; Houghton to Herter, 31 August 1959, 611.8197/8-3159; Dillon to Herter, 2 September 1959, 611.81/8-2859, and Houghton to Dillon, 3 September 1959, 611.8197/9-359, all in DF, RG 59; Norstad to White, 10 September 1959, Greece (5), CFS, LNP; Houghton to Dillon, 14 September 1959, 611.8197/9-1459, DF, RG 59. This last document illustrates the Byzantine nature of the current declassification system; a specific mandatory review request filed at the Eisenhower Library failed to dislodge it, but it was routinely declassified in full by the National Archives.

73. Some top officials did also question plans for Turkey, but there is no evidence Ike did during the key period of 15–17 June. Magill to Thurston, 30 June 1959, IRBM-Greece, box 1, RRN 57–64, OAPMA, EUR, LF, RG 59.

74. Excerpts of speeches from first closed session, 16 December 1957, *Keesing's Contemporary Archives*, 15967; Criss, "Les retombées de la crise de Cuba," 163; MemCon, 16 December 1957, 3:30–8:00 P.M., 241; summary of Zorlu's Ankara press conference, 26 January 1958, in Turkish Information Office, New York, *News from Turkey* 11 (29 January 1958): 3.

75. MemCon, 4 February 1959, 4; Houghton to Dulles, 17 January 1959 (tel. 2613), #1929, 1989, *DDRS*.

76. Merchant to Murphy, 10 July 1959, 711.56382/7-1059, and Herter to Dillon, 16 July 1959, 611.82/7-1659, both in DF, RG 59; Herter to Eisenhower, 16 September 1959, *FR* 10, pt. 2:812–13.

77. Department of State, *Khrushchev Visit, Camp David Session, September 1959*, "Reserve Briefing Papers," n.d., tab E, 34, and "Major Briefing Papers," n.d., tab E, 15; DOS, *Khrushchev Visit, Camp David, September 25-27, 1959*, "U.S. Objectives in Khrushchev Visit and Suggested Tactics for Conversation with Him," 3, 6; and DOS, *Khrushchev*

Visit, Washington, September 1959, "Major Themes of Khrushchev's Public and Private Statements and U.S. Counterarguments (Talking Paper)," 8 September 1959, 11–12, respectively #307, #303, #299, 1983, *DDRS*; Herter to Eisenhower, 16 September 1959; Dillon to Embassy Ankara et al., 17 September 1959, #305, 1987, *DDRS*.

78. Khrushchev-Reuther exchange, 20 September 1959, in *Khrushchev in America,* 129, see also 42; Beschloss, *Mayday,* 199; Herter to Embassy Ankara, 7 October 1959, Turkey (1) (June 1958–October 1959), IS, OSS, WHO, DDEL; on Khrushchev's U.S. trip, see *FR 1958–60,* 10, pt. 1:388–495. Word of the agreement had leaked on 10 October, eliciting an official "no comment"; see *NYT,* 11 October 1959, 1, 11, also 25 October 1959, 5E, and 31 October 1959, 1, and Herter to Embassy Ankara, 12 October 1959, Turkey (1) (June 1958–October 1959), IS, OSS, WHO, DDEL.

79. Houghton to Dillon, 14 September 1959, 1, Houghton to Herter, 28 September 1959, and Magill to Vest, 12 October 1959, all IRBM General (1), PFS, LNP; Norstad to Irwin, 25 September 1959, MRBM-IRBM 1957–59 (2), SS, LNP; Gates to Eisenhower, 19 October 1959, McElroy, Neil H., Secy. of Defense, 1959 (1), AS, AWF; "History, Air Force Chief of Staff for Guided Missiles," 6, 12. The MAP was the military component of the MSP. Some DOD officials wanted to cancel the third Jupiter squadron and send the fifth Thor squadron to Turkey instead, but that would have cost slightly more. In December, the administration seems to have considered providing nine of the leftover Thors to the Allied Command Europe. "NATO Thor Missiles," 23 December 1959, IRBM General [1], PFS, LNP.

80. John C. Brassell, "Jupiter: Development Aspects—Deployment," Historical Office, Office of Information, Mobile Air Material Area, Brookley AFB, September 1962, K205.0504-2, AFHRC, 1:14, 15. Indeed, a handful of Atlases achieved operational status beginning in September 1959.

81. John F. Kennedy doodles, quoted in Brugioni, *Eyeball to Eyeball,* 469; Sorensen, *Kennedy,* 3, see also 696, and Sorensen, interview by Carl Kaysen, 6 April 1964, OHC, JFKL, 65; Douglas Dillon to author, 10 September 1993; MCP, 23 December 1959 (drafted 30 December), Staff Notes December 1959, DDEDS, AWF, 2; Murphy to Herter, 6 December 1959, 765.56/12-659, DF, RG 59. Ike cited Zellerbach's comment in directing that he be replaced when the opportunity arose.

82. On Eisenhower and credibility, see Gaddis, *Strategies,* 144.

83. "History, Air Force Chief of Staff for Guided Missiles," 4, 9; for references to the disposal problem as spur for deployment, see Killian, *Sputnik, Scientists, and Eisenhower,* 113; John McCone, interview by Joe B. Frantz, 19 August 1970, OHC, JFKL, 13; also Dillon, cited in Sorensen, *Kennedy,* 3, and Dean Rusk, interview by Dennis J. O'Brien, 21 August 1970, OHC, JFKL, 366.

84. Eisenhower revisionism is now so prevalent in the scholarly literature that it hardly merits the term *revisionism.* Its key works include Ambrose, *Eisenhower;* Greenstein, *Hidden-Hand Presidency;* and Divine, *Eisenhower and the Cold War;* for Eisenhower "postrevisionism," see Pach and Richardson, *Presidency of Dwight D. Eisenhower.* For Dulles revisionism, see Immerman, *John Foster Dulles.*

85. Wollemborg, *Stars, Stripes, and Italian Tricolor,* 49; Newhouse, *De Gaulle and the Anglo-Saxons,* 23.

86. Greenstein, *Hidden-Hand Presidency,* 135; Gaddis, *Strategies,* 163; Trachtenberg, *History and Strategy,* 42 n. 92. Greenstein's point illustrates the danger in relying on a single document in the absence of context.

87. The quotation is from Eisenhower's diary, 24 January 1958. Ferrell, *Eisenhower Diaries,* 350.

88. Gaddis, "Unexpected John Foster Dulles," 76, and Pruessen, "John Foster Dulles," 25, see also 43; Marks, *Power and Peace,* 147.

89. Dulles speech, 19 December 1957, *DSB* 38 (13 January 1958): 53.

Chapter Three

1. Brassell, "Jupiter," 57–58, 15–17; Nuti, "L'Italie et les missiles *Jupiter*," 128–31, and see 132 for a map depicting the ten Italian launch-position sites.

2. Strother to AFCCS, 10 February 1961, 4–5 Missiles, Chief of Staff, TDWP, attachment.

3. MCP, 6 December 1959, *FR* 10, pt. 2:824.

4. "History, Air Force Chief of Staff for Guided Missiles," 13; Neufeld, *Ballistic Missiles*, 225; Brassell, "Jupiter," 18; Douglas to Eisenhower, 27 May 1960, Gates, T S Jr., 1959–61 (4), AS, AWF, attachment, 3. The location of launch positions in Turkey remains classified; as in Italy, presumably they were widely dispersed, at least eight miles apart.

5. Brassell, "Jupiter," 19–20; Strother to AFCCS, 10 February 1961, attachment. Tocchet, "Sending Nuclear Weapons to Europe," 2–3, 18, and Bernstein, "Reconsidering the Cuban Missile Crisis," 60, 109–10 n. 22, suggest that Eisenhower for some reason intentionally delayed delivery of the missiles to Turkey, but this is unsubstantiated.

6. Much has been written on the nuclear strategists, but in particular see Kaplan, *Wizards of Armageddon*; Herken, *Counsels of War*; Baylis and Garnett, *Makers of Nuclear Strategy*; and Trachtenberg, *History and Strategy*, 3–46.

7. Kennan, *Russia, the Atom, and the West*, 86–88; Kennan testimony, 4 February 1959, SCFR, Subcommittee, *Disarmament and Foreign Policy*, 204–5, 238. On the Reith Lectures, see also Kennan, *Memoirs, 1950-1963*, 229–66; Hixson, *George F. Kennan*, 171–93; and Mayers, *George Kennan*, 230–39.

8. Albrook, "How Good Are Our Missiles?"

9. Gavin, *War and Peace in the Space Age*, 6, 9–10, 147; Taylor, *Uncertain Trumpet*, 139–42; see also Taylor testimony, 4 February 1960, PIS, SCAS and Senate Committee on Aeronautical and Space Sciences, *Missiles, Space, and Other Major Defense Matters*, 187, 205–6. Gavin had been the army's chief of research and development until January 1958; Taylor had been army chief of staff, 1955–59.

10. *Time*, 13 April 1959, 24, 22; Murphy, "Is the Defense Budget Big Enough?" 282; see also Murphy, "NATO Alliance Goes Nuclear" and "Embattled Mr. McElroy," 246. *Time* borrowed the equation from a French newspaper it had quoted at the time of the December 1957 summit; see *Time*, 23 December 1957, 17–18. For a glimpse of Murphy's cozy relationship with Norstad and eagerness to promote the IRBM deployments, see Murphy to Norstad, 18 November 1957 and 22 December 1958, respectively Murphy, Col. Charles J. V. (5), and Murphy, Col. Charles J. V. (4), both in LNP. For a journal of opinion that raised questions about the IRBMs, see *Nation*, 8 March 1958, 197, and 29 November 1958, 397.

11. Baldwin, *Great Arms Race*, 58, 19; see also Divine, *Sputnik Challenge*, 175–76.

12. Report II, "International Security: The Military Aspect," 6 January 1958, and Report I, "The Mid-Century Challenge to U.S. Foreign Policy," 8 December 1959, both in Rockefeller Brothers Fund, *Prospect for America*, 150, 44–45.

13. Kissinger, *Nuclear Weapons and Foreign Policy*, 123, 312; Kissinger, "Missiles and the Western Alliance," 388–94 and passim; Kissinger, *Necessity for Choice*, 118–21. After the IRBMs' withdrawal, the two Kissingers reconciled by discussing them in neutral terms; see Kissinger, *Troubled Partnership*, 97–98, 103–4.

14. Kaplan, *Wizards of Armageddon*, 144–45.

15. Wohlstetter, "Delicate Balance of Terror," esp. 224–30; Trachtenberg, *History and Strategy*, 20, and broadly 17–25; see also Wohlstetter, "On the Value of Overseas Bases," esp. 4, 5, 8, 14–16. Wohlstetter later reiterated his critique of dual control. See Wohlstetter, "Nuclear Sharing," 372–77. For a mathematical "attempt to formalize" Wohlstetter's argument that likewise disparages the IRBMs, see Ellsberg, "Crude Analysis of Strategic Choices," 472–78.

16. Brodie, *Strategy in the Missile Age*, 342–47; Kahn, *On Thermonuclear War*, 283,

435, 459; see also Hoag, "On NATO Pooling," 478–79; Hoopes, "Overseas Bases," 76–77; Ransom, "NATO Military Strategy," 54; Gordon, "NATO in the Nuclear Age," 329; Rathjens, "NATO Strategy," 78–81; Knorr, "Aspects of NATO Strategy," 321. At least one scholar, although mindful of the IRBMs' drawbacks, deemed them somewhat useful *because* a first-strike capability was useful; see Snyder, *Deterrence and Defense*, 88, 93–94, 110.

17. MCP, 16 August 1960 (drafted 19 August), *FR 1958–60*, 7, pt. 1:612. Although it focuses on the origins of Permissive Action Links, the best account of the JCAE review and tour is Feaver, *Guarding the Guardians*, 172–93; see also Stein and Feaver, *Assuring Control of Nuclear Weapons*, 28–32, and Anderson, *Outsider in the Senate*, 170–73.

18. Larus, *Nuclear Weapons Safety*, 80–83; Feaver, *Guarding the Guardians*, 181–82; Anderson, *Outsider in the Senate*, 171–72; Ad Hoc Subcommittee, JCAE, "The Study of United States and NATO Nuclear Weapons Arrangements," 11 February 1961, courtesy NSA, 32–33 (hereafter cited as "Study of Nuclear Weapons Arrangements"). One RAF officer later recalled a simulated Thor launch in which, as the countdown neared zero and the USAF launch control officer failed to arrive with his key, another RAF officer's "adroit use of a screw-driver in the other key hole enabled the simulated launch to take place." Quoted in Duke, *US Defence Bases*, 233 n. 19.

19. Ramey quoted in Lang, *Inquiry into Enoughness*, 194–95; Transcript, JCAE Executive Session, 20 February 1961, Unclassified Executive Session Hearings, 1960–1961, Records of the JCAE, 1946–1977, RG 128, 72–73; Moss, *Men Who Play God*, 276. One of the IAF Jupiter commanders believed that were IAF launch control personnel to hesitate in the midst of a crisis, USAF officers would shoot them to get their keys. Another Italian officer, asked by a USAF general "if he would be able to fire [his Jupiter] even if he was deranged," lashed out at the general, "saying that his family went back to 1200 AD and there had never been anyone deranged in all those years." Nuti, "L'Italie et les missiles *Jupiter*," 134 n. 45; Leon Johnson, in Kohn and Harahan, *Strategic Air Warfare*, 94.

20. Transcript, JCAE Executive Session, 56, 71–72, 74–75; "Study of Nuclear Weapons Arrangements," 7–8; Feaver, *Guarding the Guardians*, 176.

21. "Study of Nuclear Weapons Arrangements," 35–36; Holifield interview, 107–8; Alan James, "Report on Visit to Jupiter Sites in Italy," 18 September 1961, 1961-Italy-Weapons, box 5, Country and Subject Files Relating to Atomic Energy, 1950–62, Special Assistant for Atomic Energy, LF, RG 59, 2.

22. McNamara testimony, 30 January 1963, HCAS, *Hearings on Military Posture*, 278–79; see also Transcript, JCAE Executive Session, 66, 76–77, and Holifield interview, 106–7.

23. "Study of Nuclear Weapons Arrangements," 30.

24. Ibid., 30–31, 42–44, 52–56, 60–62; McNamara testimony, 30 January 1963, 279; Holifield to JFK, 15 February 1961, Ltrs. to the President, GC, RG 128. At another point in the report, however, the authors wrote that the Italian Jupiters "should be replaced" by more modern systems; they probably meant ultimately, not immediately, since they specifically urged shielding those Jupiters as well. "Study of Nuclear Weapons Arrangements," 43. McNamara read into the public record key portions of the study that censors nonetheless excised when declassifying it in 1992, almost thirty years later. Important paragraphs concerning Turkey, however, remain unavailable. In 1959, a USAF officer had volunteered to Senator Stuart Symington that the Thors were vulnerable to rifle fire. Douglas testimony, 26 May 1959, SCA, Subcommittee, *Department of Defense Appropriations for 1960*, 705.

25. Dwight D. Eisenhower, "Annual Budget Message to the Congress: Fiscal Year 1962," 16 January 1961, *PPP*, 1960, 951; see also Eisenhower, "Annual Message to the Congress on the State of the Union," 12 January 1961, *PPP*, 1960, 918, and "Secretary Gates Answers Questions on National Defense," 10 March 1960, *DSB* 42 (11 April 1960): 557.

26. On the origins of the MLF under Eisenhower, see Winand, *Eisenhower, Kennedy,*

and the United States of Europe, 213–22; Steinbruner, *Cybernetic Theory*, 173–91; and Schwartz, *NATO's Nuclear Dilemmas*, 82–87; on Herter's 1960 MRBM proposal, see *FR 1958–60*, 7, pt. 1:611–83.

27. MCP, 13 January 1961. It is unclear to which "decision to urge" IRBMs on Italy Ike was referring, although he may merely have meant the decision to deploy IRBMs generally.

Chapter Four

1. Gaddis, *Strategies*, 198–99. A good argument for continuity is Nelson, "President Kennedy's National Security Policy." On Kennedy and the Jupiters before the missile crisis, see also Bernstein, "Reconsidering the Cuban Missile Crisis," 60–64.

2. Beschloss, *Crisis Years*, 98–99.

3. John F. Kennedy, "Kennedy Wants U.S. to Sacrifice"; JFK speech, 14 August 1958, interview by John Fischer, 9 December 1959, and speech, 14 June 1960, all in JFK, *Strategy of Peace*, 36, 215–16, preface; JFK speech, 29 February 1960, in *John Fitzgerald Kennedy: A Compilation of Statements and Speeches*, 917.

4. Taylor, *Uncertain Trumpet*, 6. Taylor's ideas meshed neatly with and "helped to shape" Kennedy's views. John F. Kennedy to Taylor, 9 April 1960, Books 4/60, Senate—Legislation 1960, Pre-Presidential Files, JFKL.

5. Analysts from RAND secretly aided Kennedy's presidential campaign, and a draft of Wohlstetter's "Delicate Balance of Terror" formed the basis of his first missile gap speech. Kaplan, *Wizards of Armageddon*, 249–50; Ball, *Politics and Force Levels*, 39–40.

6. *International Affairs* (Moscow) (October 1959): 49–54; *Izvestia* article, 8 February 1961, *CDSP* 13 (8 March 1961): 33; *Baltimore Sun*, 25 February 1961, Box 2, CN; see also Cowles to Rusk, 5 February 1961, *FR 1961–63*, 16:692. For complaints about the IRBMs in general, see also articles in *International Affairs* (Moscow) (July 1960): 17–22, (October 1960): 31, and (November 1960): 58; regarding Italy, see *NYT*, 7 July 1960, 1, and 8 July 1960, 17; *Pravda* article, 17 March 1961, *CDSP* 13 (12 April 1961): 24; and regarding Turkey, *International Affairs* (Moscow) (January 1960): 77–78, (July 1960): 45, (March 1961): 92–93, (April 1961): 94, and (May 1961): 119; *NYT*, 28 May 1961, 8.

7. MemCon, 30 March 1961, folder 11, box DA1, JJMP, 3; Acheson, "Memorandum," 4 April 1961, #410, 1993, *DDRS*, 1 (these may describe the same meeting but differ in content); Khrushchev to JFK, 22 April 1961, *NYT*, 23 April 1961, 25; Beschloss, *Crisis Years*, 131–32.

8. Rusk testimony, 28 February 1961, *ESSFRC* 13, pt. 1:219–20; Schlesinger to JFK, 13 May 1961, *CMC*, attachment, 3; Krock, *Memoirs*, 371; see also Rusk testimony, 1 May 1961 *ESSFRC* 13, pt. 1:349–50. That same year, at least one European drew the Cuba-Turkey analogy as well; see Helmut Schmidt, quoted in Sharp, "Arms Control and the Atlantic Alliance," 31.

9. Quotations from McCloy to Sorensen, 27 April 1961, folder 35, box DA1, JJMP; Bowles to JFK (marked "never sent"), 22 April 1961, Chester Bowles Papers, Yale University Library, New Haven, Conn., 12–13, courtesy Barton Bernstein; see also Rusk testimony, 3 May 1961 *ESSFRC* 13, pt. 1:472–73.

10. Feaver, *Guarding the Guardians*, 191–92; JFK to Holifield, 20 February 1961, Ltrs to Pres (1960–63), GC, RG 128; Anderson, *Outsider in the Senate*, 173; see also Komer to Bundy, 24 February 1961, Staff Memoranda, Robert W. Komer, 1/1/61–3/14/61, MM, NSF. In early 1963, portraying the Jupiter withdrawal then under way as the culmination of an effort begun in 1961, Secretary McNamara testified before the Senate Armed Services Committee that the JCAE report "was the foundation for the action that [the United States has] been taking since that time," although he may have been attempting to shift some of the responsibility for removal onto Congress and to flatter it at the same

time (especially considering McNamara's audience, some of whom also sat on the JCAE). McNamara testimony, 19 and 21 February 1963, SCAS, *Military Procurement Authorization Fiscal Year 1964*, 7–8, 314; McNamara testimony, 30 January 1963, *Hearings on Military Posture*, 278–79, 281, 283; see chapter 6.

11. "A Review of North Atlantic Problems for the Future," [24] March 1961, NATO, NSC-6017 Acheson Report, box 107, Records Relating to State Department Participation in the Operations Coordinating Board and the National Security Council, 1947–63, LF, RG 59, 6, 8, 61–62; Bowles to Hare, 20 April 1961, *FR 1961–63*, 16:695–96.

12. McNamara to Secretaries of the Military Departments et al., 1 March 1961, Defense, 1/61–3/61, Departments and Agencies, POF, attachment; Trewhitt, *McNamara*, 22; Weiss to Bell, 31 March 1961, 740.5/3-3161, DF, RG 59, 1; the only references to McNamara's recommendation are Schlesinger, *Thousand Days*, 807, and *WP*, 25 March 1963, box 14, *CN*. Its date is unknown but was probably March. One of only two or three works McNamara had read on nuclear strategy before taking over at the Pentagon was Wohlstetter's "Delicate Balance of Terror," with its sustained criticism of IRBMs. Herken, *Counsels of War*, 146; see also, however, Ball, *Politics and Force Levels*, 187.

13. George McGhee, interview by Martin J. Hillenbrand, 13 August 1964, OHC, JFKL, 11; "Record of Actions by the National Security Council at Its Four Hundred and Seventy-seventh Meeting held on March 29, 1961" (approved by JFK 5 April), box 313, NSF, 3; Bundy, NSAM 35, "Deployment of IRBM's to Turkey," 6 April 1961, *FR 1961–63*, 16:695. Claims that "Kennedy decided early in his Administration to take the missiles out" or "instructed Rusk to take steps to remove" them are thus incorrect. Dean Rusk, in Blight and Welch, *On the Brink*, 173; Newhouse, *War and Peace*, 178. The Atomic Energy Commission was also "concerned" about the Jupiters. Bowles to JFK, 7 April 1961, #41, *CMC*, attachment, 5; JFK approved the amended Acheson Report as official policy on 21 April (NSAM 40); see "NATO and the Atlantic Nations," 20 April 1961, *FR 1961–63*, 13:285–91; see also Brinkley, *Dean Acheson*, 117–24, and Steinbruner, *Cybernetic Theory*, 202–4.

14. Bowles to Embassies in London and Rome, 20 April 1961, *FR 1961–63*, 16:695–97; Bruce to Rusk, 22 April 1961, and Reinhardt to Rusk, 24 April 1961, both in Turkey, box 160, RPPS 57–61, LF, RG 59; Fessenden to Kohler, 23 May 1961, 782.56311/5-2361, DF, RG 59. One wonders if the Rome embassy did not exaggerate the Italians' attachment to their Jupiters; see below.

15. Norstad to McNamara, Lemnitzer, and Rusk, 25 April 1961, *FR 1961–63*, 16:697–99. Two weeks later, an estimate of savings from cancellation of IBRAHIM II was reduced from $35 million to $16 million, but whether this latter amount was "insignificant" is a matter of taste. Smith to Fessenden et al., 9 May 1961, 40. NATO Standing Group—Weekly Meetings, box 2, Records of the NATO Advisor, 1957–61, RA, EUR, LF, RG 59.

16. Owen to McGhee, 1 May 1961, HO Chron—January–June 1961, box 183, RPPS 57–61, LF, RG 59.

17. Rusk, *As I Saw It*, 239; Rusk to Blight, 25 February 1987, #3322, *CMC*, 1–2; Rusk, in *Presidential Recordings*, Cuban Missile Crisis Meetings, 27 October 1962, POF, 43; Rusk, quoted in Newhouse, *War and Peace*, 178; Bundy, *Danger and Survival*, 433; McGhee interview, 11; Gavin to Rusk, 14 May 1961, *FR 1961–63*, 16:700. Note, however, in addition to the objection based on Turkish funding having just been approved, the different emphasis on the Polaris question in an early interview of Rusk: "[Sarper said] it would be important for us to substitute Polaris submarines . . . if we were not to cause serious morale problems in Turkey." Rusk, interview by Dennis J. O'Brien, 19 February 1970, OHC, JFKL, 1, pt. 3:132. Rusk, along with Paul Nitze, may have tried again with the Turks at the Oslo NATO ministerial meeting, 8–10 May 1961; see Nitze, *Hiroshima to Glasnost*, 233.

18. Department of State, "Soviet Positions on Various Disarmament Questions," 25

May 1961, "President's Meeting with Khrushchev, Vienna, June 3–4, 1961: Briefing Papers," tab I, Vienna Meeting, Background Documents, 1953–61 (G-3) Briefing Material, Background Papers, Countries-USSR, box 126, POF, 7–10, emphasis in original.

19. MemCons, 3 June 1961, luncheon and 3:00 P.M., Vienna Meeting, Memos of Conversations, 6/61 (I), Countries-USSR, box 126, POF, respectively 2 and 3–4.

20. Ibid., 3:00 P.M., 5, 13.

21. Department of State, Daily Staff Summary, 8 June 1961, Daily Staff Summary, 1959–61, Records of the Executive Secretariat, LF, RG 59, 5; MemCon, 13 June 1961, FR 1961–63, 16:702–3; McGhee to Bundy, 22 June 1961, in Chang and Kornbluh, *Cuban Missile Crisis*, 15; see also Nitze, *Hiroshima to Glasnost*, 233. Concern about an unauthorized launch of Turkish Jupiters persisted and continued to fuel efforts to install PALs on alliance nuclear weapons. See Tyler, Talbot, and Morgan to Bowles, 19 July 1961, Turkey, box 142, RPPS 57–61, LF, RG 59, and attachment.

22. Bernstein, "Reconsidering the Cuban Missile Crisis," 62; Lebow and Stein, *We All Lost the Cold War*, 45; Roswell Gilpatric, interview by Dennis J. O'Brien, 30 June 1970, OHC, JFKL, 77; see also Abel, *Missile Crisis*, 192, and Hilsman, *To Move a Nation*, 202. Gilpatric did not specify which of Khrushchev's demands he meant, whether on Berlin, the Jupiters themselves, or both.

23. Bundy, "Presidency and the Peace," 356. For suggestions that the Eisenhower administration alone put the Jupiters in Europe, see Schlesinger, *Thousand Days*, 500, 807, 850; Sorensen, *Kennedy*, 3, 609, 696; Gaddis, *Russia, the Soviet Union, and the United States*, 250–51; and Bundy, in Allyn, Blight, and Welch, *Back to the Brink*, 44; for suggestions that the Kennedy administration did away with the IRBMs just as it did other vulnerable systems, see Sorensen, *Kennedy*, 696 n; Enthoven and Smith, *How Much Is Enough?*, 169; Kahan, *Security in the Nuclear Age*, 97.

24. Kinross, *Ottoman Centuries*, 313–18. I thank Nur Bilge Criss for drawing my attention to Sultan Ibrahim. It is unknown whether it was Turks or Americans who suggested the code name.

25. Brassell, "Jupiter," 70, 73; Orr testimony, 19 February 1962, HCA, Subcommittee, *Department of Defense Appropriations for 1963*, pt. 3, 475; Office of the Historian, HQ SAC, *SAC Missile Chronology*, 34 (hereafter cited as "SAC Missile Chronology"); Kitchen to Rusk and McNamara, 27 December 1961, #125, *CMC*, 5. On the language problem and its possible safety implications, see "Study of Nuclear Weapons Arrangements," 36–37.

26. *NYT*, 21 January 1962, 1, 20; 22 January 1962, 2; 23 January 1962, 7; and 26 January 1962, 2, all in box 8, *CN*.

27. Embassy Rome to DOS, 10 July 1961, 765.56311/7-1061, DF, RG 59; James, "Report on Visit to Jupiter Sites"; Reinhardt to Rusk, 23 April 1962, 765.56311/4-2362, DF, RG 59; Nuti, "L'Italie et les missiles *Jupiter*," 134 n. 41; Reinhardt to Rusk, 22 May 1962, 765.56311/5-2262, DF, RG 59; Intervista di Leopoldo Nuti al generale Giulio Cesare Graziani, M.O., 11 March 1992 (provided and translated by Nuti). James's "Report" is by far the best description available of the Jupiter program in operation.

28. *New York World Telegram*, 8 March 1962, box 8, *CN*; *CSM*, 10 March 1962, 11; MemCon, 12 June 1961, *FR* 1961–63, 13:807–8 (see also MemCon, 17 July 1961, ibid., 13:815); Finletter to Rusk, 30 June 1961, #3442, 1993, *DDRS*, 4; MemCon, 23 March 1962, 11:30 A.M., *FR* 1961–63, 13:836; MemCon, 20 March 1962, 765.5/3-2062, DF, RG 59; File cross-reference sheet re: Finletter to DOS, 19 June 1962, IRBM General (1), PFS, LNP.

29. Reinhardt to Rusk, 26 October 1962, *CMC*, #1463, pt. 1, 2, pt. 2, 1; Rusk to JFK, 9 November 1962, #3161, 1991, *DDRS*, attachment, 3–4; see also Nitze, *Hiroshima to Glasnost*, 220 n. 3. During the missile crisis, McNamara recalled that Andreotti had indicated the Italians "would be happy to get rid of" their Jupiters if the United States so desired. *Presidential Recordings*, 27 October, 39.

30. Replies by Adm. S. G. Gorshkov to correspondent's questions, *Pravda*, 2 February 1962, *CDSP* 14 (28 February 1962): 28; *NYT*, 25 June 1962, 7 (see also Dinerstein, *Making of a Missile Crisis*, 166–68); *Izvestia* articles, 28 May 1961 and 15 July 1961, *CDSP* 13 (21 June 1961): 15, and (9 August 1961): 23; *International Affairs* (Moscow) (September 1962): 93; see also ibid., (October 1962): 45–47.

31. Salinger to JFK, 8 August 1961, Countries, USSR—Security, 6/61–8/61, POF, 2; *WP*, 28 August 1961, A10; Dutton to Fulbright, 10 September 1962, enclosure, "Soviet Public Statements with Respect to Cuban Security," in *ESSFRC* 14: Appendix C, 823 (see also Sulzberger, *Last of the Giants*, 795–96, 802); Dobrynin, *In Confidence*, 52. On Khrushchev and capitalist encirclement, see Rubinstein, *Foreign Policy of the Soviet Union*, 14.

32. Luvie Moore Pearson, "My 36 Hours with Khrushchev," *Saturday Evening Post*, 7 April 1962, 72; Alexei Adzhubei, interview, in British Broadcasting Corporation, *Cuban Missile Crisis*, pt. 1, "Defying Uncle Sam."

33. Burlatsky, in Allyn, Blight, and Welch, *Back to the Brink*, 46; Lebow and Stein, *We All Lost the Cold War*, 72–73, 411–12 n. 49, see also 86, 90; Khrushchev speech at Varna, 16 May 1962, *Pravda*, 17 May, *CDSP* 14 (13 June 1962): 3; see also Gribkov and Smith, *Operation ANADYR*, 12.

34. Szulc, *Fidel*, 645; Jorge Risquet in Allyn, Blight, and Welch, *Back to the Brink*, 70; Castro quoted in Schlesinger, "Four Days with Fidel," 24; see also Lockwood, *Castro's Cuba, Cuba's Fidel*, 224. On Castro's decision to accept the Soviet missiles, see Brenner, "Thirteen Months"; Lebow and Stein, *We All Lost the Cold War*, 74–77; Blight, Allyn, and Welch, *Cuba On the Brink*, 344–48.

35. Khrushchev, *Khrushchev Remembers: The Glasnost Tapes*, 174, also 175; Khrushchev, *Khrushchev Remembers*, 494, also 493; Lebow and Stein, *We All Lost the Cold War*, 77–78; Sergo Mikoyan, in Blight and Welch, *On the Brink*, 238; see also Dobrynin, *In Confidence*, 72; Garthoff, *Reflections on the Cuban Missile Crisis*, 15; and Beschloss, *Crisis Years*, 557 n. The best discussion of Khrushchev's decision is Lebow and Stein, *We All Lost the Cold War*, 67–93; see also Beschloss, *Crisis Years*, 370–93, Zubok and Pleshakov, *Inside the Kremlin's Cold War*, 258–61, and Garthoff, *Reflections on the Cuban Missile Crisis*, 6–42. The wonderment of some over Khrushchev's intention to use MRBMs and IRBMs to defend Cuba is itself rather puzzling. Reliance on nuclear weapons capable of reaching the other superpower's own territory to deter a conventional attack against a client state had long been central to U.S. defense measures in Europe (including the NATO IRBMs); see Allison, *Essence of Decision*, 49, and Schlesinger, *Robert Kennedy*, 542–43; on this peculiarity, see Hershberg, "Before 'The Missiles of October,'" 278 n. 116.

36. "Extracts from GAO Draft Report on the THOR Program," 27 January 1961, 1961—United Kingdom—Weapons, box 5, Country and Subject Files Relating to Atomic Energy, 1950–62, Special Assistant for Atomic Energy, LF; Barbour to Rusk, 21 January 1961, 741.56311/1-2161, DF; Rusk to Barbour, 26 January 1961, 741.56311/1-2161, DF; and Rusk to Barbour, 3 February 1961, 741.56311/1-2761, DF, all in RG 59.

37. *Hansard* 652 (31 January 1962): 1073–74; *Times* (London), 31 January 1962, 10; *NYT*, 24 February 1962, 2; for earlier opposition criticism, see *Hansard* 622 (4 May 1960): 1076–77; 624 (25 May 1960): 418–19; and 640 (17 May 1961): 1366–67.

38. Lemnitzer to McNamara, 2 January 1962, CCS 9163/4720 British Isles (UK) (4 Dec. 1961) sec. 1, box 176, CDF 1961, RG 218; McNamara testimony, 24 January 1962, HCAS, *Hearings on Military Posture and H.R. 9751*, 3228, and 29 January 1962, HCA, Subcommittee, *Department of Defense Appropriations for 1963*, 92–93; DOS, "Prime Minister Macmillan's Visit to Washington, April 27–29, 1962: NATO Strategy (Including Major Nuclear Problems)," 21 April 1962, Macmillan's Visit to Washington, 1962, April 27–29, box 42, Records of Component Offices of the Bureau of European Affairs, 1944–1962, LF, RG 59, 4; Gavin to Rusk, 19 March 1962, IRBM General (1), PFS, LNP.

39. *SAC Missile Chronology*, 34; *Hansard* 664 (1 August 1962): 557; "The President's

News Conference of August 1, 1962," *PPP* 1962, 592; on the British side of the Thor discontinuation, see Clark, *Nuclear Diplomacy*, 234–37.

40. *WP*, 31 July 1962, 15; ibid., 1 and 2 August 1962, *Aviation Daily*, 1 August 1962, and *CSM*, 1 and 4 August 1962, all in box 10, *CN*. The rumors, spawned in Paris, were fed in part by the announced reshuffling of senior U.S. military personnel: Norstad, associated with NATO's heavy reliance on nuclear weapons, was to retire; JCS chair Lemnitzer was to replace him as SACEUR; and Maxwell Taylor, champion of Flexible Response, was to replace Lemnitzer. Department of Defense officials, quite reasonably, suspected the French of spreading the rumors to help justify their independent deterrent.

41. Lebow and Stein, *We All Lost the Cold War*, 45; Abel, *Missile Crisis*, 192–93; Hilsman, *To Move a Nation*, 202–3; see also Bundy, *Danger and Survival*, 428–29, and Ball, *Past Has Another Pattern*, 306, 500–502 n. 2, which relies on the work of Bernstein and Chayes in supporting this version.

42. MemCon, 21 August 1962, 12:00 P.M., and MCP, 23 August 1962, both in *CIADCMC*, 22, 28.

43. Bundy, NSAM 181, 23 August 1962, in Chang and Kornbluh, *Cuban Missile Crisis*, 61 (this, Bundy's copy of the document, has "Nitze" handwritten in the margin next to No. 1, to whom responsibility for the item was presumably given); for reference to an August "order," see O'Donnell, *"Johnny, We Hardly Knew Ye,"* 337, Hilsman, *To Move a Nation*, 203, and Abel, *Missile Crisis*, 193; for reference to the NSAM as an order, see Abel, *Missile Crisis*, 193, and Allison, *Essence of Decision*, 141–42. It is also worth noting that during the missile crisis, Kennedy's only references to the Jupiters in a pre-crisis context contain no mention of an "order." Rather, he said, "We *tried* last year to get the missiles out of there," and the minutes of a different point in the discussions read, "The President recalled that over a year ago we *wanted* to get the Jupiter missiles out of Turkey." Again, one would expect reference here to an order had Kennedy issued one. *Presidential Recordings*, 27 October 1962, 2–3, emphasis mine; MemCon, 27 October 1962, 10:00 A.M., ExComm Meetings, box 316, NSF, 4, emphasis mine.

44. NSAM 181, 62; Bernstein, "Reconsidering the Cuban Missile Crisis," 64, 111 n. 35; York, *Race to Oblivion*, 101.

45. Bundy to JFK, 31 August 1962, NSAM 181 Cuba (A) 8/23/62, MM, box 338, NSF, 2; Rostow to JFK, 3 September 1962, attachment, in Chang and Kornbluh, *Cuban Missile Crisis*, 69, see also 70.

46. JFK statement, 4 September 1962, and TASS statement, 11 September 1962, both in Larson, *"Cuban Crisis"* of 1962, 3, 14, see also 13; Rusk testimony, 17 September 1962, *ESSFRC* 14:762–63; Roberts, *First Rough Draft*, 203; "Secretary Discusses Cuban Situation on 'News and Comment' Program," aired on ABC 30 September 1962, *DSB* 47 (22 October 1962): 598; see also Hilsman to Rusk, 1 September 1962, NSAM 181 Cuba (B) 9/62, MM, box 338, NSF, 4. For invocation of the Cuban analogy in connection with Soviet concern over missiles in Iran, see Komer to Bundy, 14 September 1962, *FR* 1961–63, 18:97–98; for a Turkish rejection of the analogy during this period, see MemCon, 1 October 1962 (drafted 2 October), 601.8211/10-162, DF, RG 59, 2. On 6 September, Khrushchev again complained to a guest, this time Kennedy's secretary of the interior, Stewart Udall, about U.S. military bases surrounding the USSR. "Now as to Cuba," the premier remarked in the same conversation, "—here is an area that could really lead to some unexpected consequences." MemCon, 6 September 1962, 1:00 P.M., #363, *CMC*, 9.

47. Although Bernstein first convincingly refuted it in 1980 with his "Cuban Missile Crisis: Trading the Jupiters in Turkey?" and although numerous subsequent works are accurate on this point, the removal-order myth has led a robust afterlife. See, for examples only from the last decade, Cohen, "Why We Should Stop Studying the Cuban Missile Crisis," 4; Medland, *Cuban Missile Crisis*, 58 n. 30; Ferrell, *American Diplomacy*, 337–38; Salinger, "Gaps in the Cuban Missile Crisis Story"; Falcoff, "Learning to Love

the Missile Crisis," 67; Hilsman, *Politics of Policy Making*, 4, 58, 136; Sherwood, *Allies in Crisis*, 117; Raskin, *Essays of a Citizen*, 113; Brugioni, *Eyeball to Eyeball*, 466–67; and Powaski, *Entangling Alliance*, 65. Ironically, one of the first exponents of the removal-order story, Walt Rostow, also provided the first published account casting doubt on it; see Walt W. Rostow, interview by Richard Neustadt, 11 April 1964, OHC, JFKL, 106; Rostow, *Diffusion of Power*, 663 n. 21, also 258. Another early believer was Llewellyn Thompson; see interview by Elizabeth Donahue, 25 March 1964, OHC, JFKL, 12. On the possibility of withdrawing the warheads, compare Bundy, *Danger and Survival*, 435.

48. Abel, *Missile Crisis*, 193; RFK, *Thirteen Days*, 95; these two accounts, virtually identical, seem to stem from RFK's notes.

49. Fessenden to Kohler, 23 May 1961.

50. McGhee to Rusk, 20 April 1961, Owen, H., Chron, box 204, attachment, 2, and Morgan to Rusk, 26 May 1961, Turkey, box 142, both in RPPS 57–61, RG 59; Nalle to DOS, 9 August 1962, 782.56311/8-962, DF, RG 59; JFK, "Address before the Canadian Parliament in Ottawa," 17 May 1961, *PPP 1961*, 385. One must also be careful to draw temporal distinctions: cancellation of the Turkish deployment before base construction had actually begun (spring 1961) would have been far easier than when construction was already under way (1961–62), which in turn would have been easier than withdrawal of the missiles after construction was complete (spring 1962). Cancellation and then removal became increasingly difficult over time, and to the extent that Kennedy missed an opportunity, it presented itself in spring 1961. In the Italian case, by contrast, the U.S. prospects of securing the Jupiters' removal gradually improved over the 1961–62 period.

51. *Newsweek*, 29 October 1962, 15; Kohler to Rusk, 16 October 1962, tel. 970, 1, and tel. 978, 2, both courtesy Bernstein. Neither these nor the other four cables reporting the conversation (tels. 973, 974, and 977, courtesy Bernstein, and 981, in *FR 1961–63*, 15:359–62) contain any specific reference by Khrushchev to Jupiter missiles, unlike the best secondary account, Beschloss, *Crisis Years*, 8–9, 438–39; see also Sorensen, *Kennedy*, 691. Garthoff, in *Reflections on the Cuban Missile Crisis*, 60, also 28 n. 46, does not support his contention that the transfer of the first launch position to Turkish control on 22 October "explains" why Khrushchev raised the Jupiter issue with Kohler on the 16th.

Chapter Five

1. Gromyko quoted in Rusk, *As I Saw It*, 360; this was his version of "eyeball to eyeball," which he produced in a toast some time after October 1962. We still lack a credible, comprehensive history of the missile crisis that makes full use of primary sources. The best studies are Beschloss, *Crisis Years*, 431–568; Nathan, *Cuban Missile Crisis Revisited*; and White, *Cuban Missile Crisis*; see also Lebow and Stein, *We All Lost the Cold War*, 19–145 and 291–376 passim. The only recent examinations of the Jupiters in the missile crisis are Bernstein, "Reconsidering the Cuban Missile Crisis"; its precursor, the path-breaking "Cuban Missile Crisis: Trading the Jupiters in Turkey?"; and my own "Nuisance of Decision," from which I have drawn portions of this chapter. For a brief acknowledgment of the Jupiters' importance in the crisis, see Bird, *The Chairman*, 734 n. 18.

2. *Presidential Recordings, Transcripts*, Cuban Missile Crisis Meetings, "Off-the-Record Meeting on Cuba," 16 October 1962, 11:50–12:57 P.M. (midday), POF, 21; ibid., 6:30–7:55 P.M. (evening), 26, emphasis in original. ExComm was not formally inaugurated until 23 October. If JFK momentarily lost track of the IRBMs, he was not the first to have done so; in 1961, McGeorge Bundy had referred to "the longest range ballistic missiles already committed for NATO deployment, i.e., Pershings." During the crisis, Kennedy may have believed the Jupiters had been deployed before he entered office; he was quoted as saying on 20 October that the Turkish missiles "should have been taken out of there back in the Eisenhower administration." By "five years ago" he may have

meant the 1957 NATO decision to deploy, and he may have been confusing decision and execution. Bundy to Rusk et al., 7 July 1961, *FR 1961–63*, 14:177; O'Donnell, *"Johnny, We Hardly Knew Ye,"* 324.

3. Sorensen memorandum, 17 October 1962, Chang and Kornbluh, *Cuban Missile Crisis*, 114. The Soviets planned to deploy thirty-six SS-4 MRBMs (1,020-mile range) with thirty-six warheads but only twenty-four launchers, and twenty-four SS-5 IRBMs (2,200-mile range) with twenty warheads but only sixteen launchers. They also sent six practice SS-4 missiles and four practice SS-5s. All forty-two SS-4s, the twenty-four SS-4 launchers—all of which had achieved operational status by 28 October—and all sixty SS-4 and SS-5 warheads reached Cuba before establishment of the U.S. blockade. None of the SS-5 missiles did. Lebow and Stein, *We All Lost the Cold War*, 76; Gribkov and Smith, *Operation ANADYR*, 45–46.

4. Thomas C. Sorensen, "Information Policy Guidance on Cuba," 21 October 1962, Cuba-Subjects, GHI, box 48, CSF, TCSP, 3, emphasis in original. Thomas Sorensen, Ted's brother, was USIA deputy director (Policy and Plans).

5. Allyn, Blight, and Welch, "Essence of Revision," 144 n. 22.

6. *Presidential Recordings*, 16 October, midday, 14, 15; MemCon, 17 October 1962, 8:30 A.M., McCone, "Memorandum for Discussion Today," 17 October 1962, and Mem-Con, 17 October 1962, 8:30 A.M. and 4:00 P.M. (drafted 19 October), all in *CIADCMC*, 160, 162, 170; see also Bohlen, "Possible Soviet Reactions to the Following Alternatives," 17 October 1962, Countries-Cuba, Cuba-Security 1962, box 115, POF. On the 16th one adviser, perhaps George Ball, suggested that the Cuban move might be a "trading ploy" for Berlin. *Presidential Recordings*, 16 October, evening, 26–27. On 20 September, McCone had speculated that the Soviets might install missiles in Cuba in order to gain a "most important and effective trading position in connection with all other critical areas." McCone memorandum, "Soviet MRBMs in Cuba," 31 October 1962, in *CIADCMC*, 16.

7. *Presidential Recordings*, 16 October, midday, 21, and evening, 50 (the transcriber supposed the speaker to be Roswell Gilpatric); MemCon, 17 October 1962, 8:30 A.M. and 4:00 P.M., 172; n.a. [Llewellyn Thompson], memorandum, 19 October 1962, *CIADCMC*, 195; see also Bohlen to Rusk, 18 October 1962, reprinted in Bohlen, *Witness to History*, 491.

8. Central Intelligence Agency Information Report, "Soviet Threats of Retaliation," 23 October 1962, #41, 1990, *DDRS*; McCone to USIB Members, 19 October 1962, *CIADCMC*, 194; I. M. Tobin, "Attempts to Equate Soviet Missile Bases in Cuba with NATO Jupiter Bases in Italy and Turkey," 10 October 1962, Countries-Cuba, box 36, JFKL, 1, 3; *Presidential Recordings*, 27 October, 67. Blight and Welch cite JFK's 16 October comment in arguing that he "*missed* the symmetry" of the Cuban and Turkish deployments. *On the Brink*, 365 n. 70, emphasis mine.

9. Sorensen draft, 18 October 1962, Cuba-General, box 48, CSF, TCSP, JFKL, 2; Mem-Con, 26 October 1962, 10:00 A.M., Chang and Kornbluh, *Cuban Missile Crisis*, 181–82.

10. Tobin, "Attempts to Equate Soviet Missile Bases," 1; Frank A. Sieverts, "The Cuban Crisis, 1962," [August] 1963, #1910, 1993, *DDRS*, 50. Sieverts was special assistant to the assistant secretary of state for public affairs. Although helpful, his report is somewhat unreliable and should be used cautiously.

11. Tobin, "Attempts to Equate Soviet Missile Bases," 1; official replies to reporters' questions, *CSM*, 25 October 1962, 1; Thomas Sorensen, "Information Policy Guidance on Cuba," 3; MemCon, 22 October 1962, 5:00 P.M. (drafted 24 October), *CIADCMC*, 277. Bundy also drew the offensive-defensive distinction privately; see *Presidential Recordings*, 16 October, midday, 15.

12. Kelley, *First Book of Timothy*, 7; JFK, "Radio and Television Report to the American People on the Soviet Arms Buildup in Cuba," 22 October 1962, *PPP 1962*, 807; Tobin, "Attempts to Equate Soviet Missile Bases," 3; Sorensen and Bundy in Allyn, Blight, and Welch, *Back to the Brink*, 20; Sorensen, in Blight and Welch, *On the Brink*, 246; Gart-

hoff, *Reflections on the Cuban Missile Crisis*, 24. Sorensen and Ball claim that the Soviet secrecy and deception were an actual motive behind Kennedy's response, rather than a mere justification. "Now we know where we stand with these people," one ExComm member commented on the duplicity after the crisis, obviously embellishing for the interviewer's benefit. "They're gangsters—and you can't trust a word they say." Sorensen in Allyn, Blight, and Welch, *Back to the Brink*, 19; Ball in HCT, 12; anonymous ExComm member quoted in Alsop and Bartlett, "In Time of Crisis," 19; see also Sorensen, *Kennedy*, 683.

13. JFK, quoted in Salinger, *With Kennedy*, 328–29; "Background Briefing on Cuban Situation," 22 October 1962, 8:00 P.M., *Public Statements of Secretary of Defense Robert S. McNamara, 1962*, JFKL, 4:1877, also 1884; see also Rusk Circular 743, 24 October 1962, Planning Subcommittee, 10/62–11/62, Cuba-General, Countries, NSF; Stevenson statement before the United Nations Security Council, 23 October 1962, 4:00 P.M., in Johnson, *Ambassador*, 316, 319–20; *WP*, 24 October 1962, A23. McNamara misspoke, technically; the United States had *not* "armed the Turks and Italians with certain nuclear weapons."

14. Allyn, Blight, and Welch, "Essence of Revision," 144 n. 22, 147; see also Blight and Welch, *On the Brink*, 356 n. 30; Lebow and Stein, *We All Lost the Cold War*, 417 n. 96. If one counts the thirty Italian Jupiters or the sixty British Thors, however, the NATO and Cuban deployments were more comparable in size. Although Allyn, Blight, and Welch claim the symmetry was "far from obvious" to ExComm members, Welch and Blight conceded in 1987 that the "symmetry did not go unnoticed." And, while there was a "compelling superficial symmetry" between Cuba and Turkey, they added, an "important asymmetry . . . [was] that the Jupiters were in Turkey under a treaty of mutual defense, whereas no such treaty obligation existed between Cuba and the Soviet Union." Welch and Blight, "Eleventh Hour," 13, 13 n. 19. Why this asymmetry was "important," they do not say.

15. Betts, *Nuclear Blackmail*, 113–14; Chayes in Blight and Welch, *On the Brink*, 40, emphasis in original.

16. Some ExComm veterans have recently acknowledged that precrisis Soviet and Cuban fears of an invasion were legitimate; see McNamara in Blight and Welch, *On the Brink*, 250, Allyn, Blight, and Welch, *Back to the Brink*, 7, and Bundy, *Danger and Survival*, 416.

17. *NYT*, 26 October 1962, 17, and 29 October 1962, 14; Richard M. Montgomery, interview by Mark C. Cleary, 28 and 30 June 1983, K239.0512-1526, USAFOHP, AFHRC, 229; Truman H. Landon, interview by Hugh N. Ahmann, 31 May–3 June 1977, K239.0512-949, USAFOHP, AFHRC, 488–89; for a sense of the Turkish concern for secrecy, see Hare to Rusk, 19 January 1962, *FR 1961–63*, 16:722, and Hare to Rusk, 2 October 1962, 782.5/10-262, DF, RG 59.

18. Stimson quoted in Treverton, *Covert Action*, 11.

19. Feaver, *Guarding the Guardians*, 192–93, 193 n. 51; Gilpatric to CJCS, 18 September 1962, CCS 4615 Use of Custody (11 Jan 1961) sec. 8, JCS 1961, RG 218; Sagan, *Limits of Safety*, 109 n. 160; McNamara, in Blight and Welch, *On the Brink*, 56; see also, however, Hansen, *U.S. Nuclear Weapons*, 197. For one indication that the warheads remained mounted throughout the crisis, see "Message to the North American [*sic*] Council and the Governments of all NATO Countries," n.d. [27 October 1962], Subjects-NATO, General, 4/62–11/63, box 103, POF, 3.

20. *Time*, 2 November 1962, 35; Sagan, *Limits of Safety*, 103–6; *Presidential Recordings* (cassette 32.2), 22 October 1962, 11:45 A.M., JFKL. On predelegation, see Rosenberg, "Nuclear War Planning," esp. 172; for an explanation of the DEFCON system, see Sagan, *Limits of Safety*, 64–65. Any Soviet aircraft headed for the Jupiters would have been detected by NATO radar, but they would have met spotty antiaircraft missile defenses and "no late model air defense planes"; see Polk to Rostow and Owen, 22 October 1962, Polk, W. R., Chronology, box 233, RPPS 1962, LF, RG 59.

21. Sieverts, "Cuban Crisis," 89, 110; Historical Division, Joint Secretariat, JCS, "Chro-

nology of JCS Decisions Concerning the Cuban Crisis," 21 December 1962, reprinted in Gribkov and Smith, *Operation ANADYR*, 215. Between early 24 October and early 26 October, thirty-seven of the forty-five Jupiters, that is, at least seven of fifteen in Turkey, were on alert. JCS to Rusk, 24, 25, and 26 October, respectively 611.3722/10-2462, DF, RG 59, pt. 3, 2; Cables 10/25/62 pt. 1, Countries-Cuba, box 41, NSF, pt. 4, 2; and 611.3722/10-2462, DF, RG 59, pt. 2, 2.

22. Untitled document, n.d. [22 October], NATO-Weapons, Cables-Turkey, box 226, RSF, NSF, emphasis added; *Presidential Recordings*, 27 October, 55, emphasis in original; compare Bernstein, "Reconsidering the Cuban Missile Crisis," 90. President Kennedy actually read *Fail-Safe*—published in October 1962—probably just after the crisis; we do not know what he thought of it. Sulzberger, *Last of the Giants*, 935.

23. Robert F. Kennedy, *Thirteen Days*, 108–9.

24. White, *Cuban Missile Crisis*, 121; Stevenson to JFK, 17 October 1962, in Chang and Kornbluh, *Cuban Missile Crisis*, 119–20, emphasis in original; Sorensen memorandum, 17 October, 114. Kennedy found Stevenson's memo annoyingly contradictory; he asked Sorensen, "Tell me which side he is on?" Sorensen, *Kennedy*, 695; Sorensen, interview by John B. Martin, October 1966, box 2, JBMFAES, 5. On U.S. discussion of a trade, see also Bernstein, "Reconsidering the Cuban Missile Crisis," 71–79, 83–96.

25. Sieverts, "Cuban Crisis," 46; *Presidential Recordings* (cassette 30A.1), 18 October 1962, 11:00 A.M., JFKL; MemCon, 18 October 1962, 11:00 A.M. (drafted 19 October), *CIADCMC*, 184–85; Sorensen draft, 18 October, 1–2.

26. Gromyko to Central Committee, CPSU, 20 October 1962, in *CWIHP Bulletin*, no. 5 (Spring 1995): 67–68; see also MemCon, 18 October 1962, *FR 1961–63*, 15:385. On the JFK-Gromyko meeting, see Beschloss, *Crisis Years*, 455–57; Gromyko MemCon, 18 October 1962 (drafted 20 October), in *International Affairs* (Moscow) (October 1993): 75–79; and MemCon, 18 October 1962, 5:00 P.M., *FR 1961–63*, 15:370–76.

27. MemCon, 19 October 1962, 11:00 A.M., Chang and Kornbluh, *Cuban Missile Crisis*, 126. In fact, the previous day, when JFK speculated that Khrushchev would threaten to take Berlin in response to an attack on Cuba, McNamara "surmised perhaps that was the price [the United States] must pay and perhaps [it would] lose Berlin anyway." MemCon, 18 October 1962, 11:00 A.M., 185.

28. MemCon, NSC meeting, 2:30–5:10 P.M., 20 October 1962, portions quoted in Schlesinger, *Robert Kennedy*, 515, and in Bernstein, "Reconsidering the Cuban Missile Crisis," 73; Bernstein, ibid., 72–73; Nitze, *Hiroshima to Glasnost*, 227; Schlesinger, *Robert Kennedy*, 515; Sieverts, "Cuban Crisis," 75; Sorensen, *Kennedy*, 696; Martin, *Adlai Stevenson*, 722–24; see also Stevenson, "Political Program to Be Announced by the President," 20 October 1962, Johnson, *Ambassador*, 301–2. The hawkish advisers who attacked Stevenson and opposed a missile trade—but who perhaps were unwilling to voice that opposition fully when anyone else, especially the president, spoke of a trade—may have seized the moment as a uniquely safe opportunity to cut loose. Robert Kennedy recalled that "Guantánamo was more responsible for Stevenson's reputation as a dove than was his proposal about the Turkish bases." RFK, interview by John B. Martin, 7 December 1966, box 1, JBMFAES, SGML, 5.

29. Stevenson memo, n.d. [21 October 1962], Johnson, *Ambassador*, 303–6 (this proposal may actually have been commissioned by ExComm; see Martin, *Adlai Stevenson*, 724); Sieverts, "Cuban Crisis," 69; Chayes, *Cuban Missile Crisis*, 81–82, 95; Doodle transcript, KP-156, 1962, box 42, Doodles, Personal Papers, John F. Kennedy Papers, JFKL. This virtual consensus may explain McCone's 27 October reference to a trade: "We sat for a week, and everybody was in favor of it." At one point during 20–21 October, Stevenson did advocate an air strike. Further testimony to the widespread consideration of a trade at this point is the Joint Chiefs' submission of a (still classified) memo on 21 October exploring the implications of a trade. *Presidential Recordings*, 27 October, 57; Burris to

LBJ, 21 October 1962, #524, 1993, *DDRS*, 1; Records Transmittal Sheet, DOD "Sensitive Records on Cuba," 20 October 1970, courtesy CWIHP, 21.

30. Schlesinger journal, quoted in Schlesinger, *Robert Kennedy*, 516 (see also Schlesinger, *Thousand Days*, 811); Harriman, "Memorandum on Kremlin Reactions"; Sorensen, "Synopsis of President's Speech," n.d. [ca. 22 October 1962], #772, *CMC*, 3.

31. MemCon, 507th NSC meeting, 22 October 1962, 3:00 P.M., NSC Meetings, 1962, MM, box 313, NSF, 1, 4; Sieverts, "Cuban Crisis," 97; Ormsby-Gore to Macmillan, 23 October 1962.

32. Sieverts, "Cuban Crisis," 125–26; Rusk to JFK, 26 October 1962, Countries-Cuba, box 36, NSF, 3–4.

33. Rostow to Rusk et al., "Negotiations about Cuba," 25 October 1962, Countries-Cuba, General, box 36, NSF, 2; Rusk to Embassy Ankara et al., 25 October 1962, Cables 10/25/62, pt. 2, Countries-Cuba, box 41, NSF; Nitze Debrief of 3 Meetings re: Cuba (#15), 25 October 1962, NASD, LMP, 2; Klein to Bundy, 25 October 1962, Staff Memoranda, David Klein 8/3/62–8/29/63, MM, box 321, NSF; Dillon group discussion paper, "Scenario for Airstrike against Offensive Missile Bases and Bombers in Cuba," 25 October 1962, in Chang and Kornbluh, *Cuban Missile Crisis*, 168; Dean to Foreign Office, 25 October 1962, quoted in White, *Cuban Missile Crisis*, 203.

34. MemCon, 26 October, 10:00 A.M., 181, 182; Bird, *The Chairman*, 529; see also Rusk, *As I Saw It*, 240.

35. Sieverts, "Cuban Crisis," 178–79, emphasis in original; see also Hilsman to Rusk, "Implications of the Soviet Initiative on Cuba," 27 October 1962, 10/26/62–11/1/62, GHI, Cuba-Subjects, box 48, CSF, TCSP, 3; Bernstein, "Reconsidering the Cuban Missile Crisis," 118 n. 103; Abel, *Missile Crisis*, 185.

36. Khrushchev to JFK, 27 October 1962, in Chang and Kornbluh, *Cuban Missile Crisis*, 197–99; Porter to Rusk, 26 October 1962, #1458, *CMC*; *Manchester Guardian*, 24 and 23 October 1962, quoted in, respectively, Detzer, *The Brink*, 203, and Schlesinger, *Thousand Days*, 816; *WP*, 23 October 1962, A17, and 25 October 1962, A25; Steel, *Walter Lippmann*, 534–36; see also the cartoon in *Punch*, 17 October 1962, 547.

37. *NYT*, 24 October 1962, 1, 20, and 25 October 1962, 20; Lebow and Stein, *We All Lost the Cold War*, 133–34. A reader also proposed a trade in his letter to the editor, and columnist James Reston wrote that after a U.S. attack on Cuba, the Soviets might invoke the analogy and arrange a deal through the UN (both in *NYT*, 24 October 1962, 38).

38. Malinovsky quoted in *Newsweek*, 12 November 1962, 26; Hilsman to Rusk, 26 October 1962, #254, 1983, *DDRS*; NIC, "The Soviet Bloc Armed Forces and the Cuban Crisis: A Chronology: July–November 1962," 18 June 1963, #3130, *CMC*, 63. On 27 October, *Red Star* repeated its demand (indeed, broadened to *all* U.S. bases around the USSR)—in an article written, obviously, the previous day, at which point Khrushchev had been asking only for a no-invasion pledge. Garthoff, *Reflections on the Cuban Missile Crisis*, 75.

39. Scali to Rusk, 27 October 1962, quoted in Salinger, *With Kennedy*, 345; Beschloss, *Crisis Years*, 529–30; Steel, *Walter Lippmann*, 535. In his discussions with Castro soon after the crisis, Mikoyan implied that the Lippmann article was an indication of U.S. interest in a trade, but this was in the context of an attempt to assure the Cubans that the trade idea was first advanced by the United States; Mikoyan, understandably, was trying to downplay the extent to which the Soviet Union had acted in its own narrow interest. MemCon, 4 November 1962, in *CWIHP Bulletin*, no. 5 (Spring 1995): 98. Just after the crisis, Scali explained to Fomin, "Everything Mr. Lippmann writes does not come straight from the White House." Scali to Rusk, 29 October 1962, quoted in Salinger, *With Kennedy*, 347. On the Scali-Fomin meetings, see Fursenko and Naftali, "Using KGB Documents," 58, 60–62.

40. *Presidential Recordings*, 27 October, 6, 11, 62, 65; Troyanovski, "Caribbean Crisis,"

153; Lebow and Stein, *We All Lost the Cold War*, 134–35; Beschloss, *Crisis Years*, 526; see also Aleksandr Alekseev in Allyn, Blight, and Welch, *Back to the Brink*, 13.

41. *Presidential Recordings*, 27 October, 3, 4, 5, 11, 13, 6, see also 9; MemCon, 27 October, 10:00 A.M., 4. The 27 October audio tape transcript encompasses all three ExComm meetings held that day; pages 1–13 are from the 10:00 A.M. meeting (although these do not cover the latter part of the meeting, for which see MemCon, 27 October 1962, 10:00 A.M., 4–5), pages 14–67 from the 4:00 P.M. meeting, and pages 68–82 from the 9:00 P.M. meeting. On page 20, transcriber McGeorge Bundy writes that he chose not to transcribe thiry minutes of discussion at that juncture because "the President was not present" (for those thirty minutes, see MemCon, 27 October 1962, 4:00 P.M., ExComm Meetings, box 316, NSF, 2). On pages 58–64, however, Bundy did transcribe discussion held in JFK's absence.

42. *Presidential Recordings*, 27 October, 10–11, emphasis in original; MemCon, 27 October, 10:00 A.M., 5.

43. Abel, *Missile Crisis*, 196–97; Gilpatric, interview by O'Brien, 52. Gilpatric may have already been working on this scenario late on 26 October. Interview by O'Brien, 52.

44. *Presidential Recordings*, 27 October, 27, 31, 43; see also 15, 19, 25, 28, and 67, as well as MemCon, 27 October, 10:00 A.M., 4–5.

45. *Presidential Recordings*, 27 October, 19, 22, 24, 26, 56; MemCon, 27 October, 4:00 P.M., 2. Departing JCS chair Lyman Lemnitzer met with JFK at 5:00 P.M. and argued that the Jupiters were "a NATO—not a U.S.—matter." The ExComm subcommittee on Berlin (one of three subcommittees), headed by Paul Nitze, had agreed at its 11:00 A.M. meeting that "the door should be closed as quickly as possible" on the idea of a trade. Lemnitzer quoted in Brugioni, *Eyeball to Eyeball*, 471; Berlin subcommittee, Record of Meeting No. 4, 27 October 1962, #1545, *CMC*.

46. *Presidential Recordings*, 27 October, 23, 50, 55, 52, emphasis in original (see also 26, 53, 54–55; MemCon, 27 October, 4:00 P.M., 2); McCone MemCon, 21 October 1962, 8:30 P.M. (drafted 22 October), *CIADCMC*, 245.

47. *Presidential Recordings*, 27 October, 36, 63, 64–65, see also 44; RFK, *Thirteen Days*, 101–2; JFK to Khrushchev, 27 October 1962, in Chang and Kornbluh, *Cuban Missile Crisis*, 223–25. The Trollope ploy was named for the author Anthony Trollope, in whose books a wishful woman would interpret a handshake as a marriage proposal.

48. Rusk quoted in Ghent, "Canada, the United States, and the Cuban Missile Crisis," 182. On the consultation issue, see Costigliola, "Kennedy, the European Allies, and the Failure to Consult."

49. Hare to Rusk, 23 October 1962 (tel. 578), NATO-Weapons, Cables-Turkey, box 226, RSF, NSF; Hare to Rusk, 24 October 1962, #1260, *CMC*; *Time*, 9 November 1962, 27; Garthoff, *Reflections on the Cuban Missile Crisis*, 79; see also NIC, "Soviet Bloc Armed Forces," 63. For a similar example of Soviet-Turkish "diplomacy," see Hare to Rusk, 27 October 1962, 661.82/10-2762, DF, RG 59.

50. Joint Chiefs of Staff to Rusk, 25 October 1962, pt. 1, 2; Hare to Rusk, 23 October 1962 (tel. 576), and Rusk to Embassy Ankara, 25 October 1962 (tel. 448), both in NATO-Weapons, Cables-Turkey, box 226, RSF, NSF, 1; Wiebes and Zeeman, " 'I Don't Need Your Handkerchiefs,' " 98.

51. Rusk to Hare and Finletter, 24 October 1962, NATO-Weapons, Cables-Turkey, box 226, RSF, NSF. Rusk's cable to Reinhardt is unavailable.

52. Reinhardt to Rusk, 26 October 1962. The Italian government might also, Reinhardt speculated, "find attractive" a chance to present a Jupiter withdrawal as an "Italian contribution to [the] relaxation [of] East-West tensions."

53. Sulzberger, *Last of the Giants*, 921–22; Finletter to Rusk, 25 October 1962, *FR 1961–63*, 16:730–33. Finletter also felt that deployment of a U.S. Polaris submarine off Turkey would not satisfy the Turks because, in contrast to the Jupiters, they would not share control over its SLBMs.

54. Hare, interview by Dennis O'Brien, 19 September 1969, OHC, JFKL, 24; Hare to Rusk, 26 October 1962, NATO-Weapons, Cables-Turkey, box 226, RSF, NSF.

55. *Presidential Recordings*, 27 October, 2, 19, 22, 27–28, 39–40, 43.

56. Ibid., 3, 19, emphasis in original.

57. Ormsby-Gore to Lord Home, 27 October 1962, PREM 11/3691, MemCon, 26 October 1962, 11:15 P.M. (London time), PREM 11/3690, and Macmillan to JFK, 27 October 1962, PREM 11/3690, all courtesy Zelikow; Erkin quoted in *NYT*, 28 October 1962, 30; Bernstein, "Reconsidering the Cuban Missile Crisis," 79–83; *Presidential Recordings*, 18 October. Kennedy responded to Macmillan's Thor idea, "We don't want to have too many dismantlings but it is possible that that proposal might help." MemCon, 26 October 1962, 11:15 P.M..

58. Bundy, *Danger and Survival*, 432–35; Rusk, *As I Saw It*, 240. As Bundy recalls, the smaller group consisted of Ball, Bundy, Gilpatric, the Kennedys, McNamara, Rusk, Sorensen, and Thompson; Rusk has it as Bundy, the Kennedys, McNamara, and Rusk; Schlesinger has it as "probably" Ball, Bundy, the Kennedys, McNamara, and Rusk. Bundy, *Danger and Survival*, 432; Rusk, *As I Saw It*, 240; Schlesinger, *Robert Kennedy*, 522.

59. RFK to Rusk, 30 October 1962, #84, 1992, *DDRS*; Dobrynin cable, 27 October 1962, in Lebow and Stein, *We All Lost the Cold War*, 524–26; Sorensen in Allyn, Blight, and Welch, *Back to the Brink*, 92–93; Lebow and Stein, *We All Lost the Cold War*, 137–38; Bernstein, "Reconsidering the Cuban Missile Crisis," 94–96, 123–24 n. 176–77; Khrushchev, *Khrushchev Remembers: The Glasnost Tapes*, 179; Nuti, "L'Italie et les missiles Jupiter," 145–46; Dobrynin to MFA, 30 October 1962, courtesy CWIHP; see also Dobrynin, "Caribbean Crisis," 56–57. In RFK's memo to Rusk, the sentence beginning "If some time elapsed" has been inexplicably crossed out.

Robert Kennedy's account in *Thirteen Days* reads, "However, I said, President Kennedy had been anxious to remove those missiles from Turkey and Italy for a long period of time. He had ordered their removal some time ago, and it was our judgment that, within a short period of time after the crisis was over, those missiles would be gone." According to Sorensen, he excised the explicit-trade passage from RFK's notes because the missile trade was still a secret at the time.

A few ExComm veterans have insisted the meeting involved not a trade but rather, in the words of Rusk—who knew better—a "piece of information"; and to be fair, the other members of the smaller Oval Office group probably understood it as such when they discussed the matter before RFK met with Dobrynin. But could the Kennedys have been so naive or careless as to think that Khrushchev would not take this "piece of information" as a significant concession? If there could be no deal, why did they not simply tell Dobrynin, "Absolutely no deal. The Jupiters will remain in place indefinitely"?

Dobrynin has claimed that RFK did *not* say his brother had already ordered the Jupiters out. It is interesting in this regard that the removal-order reference is found in *Thirteen Days* but *not* in the 30 October memorandum that the book paraphrases, which only casts further doubt on the notion of a removal order. Robert F. Kennedy, *Thirteen Days*, 108–9; Rusk and McNamara in Blight and Welch, *On the Brink*, 172, 174, 191; Rusk et al., "Lessons of the Cuban Missile Crisis," 86; Johnson, *Right Hand of Power*, 380; Dobrynin in Allyn, Blight, and Welch, *Back to the Brink*, 81; see also Lebow and Stein, *We All Lost the Cold War*, 126.

60. Bernstein, "Reconsidering the Cuban Missile Crisis," 126 n. 183; *Presidential Recordings*, 27 October, 73–74, 81, emphasis in original; Sulzberger, *Last of the Giants*, 920; Norstad to JFK, 27 October 1962, Norstad Correspondence, 7/62–12/62, Subjects-NATO, box 103, POF.

61. Lebow and Stein, *We All Lost the Cold War*, 138–43; Troyanovski, "Caribbean Crisis," 154–55; MemCon, 5 November 1962 (afternoon), in *CWIHP Bulletin*, no. 5 (Spring 1995): 102.

62. Khrushchev, *Khrushchev Remembers: The Last Testament*, 512; Schlesinger, *Robert*

Kennedy, 527; Gromyko, in Allyn, Blight, and Welch, *Back to the Brink*, 87; Lebow and Stein, *We All Lost the Cold War*, 140–41; Dobrynin, *In Confidence*, 89; see also Khrushchev, *Khrushchev Remembers: The Glasnost Tapes*, 179. Regarding the trade's sequential aspect, it is interesting to note that Feklisov told a State Department official on the evening of the 27th that "his government was flexible on the details of any agreement and would not be demanding in terms of a definite time period (He mentioned specifically a year for withdrawal from Turkey)." MemCon, 27 October 1962, 28.1.1.1. Cuban Crisis October 1962, Subject Files, 1957–1963, Office of Soviet Union Affairs, EUR, LF, RG 59.

63. Rusk to Blight, 2–3; *Los Angeles Times*, 29 August 1987, 2; see also Lukas, "Class Reunion," 58, 61. White argues that the 27 October Cordier option was in fact the option reported on 25 October by the British U.N. ambassador (above) and that Rusk is thus mistaken about the date and other particulars. This is possible, but it is more likely that these represent (at least) two distinct contacts between Cordier and U.S. officials and that both Rusk's memory and the 25 October British cable are accurate. Rusk has said he did not keep the statement he dictated to Cordier. White, *Cuban Missile Crisis*, 202–3; Rusk in Blight and Welch, *On the Brink*, 173.

64. *Presidential Recordings*, 27 October, 43, 50.

65. Robert F. Kennedy, *Thirteen Days*, 109.

66. *Presidential Recordings*, 27 October, 28; see also 26, 27, 73, and Bundy, *Danger and Survival*, 437.

67. For a good counterfactual discussion of 28 October, see Bernstein, "Reconsidering the Cuban Missile Crisis," 100–101; for JFK's fears of war, see *Presidential Recordings*, 27 October, 19, 24, 25, 27, 28. In 1981, Italian prime minister Fanfani alleged that Kennedy approached him to broker a missile trade. In light of the Cordier option, Fanfani's claim is plausible, but it requires substantiation. Herken, *Counsels of War*, 378 n. 11.

68. Quotation from Neustadt and May, *Thinking in Time*, 14.

69. *Presidential Recordings*, 27 October, 57–58; Forrestal to JFK, 27 October 1962, Countries-Cuba, General, 10/26/62–10/27/62, box 36, NSF. McCloy, moreover, who had expected Stevenson to be "too soft," arrived in New York and "did not find that he had any such attitude": "I even found him tougher than I was prepared to be." McCloy, quoted in Johnson, *Ambassador*, 307 n. 222.

70. Nitze's assertion is in his *Hiroshima to Glasnost*, 219–20.

71. The first quotation comes from John McCone, quoted in Weintal and Bartlett, *Facing the Brink*, 65; Schlesinger, *Thousand Days*, 832. For this "ExComm revisionism," see Welch and Blight, "Eleventh Hour," 16; Allyn, Blight, and Welch, "Essence of Revision," 159; Kaiser, "Men and Policies," 19–21; and especially Cohn, "President Kennedy's Decision," 227–28 and passim.

72. The "Gettysburg" analogy comes from Rostow, *View from the Seventh Floor*, 19.

Chapter Six

1. On the last phase of the crisis, see Beschloss, *Crisis Years*, 546–62; on the Jupiter removal, see also Bernstein, "Reconsidering the Cuban Missile Crisis," 98–99.

2. Khrushchev to JFK, 28 October 1962, reprinted in *International Affairs* (Moscow) (Special Edition, 1992): 55–57; RFK, handwritten notes, n.d. [30 October 1962], quoted in Schlesinger, *Robert Kennedy*, 523, ellipsis in original; Dobrynin to MFA, 30 October 1962; see also Dobrynin, *In Confidence*, 90.

3. Lebow and Stein, *We All Lost the Cold War*, 143; MemCon, 6 November 1962, 6:15 P.M., and draft, JFK to Khrushchev, 6 November 1962, 4, both in Executive Committee Meetings 17–24, 11/2/62–11/12/62, box 316, MM, NSF.

4. McNamara in Sharnik, *Inside the Cold War*, 159; McNamara quoted in Bernstein, "Reconsidering the Cuban Missile Crisis," 98.

5. McNamara in Blight and Welch, *On the Brink*, 262; McNamara to author, 11 April 1994.

6. McNaughton quoted in Chayes, *Cuban Missile Crisis*, 98 n. 52. At least one member of Paul Nitze's ISA staff addressed the issue of Jupiter removal immediately after the crisis, pointing out that the Turks would want aircraft in place of the IRBMs. Nitze Debrief 9:15 A.M. [#18], 29 October 1962, NASD, LMP, 2.

7. Kennan to Rusk, 29 October 1962, 110.11-RU/10-2962, DF, RG 59.

8. Norstad to JFK, 1 November 1962, Norstad Correspondence, 7/62–12/62, box 103, Subjects-NATO, POF; JFK to Norstad, 9 November 1962, courtesy Bernstein. In early December, Norstad remarked privately that the United States should have promised in 1957 that it would not withdraw any of the nuclear weapons it was deploying in Europe. Lemnitzer, Norstad's successor as of 1 January 1963, would oppose removal as well and even report that he would "have no choice" but to side, in effect, with the Italians and Turks as to the advisability of the move. Sulzberger, *Last of the Giants*, 936–37; Bohlen to Rusk, 11 January 1963, 740.5611/1-1163, DF, RG 59.

9. Tyler to Rusk, 9 November 1962, #1342, 1992, *DDRS*, emphasis in original; Rusk to JFK, 9 November 1962, attachment. The attachment—drafted by Raymond Garthoff—concluded that "for political and psychological reasons, supported by less significant but real military reasons as well, it would not be in the US interest to propose the removal of Turkish and Italian IRBM's in the immediate future," although removal at a later time, in conjunction with a multilateral or other substitute force, would be "entirely feasible."

10. Rusk to JFK, 9 November 1962.

11. Kitchen to Komer, 10 November 1962, and Komer to Bundy, 12 November 1962 and attachment, respectively boxes 230 and 226, NATO-Weapons, Cables-Turkey, RSF, NSF; see also ISA draft, "Some Lessons From Cuba," 14 November 1962, in Chang and Kornbluh, *Cuban Missile Crisis*, 317, and Komer to JFK, 9 January 1963, box 125, Countries-Turkey, 1961–1963, POF.

12. "Notes Taken from Transcripts of Meetings of the Joint Chiefs of Staff, October–November 1962, Dealing with the Cuban Missile Crisis," 1976, courtesy NSA; Kitchen to Rusk, 3 January 1963 and attachment, George W. Ball Papers, SGML, courtesy Marc Trachtenberg; Schlesinger, *Thousand Days*, 903.

13. NIC, "Soviet Bloc Armed Forces," 78; Beschloss, *Crisis Years*, 546 n, 553, see also 547 n; *WP*, 31 October 1962, box 11, *CN*; *Time*, 9 November 1962, 29; Stevenson to Rusk, 1 November 1962, #1841, *CMC*; McCloy quoted in Beschloss, *Crisis Years*, 554 n; see also Blair to Rusk, 15 November 1962, 782.56311/11-1562, DF, RG 59; Martin, *Adlai Stevenson*, 737–40. During this period, telegrams among top Soviet diplomats did contain discussion of the Jupiter issue, including alternating instructions not to raise the issue, to raise the issue later in general disarmament talks, and to threaten to raise the issue, but they contain no indications that a formal trade had already been concluded; see Kuznetsov and Zorin to MFA, 30 October 1962; Gromyko to Kuznetsov and Zorin, 1 November 1962; Dobrynin to MFA, 1 November 1962; Zhukov to Central Committee CPSU, 2 November 1962; Gromyko to Kuznetsov and Zorin, 5 November 1962, all courtesy CWIHP.

14. MemCon, 29 November 1962 (drafted 30 November), in *International Affairs* (Moscow) (October 1993): 82. Kennedy again invoked the Finland analogy in a January meeting with Kuznetsov, who confined his response to pointing out the existence of "numerous US bases" around the USSR "which certainly could not contribute to greater confidence" internationally. MemCon, 9 January 1963, in ibid., 84.

15. McNamara testimony, 21 February 1963, 314; Rusk testimony, 25 January 1963, *ESSFRC* 15:106; see also McNamara testimony, 30 January 1963, 264; 6 February 1963, HCA, Subcommittee, *Department of Defense Appropriations for 1964*, pt. 1, 409–10; and 20 February 1963, SCAS, *Military Procurement Authorization Fiscal Year 1964*, 147; Rusk testimony, 11 January 1963, *ESSFRC* 15:10–11; Bundy, *Danger and Survival*, 434.

16. McNamara testimony, 21 February 1963, 313, 312; Rusk testimony, 25 January 1963, 105; Yarmolinsky to Bundy, 26 February 1963 and attachments, Countries-Cuba, General, 2/63, box 37A, NSF; "Secretary Rusk Appears on 'Meet the Press,'" 27 January 1963, and "Secretary Rusk Holds Press and Radio News Briefing at Houston," 26 February 1963, both in *DSB* 48, respectively (18 February 1963): 247-48 and (18 March 1963): 391; Rusk to Fulbright, 23 January 1963, 740.5612/1-2163, DF, RG 59; see also "The President's News Conference of January 24, 1963," *PPP* 1963, 98.

17. McNamara testimony, 30 January 1963, 277-81; 19 February 1963, 7-8; 20 February 1963, 147; see also Rusk testimony, 25 January 1963, 103-5. McNamara also said the JCAE report had "strongly recommended" withdrawal of the Italian Jupiters, a gross distortion at best. Part of the official story was so bold as to assert that far from accelerating the Jupiter removal, the Cuban crisis had actually slowed it down—because, of course, the process could not move ahead under Soviet pressure (see, for example, *WP*, 19 January 1963, A9).

18. Robert F. Kennedy speech, Columbia, S.C., 25 April 1963, Speeches, 1961-1964, Attorney General's Files, Robert F. Kennedy Papers, JFKL, 1; Dobrynin cable, 27 October, 526; see also Khrushchev, *Khrushchev Remembers: The Glasnost Tapes*, 177, and Troyanovski, "Caribbean Crisis," 154); McNamara testimony, 6 February 1963, 30-31. This new evidence suggests that RFK's 1969 account—"I was not giving them an ultimatum but a statement of fact"—was accurate and not a case of convenient soft-peddling. In 1964, RFK did speak privately of having "delivered [to Dobrynin] some ultimatums, particularly the one that Saturday night." Bundy convincingly argues that the McNamara quotation demonstrates not the influence of nuclear superiority but rather of "nuclear danger." Robert F. Kennedy, *Thirteen Days*, 108; RFK, interviews by John B. Martin, March-May 1964, in Guthman and Shulman, *Robert Kennedy*, 261; Bundy, *Danger and Survival*, 447-48.

19. Alsop and Bartlett, "In Time of Crisis," 19. Stevenson had not mentioned the British Thor bases.

20. Martin, *Adlai Stevenson*, 741-48 (the best account of this incident); JFK to Stevenson, 5 December 1962, quoted in ibid., 745-46, emphasis in original; Johnson, *Ambassador*, 348-52; Beschloss, *Crisis Years*, 569; Broadwater, *Adlai Stevenson*, 214; compare Schlesinger, *Thousand Days*, 835-38, and see also Bundy to Stevenson, n.d. [ca. 11 December 1962], box 909B, Adlai Stevenson Papers, SGML, in which Bundy claimed that he had tried to steer Bartlett and Alsop in a different direction and that he regretted the whole affair. Bartlett later recalled that JFK seemed "not too displeased" that the Munich charge "had turned up," both because Stevenson's proposal would enter the historical record and because it had "rather shocked" him—an incredible lie considering what we now know. Other ExComm members confirmed, prepublication, the bits on Stevenson. Beschloss, *Crisis Years*, 569, 569 n. For another disingenuous disavowal of what Bartlett and other journalists wrote, see Sorensen, *Kennedy*, 315. It is too much to call Stevenson the "unsung hero" of the crisis, as Divine does, but he definitely deserves the rehabilitation he is now enjoying in recent accounts. Divine, "Alive and Well," 560.

21. Rusk testimony, 11 January 1963, 9; Sulzberger, *Last of the Giants*, 928; see also Rusk to Ball, 12 December 1962, 611.82/12-1262, DF, RG 59, and Sorensen, interview by Martin, 7.

22. Bundy to Aron, 15 May 1963, France-General, box 72, NSF, courtesy Trachtenberg.

23. U.S. Department of Defense, *Annual Report for FY 1963*, 248, emphasis added; NBC White Paper, "Cuba: The Missile Crisis," broadcast 9 February 1964, box W-6, ATD Background Material, Writings, AMSP, 41; Schlesinger, interview by John B. Martin, 14 January 1967, box 2, JBMFAES, 9 (see also Sorensen, interview by Martin, 7); Schlesinger, *Thousand Days*, 836, 827; Sorensen, *Kennedy*, 714, 696 n 3. Other early insider accounts, such as Hilsman, *To Move a Nation* (1967), and Salinger, *With Kennedy* (1966), were less direct but still contained no hint of a trade.

24. Castro quoted in, respectively, Lockwood, *Castro's Cuba, Cuba's Fidel*, 229, and

Matthews, *Fidel Castro*, 225. Robert Kennedy's account actually appeared first as "Thirteen Days"; see 170 for the RFK-Dobrynin deal. *Thirteen Days* was published in January 1969.

25. MemCon, 10 December 1962, 11:00 A.M. (drafted 13 December), Meetings with the President, 6/62–12/62, box 317a, MM, NSF.

26. Rusk to Hare and Reinhardt, 18 December 1962, *FR 1961–63*, 16:740–41; McNamara to Andreotti, 5 January 1963, contained in Ball to Reinhardt, 5 January 1963, Italy, 1/1/63–1/13/63, Subject File 1961–64, WHF, AMSP (for a sense of the portions excised, see McNamara to Sancar, 5 January 1963, contained in Ball to Hare, 5 January 1963, *FR 1961–63*, 16:744); see also Reinhardt to Rusk, 9 January 1963, *FR 1961–63*, 13:853–54.

27. Ainsworth to Rusk, 17 January 1963, #2105, 1995, *DDRS*; Nuti, "L'Italie et les missiles *Jupiter*," 149–50; MemCon, 24 January 1963, #2175, 1995, *DDRS*, 1; Kissinger, "Memorandum of Conversation with Ambassador Cattani in Rome, January 16, 1963," and "Memorandum of Conversation with Signor Segni in Rome, January 16, 1963," both 21 January 1963, Henry Kissinger, 1/63, Staff Memoranda, MM, NSF.

28. MemCon, 16 January 1963, 11:30 A.M., *FR 1961–63*, 13:858–64; Kennedy-Fanfani joint communiqué, 17 January 1963, *DSB* 48 (4 February 1963): 164; *NYT*, 18 January 1963, 1; see also G. Frederick Reinhardt, interview by Joseph E. O'Connor, November 1966, OHC, JFKL, 8–9. For a garbled reference to an Italian top-level secret envoy consulting with U.S. officials on the Jupiters, see Andreotti, *U.S.A. Up Close*, 39–40.

29. *NYT*, 25 January 1963, 1; *FR 1961–63*, 13:864 n 4; Reinhardt to Rusk, 12 February 1963, Italy 2/1/63–2/28/63, box WH-12A, Subject File 1961–1964, WHF, AMSP; *NYT*, 13 February 1963, 2; *WP*, 21 February 1963, A21.

30. Hare to Rusk, tel. 593, 28 October 1962, NATO-Weapons, Cables-Turkey, box 226, RSF, NSF, 2; Rusk to Hare and Finletter, 29 October 1962, NATO-Weapons, Cables-Turkey, box 226, RSF, NSF; Stevenson to Rusk, 1 November 1962; *NYT*, 3 November 1962, 8.

31. Rusk to Hare and Reinhardt, 18 December 1962, 741.

32. McNamara to Sancar, 5 January 1963, 743–44; Rusk to Hare, 8 January 1963, Hare to Rusk, 18 January 1963, and Rusk to Hare, 23 January 1963, all in *FR 1961–63*, 16:745–51. On the 9th, JFK briefly met with Hare, who recalled Kennedy telling him, "You can tell anyone in the Turkish government . . . that this question of the Jupiters is not part of any deal with the Russians." Hare, interview by O'Brien, 24.

33. *CSM*, 24 January 1963, 2; Hare to Rusk, 27 January 1963, 1 February 1963, and 18 February 1963, all in *FR 1961–63*, 16:752–54, 757–60; Hare to Rusk, 9 February 1963, DEF-Defense Affairs Tur-A 2/1/63, box 3743, SNF, RG 59; *FR 1961–63*, 16:757 n. 1, and 760 n. 6; OSD to Rusk, 6 February 1963, DEF-Defense Tur 2/1/63, Box 3743, SNF, RG 59. For the future military deliveries Wood was authorized to discuss with Sancar, see Rusk to Hare, 7 March 1963, NATO-Weapons, Cables-Turkey, box 226, RSF, NSF. At roughly this time, one USAF general completely ignorant about the Jupiters and their impending removal landed in Turkey and was mobbed by reporters who asked, "What about the missiles?" He had read up on Turkey before arriving, he recalled, so he "launched into a little dissertation on . . . Ataturk's greatness and dodged the subject." Arno H. Luehmann, interview by Hugh N. Ahmann, 5 November 1986, K239.0512-1731, USAFOHP, AFHRC, 113–14.

34. Finletter to Rusk, 26 January 1963, 711.5611/1-2563, DF, RG 59; "Briefing Paper for the President's Press Conference, February 7, 1963—Subject: Replacement of Jupiter Missiles," 2/7/63, Background Materials III, Press Conferences, 11/20/62–2/21/63, box 58, POF; Nuti, "L'Italie et les missiles *Jupiter*," 154–55.

35. Landon interview, 486–87; Robert J. Wood and William P. Bundy testimony, 9 May 1963, HCFA, *Foreign Assistance Act of 1963*, pt. 4, 699. For a glimpse of some of the military details of POT PIE, see Senter to various commands, 19 March 1963 and attachment, "A Plan for the Withdrawal and Disposition of the SM-78 (Jupiter) Missile

Weapon System from Italy and Turkey," K220.8630-7, AFHRC. The Italian and Turkish segments of the operation were labeled POT PIE I and POT PIE II, respectively.

36. Neufeld, *Ballistic Missiles*, 232–33; McNamara to JFK, 25 April 1963, folder 6, Countries-Turkey, box 125, POF.

37. *NYT*, 13 April 1963, 2; *Baltimore Sun*, 13 April 1963, box 14, *CN*; McNamara testimony, 8 April 1963, HCFA, *Foreign Assistance Act of 1963*, pt. 1, 74; Hare to Rusk, 17 April 1963, DEF-Defense Affairs Tur-A 2/1/63, box 3743, SNF, RG 59; Criss, "U.S. Forces in Turkey," 347.

38. Department of State, Bureau of Public Affairs, *American Opinion Summary*, No. 146, 31 January 1963, #2892, *CMC*, 1; Editorials in *CSM*, 23 January 1963, E1, and *NYT*, 31 January 1963, 6; *Newsweek*, 28 January 1963, 45; *Time*, 1 February 1963, 21; Garrison, *Heritage of Stone*, 113.

39. LeMay quoted in Herken, *Counsels of War*, 378 n. 11; HQ TUSLOG, "Report on Operations, USAFE Logistics Group (Turkey)," 7/1/62–12/31/62, 20 February 1963, #2817, *CMC*; Leon Johnson, interview, 14 April 1965, K239.0512-609, USAFOHP, AFHRC, 47–48; Coffey, *Iron Eagle*, 392; Kohn and Harahan, *Strategic Air Warfare*, 114, 115; MemCon, 23 March 1962, 11:30 A.M., 837; LeMay testimony, 25 February 1963, HCA, Subcommittee, *Department of Defense Appropriations for 1964*, pt. 2, 463, 571–74; Disosway interview, 152; see also Frank F. Everest, interview by John N. Dick Jr., 23–25 August 1977, K239.0512-957, USAFOHP, AFHRC, 163–64, and LeMay, *America Is in Danger*, 140, 142, where LeMay indirectly suggests Kennedy traded and asserts that the IRBM withdrawal helped raise questions about the "creditability" of the U.S. deterrent.

40. *Congressional Record*, 19 February 1963, 88th Cong., 1st sess., 1963, 109, pt. 2:2534–35; *Baltimore Sun*, 11 February 1963, 1; McNamara testimony, 22 February 1963, SCAS, *Military Procurement Authorization Fiscal Year 1964*, 351.

41. Gallois quoted in *U.S. News and World Report*, 25 March 1963, 58; "Accords de Nassau"; Bohlen to Rusk, 27 March 1963, DEF 12 Armaments US/NATO 2/1/63, box 3751, SNF, RG 59; *NYT*, 27 March 1963, 2.

42. Bradlee, *Conversations with Kennedy*, 131–33; JFK to William Bundy, 15 February 1963, in Claflin, *JFK Wants to Know*, 242. There had, in fact, been forty-two thousand Soviet troops in Cuba during the crisis and as many as thirty-seven thousand in February 1963. In 1960 NATO had approved establishment of the Cretan "NAMFI" (North Atlantic Missile Firing Installation), but user nations did not sign the necessary agreement until June 1964.

43. Bundy to JFK, 11 May 1963, Index of Weekend Papers, 4/63–6/63, box 318, MM, NSF.

44. *Newsweek*, 15 April 1963, box 14, *CN*; JCS to Lemnitzer, 19 January 1963, Chairman's Messages, Maxwell Taylor Papers, RG 218, 3.

45. Bundy, *Danger and Survival*, 434–35; Rusk et al., "Lessons of the Cuban Missile Crisis," 86.

46. See Kaufman, "JFK as World Leader."

47. On the MLF, see Schwartz, *NATO's Nuclear Dilemmas*, 82–135; on Skybolt, see Clark, *Nuclear Diplomacy*, esp. 338–421; on the reconnaissance satellite regime, see Gaddis, *Long Peace*, 201–6; on joint, active nonproliferation in China, see Chang, *Friends and Enemies*, 228–52; on the PALs leak, see *Newsweek*, 5 May 1969, 46–47.

Conclusion

1. Nixon to Kissinger, n.d. [18 September 1970], quoted in Kissinger, *White House Years*, 642.

2. Bundy, *Danger and Survival*, 435.

3. McMahon, "Credibility and World Power," 455 and passim.

4. Tuchman, *March of Folly*, 383.

WORKS CITED

Manuscripts

Abilene, Kansas
Dwight D. Eisenhower Library
  John Foster Dulles Papers, 1951–59
  Dwight D. Eisenhower Papers
    Ann Whitman File (Papers as president of the United States, 1953–61)
    White House Central Files, 1953–61 (Records as president)
  Lauris Norstad Papers, 1930–87
  Oral History Collection
  President's Science Advisory Committee Records, 1957–61
  Public Statements of Secretary of Defense Neil McElroy, 1957–58
  White House Office Records
    Office of the Special Assistant for National Security Affairs, Records, 1952–61
    Office of the Staff Secretary, Records, 1952–61

Amherst, Massachusetts
Amherst College Archives
  John J. McCloy Papers

Austin, Texas
Lyndon B. Johnson Library
  Lyndon B. Johnson Papers
    Vice Presidential Security File
  Lawrence McQuade Papers
    Notes as Assistant Secretary of Defense, 1961–63

Boston, Massachusetts
John F. Kennedy Library
  John F. Kennedy Papers
    Personal Papers
      Presidential Doodles
    Pre-Presidential Papers
    Presidential Papers, 1961–63
      National Security Files
      President's Office Files
  Robert F. Kennedy Papers, 1925–68
    Attorney General Files
  Oral History Collection
  Public Statements of Secretary of Defense Robert S. McNamara, 1962
  Arthur M. Schlesinger Jr. Papers, 1939–89

Theodore C. Sorensen Papers, 1953–64
U.S. Department of Defense, Records, 1961–63
  Current News

College Park, Maryland
National Archives (Archives II)
  RG 59: Records of the Department of State
  RG 218: Records of the Joint Chiefs of Staff
  RG 273: Records of the National Security Council

London, England
Public Record Office, Kew
  Records of the Prime Minister's Office (PREM 11)

Montgomery, Alabama
U.S. Air Force Historical Research Center, Maxwell Air Force Base
  Unit Histories
  United States Air Force Oral History Program

New Haven, Connecticut
Yale University Library
  Chester Bowles Papers

Princeton, New Jersey
Princeton University, Seeley G. Mudd Library
  George W. Ball Papers
  JFD-DDEL Chronological Series
  John Foster Dulles Oral History Project
  John Foster Dulles Papers
  John B. Martin Papers
  Adlai E. Stevenson Papers

Stanford, California
Hoover Institution Archives
  Ellis O. Briggs Papers
    "Proud Servant: The Autobiography of Ellis Ormsbee Briggs, Ambassador to Seven
    Countries and Career Ambassador of the United States of America," typescript,
    1975.

Washington, D.C.
Georgetown University, Lauinger Library
  Foreign Affairs Oral History Program
Library of Congress, Manuscript Division
  Nathan F. Twining Papers
  Thomas D. White Papers
National Archives
  RG 128: Records of Congressional Committees
National Security Archive
  Miscellaneous Declassified Documents

Published Primary Sources

Chang, Laurence, and Peter Kornbluh, eds. *The Cuban Missile Crisis, 1962: A National
  Security Archive Documents Reader*. New York: New Press, 1992.

Claflin, Edward B., ed. *JFK Wants to Know: Memos from the President's Office, 1961–1963.* New York: Morrow, 1991.

Declassified Documents Reference System. Washington, D.C.: Carrollton, 1977–81; Woodbridge, Conn.: Research Publications International, 1982–.

Ferrell, Robert H., ed. *The Eisenhower Diaries.* New York: W. W. Norton, 1981.

Foreign Relations of the United States. Washington, D.C.: GPO, 1986–.

John Fitzgerald Kennedy: A Compilation of Statements and Speeches Made during His Service in the United States Senate and House of Representatives. Washington, D.C.: GPO, 1964.

Johnson, Walter, ed. *Ambassador to the United Nations, 1961-1965.* Vol. 8 of *The Papers of Adlai E. Stevenson.* Boston: Little, Brown, 1979.

Khrushchev in America: Full Texts of the Speeches Made by N. S. Khrushchev, Chairman of the Council of Ministers of the USSR, on His Tour of the United States, September 15-27, 1959, Translated from "Live in Peace and Friendship!" New York: Crosscurrents, 1960.

Koch, Scott A., ed. *CIA Cold War Records: Selected Estimates on the Soviet Union, 1950-1959.* Washington, D.C.: History Staff, Central Intelligence Agency, 1993.

Larson, David L., ed. *The "Cuban Crisis" of 1962: Selected Documents and Chronology.* Boston: Houghton Mifflin, 1963.

McAuliffe, Mary S., ed. *CIA Documents on the Cuban Missile Crisis, 1962.* Washington, D.C.: History Staff, Central Intelligence Agency, 1992.

Minutes of the Telephone Conversations of John Foster Dulles and Christian Herter. Washington, D.C.: University Press of America, 1980.

National Security Archive. *The Berlin Crisis, 1958-1962.* Alexandria, Va.: Chadwyck-Healey, 1991.

———. *The Cuban Missile Crisis, 1962.* Alexandria, Va.: Chadwyck-Healey, 1990.

———. *Nuclear Non-Proliferation, 1945-1990.* Alexandria, Va.: Chadwyck-Healey, 1992.

Office of Administrative Assistant, Secretary of the Air Force. *Current News.*

Public Papers of the Presidents. Washington, D.C.: GPO, 1958–64.

Trachtenberg, Marc, ed. *The Development of American Strategic Thought: Basic Documents from the Eisenhower and Kennedy Periods, Including the Basic National Security Policy Papers from 1953 to 1959.* New York: Garland, 1988.

U.S. Department of Defense. *Annual Report for FY 1963.* Washington, D.C.: GPO, 1964.

U.S. Department of State. *Foreign Ministers Meeting, May-August 1959, Geneva.* Publication No. 6882, International Organization and Conference Series 8. Washington, D.C.: GPO, 1959.

Newspapers and Periodicals

Aviation Daily
Baltimore Sun
Christian Science Monitor
Cold War International History Project Bulletin
Congressional Record
Current Digest of the Soviet Press
Department of State Bulletin
Foreign Broadcast Information Service, Daily Reports
Fortune
International Affairs (Moscow)
Keesing's Contemporary Archives
Los Angeles Times
Nation

NATO Letter
News from Turkey
Newsweek
New York Herald Tribune
New York Review of Books
New York Times
New York Times Magazine
New York World Telegram
Punch
Reporter
Saturday Evening Post
Saturday Review
Time
Times (London)
U.S. News and World Report
Washington Post

Congressional Hearings

House
Committee on Appropriations. *The Ballistic Missile Program.* 85th Cong., 2d sess., 1957.
———. *Department of Defense Appropriations for 1960.* 86th Cong., 1st sess., 1959.
Committee on Appropriations, Subcommittee. *Department of Defense Appropriations for 1959.* 85th Cong., 2d sess., 1958.
———. *Department of Defense Appropriations for 1963.* 87th Cong., 2d sess., 1962.
———. *Department of Defense Appropriations for 1964.* 88th Cong., 1st sess., 1963.
Committee on Armed Services. *Hearings on Military Posture.* 88th Cong., 1st sess., 1963.
———. *Hearings on Military Posture and H.R. 9751.* 87th Cong., 2d sess., 1962.
Committee on Foreign Affairs. *Foreign Assistance Act of 1963.* 88th Cong., 1st sess., 1963.
Executive Sessions of the House Foreign Affairs Committee.

Senate
Committee on Appropriations, Subcommittee. *Department of Defense Appropriations for 1960.* 86th Cong., 1st sess., 1959.
Committee on Armed Services. *Military Procurement Authorization Fiscal Year 1964.* 88th Cong., 1st sess., 1963.
Committee on Armed Services, Preparedness Investigating Subcommittee. *Hearings, Inquiry into Satellite and Missile Programs.* 85th Cong., 1st and 2d sess., 1957–58.
———. *Major Defense Matters.* 86th Cong., 1st sess., 1959.
Committee on Armed Services, in conjunction with Senate Committee on Aeronautical and Space Sciences. *Missiles, Space, and Other Defense Matters.* 86th Cong., 2d sess., 1960.
Committee on Foreign Relations, Subcommittee. *Disarmament and Foreign Policy.* 86th Cong., 1st sess., 1959.
Executive Sessions of the Senate Foreign Relations Committee.

Secondary Sources

Abel, Elie. *The Missile Crisis.* Philadelphia: Lippincott, 1966.
Abramson, Rudy. *Spanning the Century: The Life of W. Averell Harriman, 1891–1986.* New York: Morrow, 1992.

"Accords de Nassau." *Revue militaire d'information*, no. 347 (March 1963): 89.

Adenauer, Konrad. *Erinnerungen, 1955-1959*. Stuttgart: Deutsche Verlags-Anstalt, 1967.

Albrook, Robert C. "How Good Are Our Missiles?" *Reporter*, 6 February 1958, 21–23.

Allen, Craig. *Eisenhower and the Mass Media: Peace, Prosperity, and Prime-Time TV*. Chapel Hill: University of North Carolina Press, 1993.

Allison, Graham T. *Essence of Decision: Explaining the Cuban Missile Crisis*. Boston: Little, Brown, 1971.

Allyn, Bruce J., James G. Blight, and David A. Welch. "Essence of Revision: Moscow, Havana, and the Cuban Missile Crisis." *International Security* 14 (Winter 1989–90): 136–72.

———, eds. *Back to the Brink: Proceedings of the Moscow Conference on the Cuban Missile Crisis, January 27-28, 1989*. CSIA Occasional Paper No. 9. Lanham, Md.: University Press of America, 1992.

Alsop, Stewart, and Bartlett, Charles. "In Time of Crisis." *Saturday Evening Post*, 8 December 1962, 16–20.

Ambrose, Stephen E. *Eisenhower: The President*. Vol. 2 of *Eisenhower*. New York: Simon & Schuster, 1984.

Anderson, Clinton P., with Milton Viorst. *Outsider in the Senate: Senator Clinton Anderson's Memoirs*. New York: World Publishing, 1970.

Andreotti, Giulio. *The U.S.A. Up Close: From the Atlantic Pact to Bush*. Translated by Peter C. Farrell. New York: New York University Press, 1992.

Appleby, Charles A., Jr. "Eisenhower and Arms Control, 1953–1961: A Balance of Risks." Ph.D. diss., Johns Hopkins University, 1987.

Armacost, Michael H. *The Politics of Weapons Innovation: The Thor-Jupiter Controversy*. New York: Columbia University Press, 1969.

Baar, James, and William E. Howard. *Combat Missileman*. New York: Harcourt Brace, 1961.

Baldwin, Hanson W. *The Great Arms Race: A Comparison of U.S. and Soviet Power Today*. New York: Praeger, 1958.

Ball, Desmond. *Politics and Force Levels: The Strategic Missile Program of the Kennedy Administration*. Berkeley and Los Angeles: University of California Press, 1980.

Ball, George. *The Past Has Another Pattern: Memoirs*. New York: W. W. Norton, 1982.

Baylis, John. *Anglo-American Defense Relations, 1939-1984: The Special Relationship*. 2d ed. New York: St. Martin's. 1984.

Baylis, John, and John Garnett, eds. *Makers of Nuclear Strategy*. New York: St. Martin's, 1991.

Berding, Andrew H. *Dulles on Diplomacy*. Princeton: Van Nostrand, 1965.

Bernstein, Barton J. "The Cuban Missile Crisis: Trading the Jupiters in Turkey?" *Political Science Quarterly* 95 (Spring 1980): 97–125.

———. "Reconsidering the Cuban Missile Crisis: Dealing with the Problems of American Jupiters in Turkey." In *The Cuban Missile Crisis Revisited*, edited by James A. Nathan, 55–129. New York: St. Martin's, 1992.

Beschloss, Michael R. *The Crisis Years: Kennedy and Khrushchev, 1960-1963*. New York: HarperCollins, 1991.

———. *Mayday: The U-2 Affair*. New York: Harper & Row, 1986.

Betts, Richard K. *Nuclear Blackmail and Nuclear Balance*. Washington, D.C.: Brookings Institution, 1987.

Bird, Kai. *The Chairman: John J. McCloy and the Making of the American Establishment*. New York: Simon & Schuster, 1992.

Blight, James G., Bruce J. Allyn, and David A. Welch. *Cuba on the Brink: Castro, the Missile Crisis, and the Soviet Collapse*. New York: Pantheon, 1993.

Blight, James G., and David A. Welch. *On the Brink: Americans and Soviets Reexamine the Cuban Missile Crisis*. New York: Hill & Wang, 1989.

Bloomfield, Lincoln P., Walter C. Clemens Jr., and Franklyn Griffiths. *Khrushchev and the Arms Race: Soviet Interests in Arms Control and Disarmament, 1954-1964*. Cambridge: MIT Press, 1966.

Bohlen, Charles E. *Witness to History, 1929-1969*. New York: W. W. Norton, 1973.

Botti, Timothy J. *The Long Wait: Forging the Anglo-American Nuclear Alliance, 1945-1958*. Westport, Conn.: Greenwood, 1987.

Boutwell, Jeffrey. *The German Nuclear Dilemma*. Ithaca, N.Y.: Cornell University Press, 1990.

Bradlee, Benjamin C. *Conversations with Kennedy*. New York: W. W. Norton, 1975.

Brenner, Philip. "Thirteen Months: Cuba's Perspective on the Missile Crisis." In *The Cuban Missile Crisis Revisited*, edited by James A. Nathan, 187–217. New York: St. Martin's, 1992.

Brinkley, Douglas. *Dean Acheson: The Cold War Years, 1953-1971*. New Haven: Yale University Press, 1992.

British Broadcasting Corporation. *The Cuban Missile Crisis* (documentary). London: BBC, 1992.

Broadwater, Jeff. *Adlai Stevenson and American Politics: The Odyssey of a Cold War Liberal*. New York: Twayne, 1994.

Brodie, Bernard. *Strategy in the Missile Age*. Princeton: Princeton University Press, 1959.

Brugioni, Dino. *Eyeball to Eyeball: The Inside Story of the Cuban Missile Crisis*. New York: Random House, 1991.

Bundy, McGeorge. *Danger and Survival: Choices about the Bomb in the First Fifty Years*. New York: Random House, 1988.

———. "The Presidency and the Peace." *Foreign Affairs* 42 (April 1964): 353–65.

Chang, Gordon H. *Friends and Enemies: The United States, China, and the Soviet Union, 1948-1972*. Stanford: Stanford University Press, 1990.

Chayes, Abram. *The Cuban Missile Crisis: International Crises and the Role of Law*. New York: Oxford University Press, 1974.

Cioc, Marc. *Pax Atomica: The Nuclear Defense Debate in West Germany during the Adenauer Era*. New York: Columbia University Press, 1988.

Clark, Ian. *Nuclear Diplomacy and the Special Relationship: Britain's Deterrent and America, 1957-1962*. Oxford: Clarendon, 1994.

Clark, Ian, and David Angell. "Britain, the United States, and the Control of Nuclear Weapons: The Diplomacy of the Thor Deployment." *Diplomacy and Statecraft* 2 (November 1991): 153–77.

Coffey, Thomas M. *Iron Eagle: The Turbulent Life of General Curtis LeMay*. New York: Avon, 1986.

Cohen, Eliot A. "Why We Should Stop Studying the Cuban Missile Crisis." *National Interest*, no. 2 (Winter 1985–86): 3–13.

Cohn, Elizabeth. "President Kennedy's Decision to Impose a Blockade in the Cuban Missile Crisis: Building Consensus in the ExComm after the Decision." In *The Cuban Missile Crisis Revisited*, edited by James A. Nathan, 219–35. New York: St. Martin's, 1992.

Costigliola, Frank. "Kennedy, the European Allies, and the Failure to Consult." *Political Science Quarterly* 110 (Spring 1995): 105–23.

Couloumbis, Theodore A. *Greek Political Reaction to American and NATO Influences*. New Haven: Yale University Press, 1966.

Criss, Nur Bilge. "Les retombées de la crise de Cuba: Les *Jupiter* 'turcs.' " In *L'Europe et la Crise de Cuba*, edited by Maurice Vaïsse, 159–68. Paris: Armand Colin, 1993.

———. "U.S. Forces in Turkey." In *U.S. Military Forces in Europe: The Early Years*,

1945–1970, edited by Simon W. Duke and Wolfgang Krieger, 331–51. Boulder, Colo.: Westview, 1993.

de Gaulle, Charles. *Memoirs of Hope: Renewal and Endeavor*. Translated by Terence Kilmartin. New York: Simon & Schuster, 1971.

Detzer, David. *The Brink: Cuban Missile Crisis, 1962*. New York: Crowell, 1979.

Dinerstein, Herbert S. *The Making of a Missile Crisis: October 1962*. Baltimore: Johns Hopkins University Press, 1976.

Divine, Robert A. "Alive and Well: The Continuing Cuban Missile Crisis Controversy." *Diplomatic History* 18 (Fall 1994): 551–60.

———. *Blowing on the Wind: The Nuclear Test Ban Debate, 1954–1960*. New York: Oxford University Press, 1978.

———. *Eisenhower and the Cold War*. Oxford University Press, 1981.

———. *The Sputnik Challenge: Eisenhower's Response to the Soviet Satellite*. New York: Oxford University Press, 1993.

Dobrynin, Anatoly. "The Caribbean Crisis: An Eyewitness Account." *International Affairs* (Moscow), no. 8 (August 1992): 47–60.

———. *In Confidence: Moscow's Ambassador to America's Six Cold War Presidents*. New York: Random House, 1995.

Duke, Simon W. *US Defence Bases in the United Kingdom: A Matter for Joint Decision?* Houndsmills, Basingstroke: Macmillan, 1987.

Eisenhower, Dwight D. *Mandate for Change, 1953–1956*. Garden City, N.Y.: Doubleday, 1963.

———. *Waging Peace, 1956–1961*. Garden City, N.Y.: Doubleday, 1965.

Ellsberg, Daniel. "The Crude Analysis of Strategic Choices." *American Economic Review* 51 (May 1961): 472–78.

Enthoven, Alain C., and Wayne K. Smith. *How Much Is Enough? Shaping the Defense Program, 1961–1969*. New York: Harper & Row, 1971.

Facon, Patrick. "U.S. Forces in France, 1945–1958." In *U.S. Military Forces in Europe: The Early Years, 1945–1970*, edited by Simon W. Duke and Wolfgang Krieger, 233–48. Boulder, Colo.: Westview, 1993.

Falcoff, Mark. "Learning to Love the Missile Crisis." *National Interest*, no. 16 (Summer 1989): 63–73.

Feaver, Peter D. *Guarding the Guardians: Civilian Control of Nuclear Weapons in the United States*. Ithaca, N.Y.: Cornell University Press, 1992.

Felken, Detlef. *Dulles und Deutschland: Die amerikanische Deutschlandpolitik, 1953–1959*. Bonn: Bouvier, 1993.

Ferrell, Robert H. *American Diplomacy: The Twentieth Century*. New York: W. W. Norton, 1988.

Fursenko, Alexander, and Timothy Naftali. "Using KGB Documents: The Scali-Feklisov Channel in the Cuban Missile Crisis." *Cold War International History Project Bulletin*, no. 5 (Spring 1995): 58, 60–62.

Gaddis, John Lewis. *The Long Peace: Inquiries into the History of the Cold War*. New York: Oxford University Press, 1987.

———. *Russia, the Soviet Union, and the United States: An Interpretive History*. 2d ed. New York: McGraw-Hill, 1991.

———. *Strategies of Containment: A Critical Appraisal of Postwar American National Security Policy*. New York: Oxford University Press, 1982.

———. "The Unexpected John Foster Dulles: Nuclear Weapons, Communism, and the Russians." In *John Foster Dulles and the Diplomacy of the Cold War*, edited by Richard Immerman, 47–77. Princeton: Princeton University Press, 1990.

The Gallup Poll: Public Opinion, 1949–1958. Vol. 2 of *The Gallup Poll: Public Opinion, 1935–1971*. New York: Random House, 1972.

Garrison, Jim. *A Heritage of Stone*. New York: G. P. Putnam & Sons, 1970.

Garthoff, Raymond L. *Reflections on the Cuban Missile Crisis.* Rev. ed. Washington, D.C.: Brookings Institution, 1989.

Gavin, James. *War and Peace in the Space Age.* New York: Harper & Brothers, 1958.

Ghent, Jocelyn. "Canada, the United States, and the Cuban Missile Crisis." *Pacific Historical Review* 48 (May 1979): 159–84.

Gilpin, Robert. *American Scientists and Nuclear Weapons Policy.* Princeton: Princeton University Press, 1962.

Gordon, Lincoln. "NATO in the Nuclear Age." *Yale Review* 47 (March 1959): 321–35.

Greenstein, Fred I. *The Hidden-Hand Presidency: Eisenhower as Leader.* New York: Basic Books, 1982.

Gribkov, Anatoli I., and William Y. Smith. *Operation ANADYR: U.S. and Soviet Generals Recount the Cuban Missile Crisis.* Chicago: Edition Q, 1994.

Guthman, Edwin O., and Jeffrey Shulman. *Robert Kennedy in His Own Words: The Unpublished Recollections of the Kennedy Years.* New York: Bantam, 1988.

Hansard: House of Commons Debates, 1962.

Hansen, Chuck. *U.S. Nuclear Weapons: The Secret History.* New York: Orion, 1988.

Harrison, Michael M. *The Reluctant Ally: France and Atlantic Security.* Baltimore: Johns Hopkins University Press, 1981.

Herken, Gregg. *Counsels of War.* 2d ed. New York: Oxford University Press, 1987.

Hershberg, James G. "Before 'the Missiles of October': Did Kennedy Plan a Military Strike against Cuba?" In *The Cuban Missile Crisis Revisited*, edited by James A. Nathan, 237–80. New York: St. Martin's, 1992.

Hilsman, Roger. *The Politics of Policy Making in Defense and Foreign Affairs: Conceptual Models and Bureaucratic Politics.* 2d ed. Englewood Cliffs, N.J.: Prentice-Hall, 1990.

———. *To Move a Nation: The Politics of Foreign Policy in the Administration of John F. Kennedy.* Garden City, N.Y.: Doubleday, 1967.

Hixson, Walter L. *George F. Kennan: Cold War Iconoclast.* New York: Columbia University Press, 1989.

Hoag, Malcolm W. "On NATO Pooling." *World Politics* 10 (April 1958): 475–83.

Hoopes, Townsend. *The Devil and John Foster Dulles.* Boston: Little, Brown, 1973.

———. "Overseas Bases in American Strategy." *Foreign Affairs* 37 (October 1958): 69–82.

Immerman, Richard, ed. *John Foster Dulles and the Diplomacy of the Cold War.* Princeton: Princeton University Press, 1990.

Ireland, Timothy. "Building NATO's Nuclear Posture, 1950–65." In *The Nuclear Confrontation in Europe*, edited by Jeffrey D. Boutwell, Paul Doty, and Gregory F. Treverton, 5–43. London: Croom Helm, 1985.

Johnson, U. Alexis. *The Right Hand of Power: The Memoirs of an American Diplomat.* Englewood Cliffs, N.J.: Prentice-Hall, 1984.

Kahan, Jerome H. *Security in the Nuclear Age: Developing U.S. Strategic Arms Policy.* Washington, D.C.: Brookings Institution, 1975.

Kahn, Herman. *On Thermonuclear War.* Princeton: Princeton University Press, 1960.

Kaiser, David. "Men and Policies, 1961–69." In *The Diplomacy of the Crucial Decade: American Foreign Relations during the 1960s*, edited by Diane B. Kunz, 11–41. New Haven: Yale University Press, 1994.

Kaplan, Fred. *The Wizards of Armageddon.* Stanford: Stanford University Press, 1991.

Kaplan, Lawrence S. *NATO and the United States: The Enduring Alliance.* Boston: Twayne, 1988.

Kaufman, Burton I. "JFK as World Leader: A Perspective on the Literature." *Diplomatic History* 17 (Summer 1993): 447–69.

Kelleher, Catherine. *Germany and the Politics of Nuclear Weapons.* New York: Columbia University Press, 1975.

Kelley, Robert Eaton. *The First Book of Timothy*. Hanover, N.H.: University Press of New England, 1996.

Kennan, George F. *Memoirs, 1950–1963*. Boston: Little, Brown, 1972.

———. *Russia, the Atom, and the West*. New York: Harper & Brothers, 1958.

Kennedy, John F. "Kennedy Wants U.S. to Sacrifice." *New York Times*, 8 December 1957, 81.

———. Review of B. H. Liddell Hart's *Deterrent or Defense?*, *Saturday Review*, 3 September 1960, 17–18.

———. *The Strategy of Peace*. New York: Harper & Brothers, 1960.

Kennedy, Robert F. *Thirteen Days: A Memoir of the Cuban Missile Crisis*. New York: W. W. Norton, 1969.

———. "Thirteen Days: The Story of How the World Almost Ended." *McCall's*, November 1968, 6ff.

Khrushchev, Nikita S. *Khrushchev Remembers*. Translated and edited by Strobe Talbott. Boston: Little, Brown, 1970.

———. *Khrushchev Remembers: The Glasnost Tapes*. Translated and edited by Jerrold L. Schechter. Boston: Little, Brown, 1990.

———. *Khrushchev Remembers: The Last Testament*. Translated and edited by Strobe Talbott. Boston: Little, Brown, 1974.

Killian, James R., Jr. *Sputnik, Scientists, and Eisenhower: A Memoir of the First Special Assistant to the President for Science and Technology*. Cambridge, Mass.: MIT Press, 1977.

Kinross, Lord. *The Ottoman Centuries: The Rise and Fall of the Turkish Empire*. New York: Morrow, 1977.

Kissinger, Henry. "Missiles and the Western Alliance." *Foreign Affairs* 36 (April 1958): 383–400.

———. *The Necessity for Choice: Prospects of American Foreign Policy*. New York: Harper & Brothers, 1960.

———. *Nuclear Weapons and Foreign Policy*. New York: Harper & Brothers, 1957.

———. *The Troubled Partnership: A Re-appraisal of the Atlantic Alliance*. New York: McGraw-Hill, 1965.

———. *White House Years*. Boston: Little, Brown, 1979.

Knorr, Klaus, "Aspects of NATO Strategy: A Conference Report." In *NATO and American Security*, edited by Klaus Knorr, 307–34. Princeton: Princeton University Press, 1959.

Kogan, Norman. *A Political History of Postwar Italy*. New York: Praeger, 1966.

Kohn, Richard H., and Joseph P. Harahan, eds. *Strategic Air Warfare: An Interview with Generals Curtis E. LeMay, Leon W. Johnson, David A. Burchinal, and Jack J. Catton*. Washington, D.C.: Office of Air Force History, 1988.

Krock, Arthur. *Memoirs: Sixty Years on the Firing Line*. New York: Funk & Wagnalls, 1968.

Lagani, Irene. "U.S. Forces in Greece in the 1950s." In *U.S. Military Forces in Europe: The Early Years, 1945–1970*, edited by Simon W. Duke and Wolfgang Krieger, 309–30. Boulder, Colo.: Westview, 1993.

Lang, Daniel. *An Inquiry into Enoughness: Of Bombs and Men and Staying Alive*. New York: McGraw-Hill, 1965.

Larson, Arthur. *Eisenhower: The President Nobody Knew*. New York: Scribner's, 1968.

Larus, Joel. *Nuclear Weapons Safety and the Common Defense*. Columbus: Ohio State University Press, 1967.

Lebow, Richard Ned, and Janet Gross Stein. *We All Lost the Cold War*. Princeton: Princeton University Press, 1994.

LeMay, Curtis E., with Dale O. Smith. *America Is in Danger*. New York: Funk & Wagnalls, 1968.

Lockwood, Lee. *Castro's Cuba, Cuba's Fidel: An American Journalist's Inside Look at Today's Cuba—In Text and Picture*. New York: Vintage, 1969.

Loeb, Larry M. "Jupiter Missiles in Europe: A Measure of Presidential Power." *World Affairs* 139 (1976): 27–39.

Lucas, W. Scott. *Divided We Stand: Britain, the US, and the Suez Crisis*. London: Hodder & Stoughton, 1991.

Lukas, J. Anthony. "Class Reunion: Kennedy's Men Relive the Cuban Missile Crisis." *New York Times Magazine*, 30 August 1987, 22ff.

McMahon, Robert J. "Credibility and World Power: Exploring the Psychological Dimension in Postwar American Diplomacy." *Diplomatic History* 15 (Fall 1991): 455–71.

Macmillan, Harold. *Riding the Storm, 1956–59*. London: Macmillan, 1971.

Marks, Frederick W., III. *Power and Peace: The Diplomacy of John Foster Dulles*. Westport, Conn.: Praeger, 1993.

Martin, John B. *Adlai Stevenson and the World*. New York: Doubleday, 1977.

Matthews, Herbert L. *Fidel Castro*. New York: Simon & Schuster, 1969.

Mayers, David. *George Kennan and the Dilemmas of US Foreign Policy*. New York: Oxford University Press, 1988.

Medland, William J. *The Cuban Missile Crisis: Needless or Necessary?* New York: Praeger, 1989.

Melissen, Jan. *The Struggle for Nuclear Partnership: Britain, the United States, and the Making of an Ambiguous Alliance, 1952–1959*. Groningen: Styx Publications, 1993.

Moss, Norman. *Men Who Play God: The Story of the Hydrogen Bomb*. London: Victor Gollancz, 1968.

Murphy, Charles J. V. "The Embattled Mr. McElroy." *Fortune*, April 1959, 147ff.

———. "Is the Defense Budget Big Enough?" *Fortune*, November 1959, 144ff.

———. "The NATO Alliance Goes Nuclear." *Fortune*, February 1958, 98ff.

Nash, Philip. "Jumping Jupiters: The US Search for IRBM Host Countries in NATO, 1957–59." *Diplomacy and Statecraft* 6 (November 1995): 753–86.

———. "Nuisance of Decision: Jupiter Missiles and the Cuban Missile Crisis." *Journal of Strategic Studies* 14 (March 1991): 1–26.

Nathan, James A., ed. *The Cuban Missile Crisis Revisited*. New York: St. Martin's, 1992.

Navias, M. S. *Nuclear Weapons and British Strategic Planning, 1955–1958*. Oxford: Clarendon, 1991.

Nelson, Anna Kasten. "President Kennedy's National Security Policy: A Reconsideration." *Reviews in American History* 19 (1991): 1–14.

Neufeld, Jacob. *The Development of Ballistic Missiles in the United States Air Force, 1945–1960*. Washington, D.C.: Office of Air Force History, 1990.

Neustadt, Richard E., and Ernest R. May. *Thinking in Time: The Uses of History for Decision-Makers*. New York: Free Press, 1986.

Newhouse, John. *De Gaulle and the Anglo-Saxons*. New York: Viking, 1970.

———. *War and Peace in the Nuclear Age*. New York: Knopf, 1989.

Nitze, Paul H., with Ann M. Smith and Steven L. Rearden. *From Hiroshima to Glasnost: At the Center of Decision—A Memoir*. New York: Grove Weidenfeld, 1989.

Nixon, Richard M. *Six Crises*. New York: Doubleday, 1962.

Nuti, Leopoldo. "L'Italie et les missiles *Jupiter*." In *L'Europe et la Crise de Cuba*, edited by Maurice Vaïsse, 123–57. Paris: Armand Colin, 1993.

———. "Italy and the Nuclear Choices of the Atlantic Alliance, 1955–1963." In *Securing Peace in Europe, 1945–1962: Thoughts for the Post–Cold War Era*, edited by Beatrice Heuser and Robert O'Neill, 222–45. New York: St. Martin's, 1992.

O'Donnell, Kenneth P. *"Johnny, We Hardly Knew Ye": Memories of John Fitzgerald Kennedy*. Boston: Little, Brown, 1970.

Office of the Historian, Headquarters, Strategic Air Command. *SAC Missile Chronology, 1939–1988*. Offutt Air Force Base, Nebr.: HQ SAC, 1990.

Pach, Chester J., Jr., and Elmo Richardson. *The Presidency of Dwight D. Eisenhower.* Lawrence: University Press of Kansas, 1991.

Powaski, Ronald E. *The Entangling Alliance: The United States and European Security, 1950-1993.* Westport, Conn.: Greenwood, 1994.

Pruessen, Ronald W. "John Foster Dulles and the Predicaments of Power." In *John Foster Dulles and the Diplomacy of the Cold War,* edited by Richard Immerman, 21–45. Princeton: Princeton University Press, 1990.

Ransom, Harry H. "NATO Military Strategy in Transition." *Journal of International Affairs* 12 (1958): 44–58.

Raskin, Marcus G. *Essays of a Citizen: From National Security State to Democracy.* Armonk, N.Y.: M. E. Sharpe, 1991.

Rathjens, George W., Jr. "NATO Strategy: Total War." In *NATO and American Security,* edited by Klaus Knorr, 65–97. Princeton: Princeton University Press, 1959.

Richardson, James L. *Germany and the Atlantic Alliance: The Interaction of Strategy and Politics.* Cambridge: Harvard University Press, 1966.

Roberts, Chalmers. *First Rough Draft: A Journalist's Journal of Our Times.* New York: Praeger, 1973.

Rockefeller Brothers Fund. *Prospect for America: The Rockefeller Panel Reports.* Garden City, N.Y.: Doubleday, 1961.

Rosenberg, David Alan. "Nuclear War Planning." In *The Laws of War: Constraints on Warfare in the Western World,* edited by Michael Howard, George J. Andreopoulos, and Mark R. Shulman, 160–89. New Haven: Yale University Press, 1994.

Rostow, Walt W. *The Diffusion of Power: An Essay in Recent History.* New York: Macmillan, 1972.

———. *View from the Seventh Floor.* New York: Harper & Row, 1964.

Rubinstein, Alvin Z., ed. *The Foreign Policy of the Soviet Union.* 3d ed. New York: Random House, 1972.

Rusk, Dean, as told to Richard Rusk, *As I Saw It.* New York: W. W. Norton, 1990.

Rusk, Dean, Robert McNamara, George W. Ball, Roswell L. Gilpatric, Theodore Sorensen, and McGeorge Bundy. "The Lessons of the Cuban Missile Crisis." *Time,* 27 September 1982, 85–86.

Sagan, Scott D. *The Limits of Safety: Organizations, Accidents, and Nuclear Weapons.* Princeton: Princeton University Press, 1993.

Salinger, Pierre. "Gaps in the Cuban Missile Crisis Story." *New York Times,* 5 February 1989, E25.

———. *With Kennedy.* New York: Avon, 1966.

Scheinman, Lawrence. *Atomic Energy Policy in France under the Fourth Republic.* Princeton: Princeton University Press, 1965.

Schlesinger, Arthur M., Jr. "Four Days with Fidel: A Havana Diary." *New York Review of Books,* 26 March 1992, 22–29.

———. *Robert Kennedy and His Times.* Boston: Houghton Mifflin, 1978.

———. *A Thousand Days: John F. Kennedy in the White House.* Boston: Houghton Mifflin, 1965.

Schwartz, David N. *NATO's Nuclear Dilemmas.* Washington, D.C.: Brookings Institution, 1983.

Schwarz, Hans-Peter. *Adenauer: Der Staatsmann, 1952-1967.* Stuttgart: Deutsche Verlags-Anstalt, 1991.

Sharnik, John. *Inside the Cold War: An Oral History.* New York: Arbor House, 1987.

Sharp, Jane M. O. "Arms Control and the Atlantic Alliance." In *The Allies and Arms Control,* edited by Fen Osler Hampson, Harald von Riekhoff, and John Roper, 13–44. Baltimore: Johns Hopkins University Press, 1992.

Sherwood, Elizabeth D. *Allies in Crisis: Meeting Global Challenges to Western Security.* New Haven: Yale University Press, 1990.

Snyder, Glenn H. *Deterrence and Defense: Toward A Theory of National Security*. Princeton: Princeton University Press, 1961.

Sorensen, Theodore C. *Kennedy*. New York: Harper & Row, 1965.

Spaak, Paul-Henri. *The Continuing Battle: Memoirs of a European, 1936-1966*. Translated by Henry Fox. Boston: Little, Brown, 1971.

Steel, Ronald. *Walter Lippmann and the American Century*. Boston: Little, Brown, 1980.

Stein, Peter, and Peter Feaver. *Assuring Control of Nuclear Weapons: The Evolution of Permissive Action Links*. CSIA Occasional Paper No. 2, Cambridge: Harvard University, 1987.

Steinbruner, John. *The Cybernetic Theory of Decision*. Princeton: Princeton University Press, 1974.

Sterling, Claire. "Turkey: Menderes Gambles on Time." *Reporter*, 26 December 1957, 19–23.

Sulzberger, Cyrus L. *The Last of the Giants*. New York: Macmillan, 1970.

Szulc, Tad. *Fidel: A Critical Portrait*. New York: Avon, 1986.

Taylor, Maxwell D. *The Uncertain Trumpet*. New York: Harper & Brothers, 1959.

Tocchet, Gary. "Sending Nuclear Weapons to Europe: A Reconsideration of the Thor and Jupiter Deployment." N.d. [1985?].

Trachtenberg, Marc. *History and Strategy*. Princeton: Princeton University Press, 1991.

Treverton, Gregory F. *Covert Action: The Limits of Intervention in the Postwar World*. New York: Basic Books, 1987.

Trewhitt, Henry L. *McNamara: His Ordeal in the Pentagon*. New York: Harper & Row, 1971.

Troyanovski, Oleg. "The Caribbean Crisis: A View from the Kremlin." *International Affairs* (Moscow), nos. 4–5 (April–May 1992): 147–57.

Tuchman, Barbara W. *The March of Folly: From Troy to Vietnam*. New York: Knopf, 1984.

van der Harst, Jan. "The Storage of US Nuclear Warheads in the Netherlands and the IRBM Debate." Paper presented at the Nuclear History Program Fourth Study and Review Conference, Nice, France, 23–27 June 1993.

Wampler, Robert A. "Eisenhower, NATO, and Nuclear Weapons: The Strategy and Political Economy of Alliance Security." In *Eisenhower: A Centenary Assessment*, edited by Günter Bischof and Stephen E. Ambrose, 162–90. Baton Rouge: Louisiana State University Press, 1995.

Weintal, Edward, and Charles Bartlett. *Facing the Brink: An Intimate Study of Crisis Diplomacy*. New York: Scribner's, 1967.

Welch, David A., ed. "Proceedings of the Hawk's Cay Conference on the Cuban Missile Crisis." Working Paper 89–1, Cambridge, Mass.: Center for Science and International Affairs, 1989.

Welch, David A., and James G. Blight. "The Eleventh Hour of the Cuban Missile Crisis: An Introduction to the ExComm Transcripts." *International Security* 12 (Winter 1987–88): 5–29.

WGBH. *The Cuban Missile Crisis: At the Brink*. Episode Five of *War and Peace in the Nuclear Age* (documentary). Boston: WGBH, 1988.

White, Mark J. *The Cuban Missile Crisis*. New York: New York University Press, 1995.

Wiebes, Cees, and Bert Zeeman. " 'I Don't Need Your Handkerchiefs': Holland's Experience of Crisis Consultation in NATO." *International Affairs* (London) 66 (1990): 91–113.

Winand, Pascaline. *Eisenhower, Kennedy, and the United States of Europe*. New York: St. Martin's, 1993.

Wohlstetter, Albert. "The Delicate Balance of Terror." *Foreign Affairs* 37 (January 1959): 211–34.

————. "Nuclear Sharing: NATO and the N+1 Country." *Foreign Affairs* 39 (April 1961): 355–87.

————. "On the Value of Overseas Bases." RAND Paper P-1877, Santa Monica, Calif.: Rand Corporation, 1960.

Wollemborg, Leo. *Stars, Stripes, and Italian Tricolor: The United States and Italy, 1946–1989.* New York: Praeger, 1990.

York, Herbert. *Race to Oblivion: A Participant's View of the Arms Race.* New York: Simon & Schuster, 1970.

Zubok, Vladislav, and Constantine Pleshakov. *Inside the Kremlin's Cold War: From Stalin to Khrushchev.* Cambridge: Harvard University Press, 1996.

Zuckerman, Sir Solly. *Scientists and War: The Impact of Science on Military and Civil Affairs.* London: Hamish Hamilton, 1966.

INDEX